WRITING WITH A VENGEANCE

CAROL MOSSMAN

Writing with a Vengeance

The Countess de Chabrillan's Rise from Prostitution

UNIVERSITY OF TORONTO PRESS
Toronto Buffalo London

© University of Toronto Press Incorporated 2009
Toronto Buffalo London
www.utppublishing.com
Printed in Canada

ISBN 978-0-8020-9691-3 (cloth)
University of Toronto Romance Series

Printed on acid-free, 100% post-consumer recycled paper with vegetable-based inks.

Library and Archives Canada Cataloguing in Publication

Mossman, Carol A.
Writing with a vengeance : the Countess de Chabrillan's rise from
prostitution / Carol Mossman.

(University of Toronto romance series)
Includes bibliographical references and index.
ISBN 978-0-8020-9691-3

1. Chabrillan, Céleste Vénard de, comtesse, 1824–1909. 2. Chabrillan,
Céleste Vénard de, comtesse, 1824–1909 – Criticism and interpretation.
3. Authors, French – 19th century – Biography. 4. French literature –
19th century – Criticism and interpretation. 5. Courtesans – France –
Biography. I. Title. II. Series: University of Toronto romance series

PQ2204.C767M67 2009 843'.8 C2009-902207-9

The University of Toronto Press acknowledges the financial assistance to
its publishing program of the Canada Council for the Arts and the Ontario
Arts Council.

University of Toronto Press acknowledges the financial support for its
publishing activities of the Government of Canada through the Book
Publishing Industry Development Program (BPIDP).

To my parents, Paul and Ann; to George, Donald, and Vicky;
and to my husband, Ken, with love and gratitude

Contents

Preface

I first happened on a reference to Countess Céleste de Chabrillan while preparing an undergraduate course which included Georges Bizet's great opera *Carmen*. Chabrillan was, I learned, a good friend of his, and likely one of the women he had in mind when he created his formidable gypsy character. I was intrigued. Having spent a couple of decades or so reading French literature of the nineteenth century and studying its culture, I had not previously encountered her name. I resolved to investigate.

The next summer found me doing just that in Paris at the Bibliothèque Nationale, where I discovered not only that Chabrillan had composed two series of memoirs, but that she had a whole string of novels and plays to her credit as well. When I found that she had begun her professional life – at sixteen – as a registered prostitute and, some twenty-five years later, had taught herself to write, I realized that her story was too extraordinary not to explore in detail. I was hooked. What manner of narrative, I wondered, might issue from the imagination of a woman forced to undergo the ordeals which she doubtless had endured? More interestingly perhaps, what kind of perspective would her writing offer?

Years after beginning this project, I continue to be amazed at the resilience of this woman of indomitable spirit. Above all else, however, is the immense respect I have developed for the power of the process of writing, for its capacities to heal, to solace, and even to refashion personal identity itself.

Acknowledgments

Over the years, this book has undergone more than one iteration. I wish to thank Mary Isaacsson and Madeleine Cottonet Hage for their readings in the early phases of composition. They helped to give the book its present orientation and convinced me that the project was, in fact, worthy of being undertaken. I am more grateful than I can say for the invaluable comments and insights of Vivien Rubin and Linda Kauffman, both of whom intervened at a later stage. I am further indebted to Linda for suggesting part of this study's title. To Doris Kadish I extend particular thanks for her intellectual support over the years and for the powerful example she has set, for me and many others, of a scholar who pursues historical research of the highest calibre in a way that matters to us today. And I thank Trudy Todd for being so generous with her friendship and wisdom over the years.

I gratefully acknowledge the Graduate Research Board of the University of Maryland at College Park for granting me a semester which I could dedicate exclusively to my research, and the same University of Maryland for a sabbatical leave which was instrumental in helping me to complete this book. I thank the anonymous readers of *Writing with a Vengeance* in its manuscript form for their insightful and knowledgeable comments.

And finally I am grateful to Kenneth Kato, whose moral support and love – and plain willingness to read draft after draft – were essential to the completion of this project.

Illustrations

WRITING WITH A VENGEANCE

Introduction

The scene is nineteenth-century Paris in a working-class district near the boulevard du Temple on the Right Bank. Céleste Vénard, a young woman (a teenager really), has been fighting with her mother day in day out. Usually the disputes revolve around her mother's companion, Vincent, who has attempted to rape Céleste, although her mother refuses to believe this. Finally, a domestic crisis erupts. Céleste has just turned sixteen and she asks her mother to accompany her to the police prefecture to give the written permission which would allow her daughter to register as a prostitute in the city of Paris. A group of policemen, agents from the vice squad, would then have been brought in to memorize Céleste's features in detail, the more easily to pick her up should she become lax in fulfilling her administrative and sanitary obligations. Her name is then inscribed on the rosters of infamy. The year is 1840.

Some eleven years later, as Vénard is labouring to teach herself to write, she will begin her *Mémoires* by acknowledging that her account is about a woman whom 'everyone knows': in a word, a public woman. A century and a half later, few people remember this extraordinary figure who emerged from the masses of poor women doomed to prostitution to become a notorious courtesan. Her nom de guerre was La Mogador and she *did* know everyone – at least, the prominent men of the period. In 1854, she scandalized *le Tout-Paris* by marrying Count Lionel de Chabrillan, and together they emigrated to Australia during the gold rush.

These events would be enough for a lifetime, but her story does not stop here. In 1856, the Countess returned to Paris no better off financially but infinitely richer in experience for these years of travel. Then tragedy struck. She lost her husband Lionel to illness. From 1858 to

1909, the Countess de Chabrillan was on her own in a hostile world. As a woman without means adamantly committed to living an honourable existence, how was she going to support herself? It did not help that the forces of Parisian respectability which had seethed at the news of her marriage into the French nobility were hell-bent on restoring her to her 'proper' place. No less a personage than Théodore de Lesseps, a high-ranking official at the Foreign Ministry, acting on behalf of the Chabrillan family, would attempt to bribe the Countess to renounce her noble name in exchange for an annuity which would have guaranteed her a comfortable existence for the rest of her days.

Instead, she clung fiercely to the name 'Chabrillan,' not because it offered an instant new identity: the self-hatred and shame she felt due to her former profession were far too deep for any such immediate remedy. She absolutely refused to relinquish her married name – for her it held the promise of legitimacy. Because what really makes the Countess de Chabrillan extraordinary is less her astounding life and versatility (she had also done a stint as a trick rider at the Paris Hippodrome), but rather her sheer determination to enter the ranks of respectability, cost what it may.

Many other nineteenth-century Parisian courtesans led colourful and sensational lives. Some even wrote memoirs, though the Countess's were among the earliest. Likewise other women of modest means wrote of their travels.[1] But one would be hard pressed to find another person anywhere who rose from what is surely the deepest circle of social hell and contempt by teaching herself to write and then embarking on a career as a playwright and novelist. From 1857 to 1885, the Countess de Chabrillan wrote twenty-six plays, ten novels, several operetta libretti, and a second instalment of her memoirs.

And as she wrote, she was righting her own 'wrongs' – surely – but also the myriad wrongs which the society of nineteenth-century France perpetrated on so many of the impoverished and the vulnerable. Her fiction always makes manifest the plight of the disadvantaged. Hers is truly one of the vox populi.

Writing with a Vengeance takes as its central aim an exploration of Céleste de Chabrillan's novelistic production, paying particular attention to the opportunities to reconfigure identity afforded through the complex mediation of the writing process itself. Because Mogador is not a well-known figure today, part 1 of this book provides the biographical and historical background sufficient to allow readers to grasp the arduousness of the path upon which this determined woman embarked. Once this context has been established, part 2 moves forward to an interpretive reading of her works of fiction. As a whole, then, *Writing with a Vengeance* proposes a contextualized literary study of a woman whose writing has remained draped in an obscurity due largely to her ill-repute.

When one thinks of the world of high harlotry of nineteenth-century France, what often comes to mind are images of glamour, frivolity, and extravagance; of gilt carriages parading down the Champs-Élysées toward the Bois de Boulogne; lavish dresses in satin and silk; hair bedecked with tiaras and diamonds (sometimes the wife's); vast sums of money thrown away on an evening's entertainment; private residences worth millions; country estates; winters in Paris at the Opera, the theatre (and at orgies); summers taking the waters in the cosmopolitan spas of Germany and elsewhere. The courtesan – that diva of prostitution – began to come into prominence in the 1840s during the reign of King Louis-Philippe, rising to even greater heights over the two decades during which Napoleon III exercised power. Hers were succès de scandale, and there was no city like Paris for savouring a scandal.

The feats and fates of these women have become the stuff of legend. Cora Pearl (1835–86), the British girl who made good in the French capital, became the mistress of Prince Napoleon, the Emperor's cousin. Rumour had it that one lover, hoping to take her Troy, gave her a silver horse filled with jewels. (This would have come in handy later, for Pearl was an inveterate gambler.) Esther Guimond (b?–1879), a courtesan of Louis-Philippe's reign, claims to have been launched by Guizot, the eminent historian and later prime minister. She was simultaneously kept – so it was said – by Émile de Girardin, the man who introduced the penny press to France: the two men, whose politics clashed, evidently came to an understanding in her regard.

La Païva (1819–84) travelled far indeed to be able to lay claim to her nom de guerre. Born Thérèse Lachmann in Moscow, she migrated to Paris, where she began her career in remunerated love in the quartier du Temple where Céleste Vénard herself was raised. Eventually she married a Portuguese marquis. The marriage lasted a matter of months. The Count retreated to his native Lusitania, but there she was: a wealthy marquise in Paris, hosting a weekly salon attended by men such as Girardin, writers Théophile Gautier and Sainte-Beuve, and painter Delacroix. The private residence she had constructed for herself (which stands today) took ten years to build and featured an onyx staircase leading to the throne room – that is to say, the private chamber of Madame where a bed of legendary value had pride of place.

And the list goes on. Blanche d'Antigny was 'imported' to Russia by its Prince only to be exported by the Empress, whom she had offended by buying a dress which was supposed to have been reserved for her Royal Highness. She is considered to be the model on whom Émile Zola based his famous courtesan Nana. Léonide Leblanc (1842–94) acted at the Variétés Theatre as did Vénard. Also known as Mademoiselle Maximum for her financial acumen, she was the long-time mistress of the Duke d'Aumale, the fourth son of Louis-Philippe. For her part, Alice Ozy, a well-known actress, specialized in prominent artists and writers: Liszt, Gautier (again), Chassériau, Gustave Doré, and doubtless scores of others. Exclusivity being the prerogative of the courtesan, she refused Victor Hugo her services, entering instead into a liaison with his son Charles.

Not to be forgotten, Madame Sabatier, known as 'la Présidente,' held her salon on Sundays for fourteen years from 1847 to 1861. All of (male) literary Paris attended this salon with regularity over a period of many years: Flaubert, Baudelaire, Gautier (yet again), Maxime du Camp, and many others. Marie Duplessis (1824–47), allegedly Alexandre Dumas fils's model for the tragic Marguerite Gautier of *La dame aux camélias*, was further immortalized (if this is possible) by Verdi in his 1853 *La traviata*. It was rumoured that the Duke de Guiche spent ten thousand francs on her in six months alone (Richardson, *The Courtesans* 154). But the excesses of Parisian life became an *affaire d'état* when Empress Eugénie herself had to ask Marguerite Bellanger to cease seeing her husband, Napoleon III, for health reasons: after spending an evening with her, he would return home in a state of virtual collapse.

The splendours of nineteenth-century Paris were renowned throughout the world. The city was second to none in its spectacular urban landscapes, which were given a facelift by Baron Haussmann in the 1850s and 1860s. It boasted world exhibitions featuring all the latest exotica from the colonies and the most up-to-date technology. And it was a city where love came notoriously easily. Offenbach's fluff operetta *La vie parisienne* (1866) depicts a Scandinavian couple come to enjoy the wonders of Paris, each secretly hoping to have an amorous adventure. After many naughty antics, rendezvous made by each spouse with a love interest, whom should they encounter when at last they go to their respective assignations but each other! A happy ending, surely, since in the end, the marriage vows are respected, but the audience has had a good gander at the erotic smorgasbord which the city proposed, and the fires of conjugal love have been reignited before the couple returns to their chilly nordic home.

The world of *la grande bicherie* persisted beyond the 1871 collapse of the Second Empire, the major cataclysm resulting from the Franco-Prussian War. Some thirty years later during the belle époque, one would encounter such *grandes horizontales* as Cléo de Mérode, la Belle Otéro, and Liane de Pougy. But the generation of 1900 witnessed the decline of the reign of these queens of the boudoir. French society had changed fundamentally. More middle-class women had entered the workforce and were beginning to earn decent wages for the first time. Their presence in the public arena was becoming increasingly acceptable. As Lenard Berlanstein's discussion of actresses (those *other* public women) shows, they were far less stigmatized by century's end. Society was gradually acknowledging that women who made spectacles of themselves were not necessarily women of ill-repute. More and more, women could be seen and heard in public and still hold on to their respectability.

In a number of ways, Céleste Vénard's origins and career intersected with these other courtesans, many of whom she knew. Like her, most had come from the working classes and possessed only rudimentary educations. Like her, too, many had been *femmes de théâtre* at one of the myriad Parisian theatres, and some had even been accomplished actresses. Almost none, however, had stooped so low as to be registered with the Paris police.[2]

Writing with a Vengeance describes the attempts of a fallen woman to come to terms with herself and her past. The prospect of writing about that past, as daunting as it was, must have held the promise of relief and perspective. It was thus that, resolute in her pursuit of all things, Céleste Vénard undertook to teach herself to write. Out of this punishing ordeal, a four-volume recollection of her less-than-exemplary life emerged and was published first in 1854 and then again in 1858. This narrative and its 1877 sequel are virtually the only sources that describe the events and details of her life. They offer a unique lens through which to view the customs and values of the period.

Early in her memoirs, Céleste Mogador promises to recount her past 'as chastely as possible.' To the modern reader, Mogador's narrative hardly seems racy. Her accounts supply no salacious details whatsoever, and in general she avoids giving names of 'respectable' people whose reputations might be harmed by figuring in her story. If, to a reader of today, there is nothing shocking in what she relates, to her generation it must have been otherwise. Perhaps the simple fact that a woman would divulge, in print, her connections to the milieu of the

Parisian brothels was enough to stun the reading public. Perhaps, too, the simplicity, sincerity, and lack of sensationalism which characterize her tale were disconcerting to readers accustomed to the widely available spicy gossip columns all a-twitter with news from the social netherworld. Not to be overlooked is the possibility that male readers recognized themselves, their friends, or simply their own lifestyles in the escapades described in the *Mémoires*, while at the same time too many wives were given the occasion to wonder about their spouse's activities. Finally, perhaps the shock value of Céleste Mogador's memoirs lies precisely in their sombre realism, which smacks of a truth that her culture refused to acknowledge.

This brings us to the issue of Céleste Vénard's credibility. All autobiographies and memoirs distort. Indeed, it is impossible for any personal narrative not to do so inasmuch as it is, by definition, the writing of a self told from within. Personal narratives are also variously motivated: here one thinks of the opening gesture of Jean-Jacques Rousseau's *Confessions* in which he depicts himself brandishing his document in no less important a face than God's in a fierce gesture of self-vindication. This aggressive reclaiming of innocence sets the tone for the tale of a genius thwarted at every turn of his life by enemies visible and invisible.

So it is that every autobiographical text offers the projection of a self fashioned along the fault lines of a particular personality, a project which may be aimed simply at the writer him/herself, or at a broader public, or both. Beyond these agendas, however, a reader can often sense if an autobiographer is being grossly self-promoting, and whether she or he is exploiting the public's expectations in some way – either noisily gratifying them or ostentatiously contradicting them.

If a person is sufficiently influential in his or her time (as was Rousseau), facts and events related by the writer are likely to find corroboration or refutation in contemporary commentary. Mogador was less influential than she was notorious. To write about her implied 'knowing' her, and not all men would be prepared to implicate themselves in that way. Contemporary writings which commented on the veracity of her memoirs are non-existent to my knowledge. Snide references to her as a prostitute or courtesan exist, and there are one or two such references with respect to her as a writer, one in the Goncourt brothers' *Journal*, for example. (The Goncourts, writers themselves, are best known today for their acerbic commentary on Parisian society of the mid-nineteenth century.) Another author who speaks of Mogador in his history of Paris's Folies-Marigny Theatre, P.L. de Pierrefitte, has nothing but praise for her efforts in rehabilitating that theatre in the 1860s and describes her multiple roles as director, actress, fundraiser, and sometime playwright.

Because of *who she was*, then, virtually no corroborative documents exist by which one might gauge the 'truth value' of what she has written. This being the case, let me describe the tone of Mogador's *Mémoires* as being generally sober and sombre about the scandalous life she led. Never does she glorify her life: on the contrary, frequent are the moments in which she engages in considerable self-vilification. Many of the events and characters she describes – fellow whores, illiterate women of the proletariat, twelve-year-olds seduced and reduced to prostitution, women crippled by conjugal beatings, others used as fronts for illegal gambling operations – all testify with eloquent frankness to the daily miseries and the precarious life of the working classes in nineteenth-century France.

Mogador is also candid and forthright about her own flaws. On numerous occasions she admits to her own trivial jealousy or vanity, and sometimes to out-and-out manipulation of male rivals to serve her own ends. One does not have a sense, at any time in the *Mémoires*, of self-aggrandizement. In fact, in her memoirs, it is as if she is putting things in their right place, restoring a sense of perspective to the well-worn story of the prostitute by attempting to deflate the abundant sensationalist myths which circulated in the nineteenth century around the person of the strumpet. And, while she accepts responsibility for her life and her acts, she also points a finger – rarely at individuals but at a society without a social safety net in which the poor are virtually forced to resort to dishonesty or dishonourable acts in order to survive.

Thus, while it is difficult to take the measure of the truth of any given event described in her memoirs, there is also little reason to doubt, in a general way, the veracity of what is being recounted. For, whereas it is obvious from the opening lines of Rousseau's *Confessions* that he stands to gain his readers' sympathy in recounting his life, for Mogador, the narrative stakes are far less obvious.

In fact, as fate would have it, when Count Lionel de Chabrillan proposed marriage to her in 1853, she had just sent her manuscript in to be published. As soon as she realized how scandalized the Chabrillan family would be if the *Mémoires* were to appear in print, she used all her connections in high places to annul the contract. Nonetheless, some fifty copies had already rolled off the presses in 1854 before production could be halted. Subsequently, the publishing house sued her for breach of contract; she lost the suit, and the *Mémoires de Céleste Mogador* appeared in their four-volume entirety in 1858.[3]

In 1877, long after Lionel's death, she published a one-volume sequel, *Suite des mémoires de Céleste Mogador par la comtesse de Chabrillan*. In this chronicle, she recounts their life in Australia and her beginnings as a writer. Another edition of the first set was published in 1876. Clearly there was a substantial reading public interested in what she had to say. This brings us to the knotty problem of her readership.

It is nearly impossible to determine who the Countess's reading public actually was. Their numbers were, in any case, restricted by the fact that she never published her works in the serial format so lucrative and so popular at the time. Due to technological advances in the printing industry, newspapers partially subsidized by advertisement hit the market in 1836 with Girardin's highly successful newspaper *La Presse*. Not only did famous novelists like Hugo, Sand, and Balzac earn good money by publishing their work in instalments in these journals, the newspapers themselves earned fortunes because they featured famous writers of the day. Due to the volume of the sales and the new advertising capabilities, the cost of a copy of *La Presse* was slashed by one-half. Readership expanded accordingly.

For those who still could not afford to purchase the news under these improved conditions, there was always the *cabinet de lecture*. As of the early 1800s, these reading rooms existed in both Paris and the provinces, taking over the role of disseminating news and literature formerly held by the travelling book hawker.[4] In these reading rooms, one could rent books for short or long periods. Newspapers and magazines were also available for consultation. The *cabinet de lecture* would stock the classics as well as a good number of currently popular writers. It would even offer a collection of the much-disdained but apparently much-read 'novels for chamber maids,' romance novels whose authors were frequently women.

No matter how much the Countess de Chabrillan would have liked to publish in serial form, she did not. She claims that her friend Girardin had promised to serialize one of her novels until the intervention of the Chabrillan family, outraged that she still bore their name, and no doubt fearful lest it appear day after insulting day at the bottom of a newspaper column. As to how Céleste de Chabrillan's novels were read and where, we know that they first appeared in book form (one-half of her books were published by Michel Lévy, later Calmann-Lévy) and perhaps marketed at la Libraire nouvelle, the publisher's successful bookstore/literary salon located in the fashionable boulevard district on the

Right Bank. Her novels were also stocked in some of Paris's *cabinets de lecture*: the 1896 catalogue of 'Aux bibliophiles' *cabinet* indicates that they held seven of her novels; Delorme's 1871 catalogue features six of her novels along with the first series of her memoirs (the second had not yet appeared); and the 1863 catalogue of the 'Cinq mille volumes' *cabinet* held two of the four novels she had published by that date.

Evidence also suggests that her works were read by all rungs of society. In the 1920s, Marcel Proust lamented the disappearance of that unique phenomenon, the *cabinet de lecture* 'où il y avait des livres qu'on ne trouvait plus là (les romans de la comtesse d'Asche et de Céleste Mogador [...])' (*Essais* 606) (where one could find books no longer around [the novels of the Countess d'Asche and Céleste Mogador [...]). And in a draft excerpt from his *À la recherche du temps perdu*, the narrator describes with nostalgia the library belonging to the father of the Count de Guermantes which contained works by 'Balzac, d'Alphonse Karr, de Céleste de Chabrillan, de Roger de Beauvoir and d'Alexandre Duval,' all bound in the same style (*Contre Sainte-Beuve* 282).

That Céleste de Chabrillan managed to write, to be published, and to be read at all is a tribute to her tenacity, her indomitable will, and, as this book will show, her urgent need to redeem herself in her own eyes and in those of her contemporaries. For a host of reasons, most cultures (and certainly nineteenth-century France) have a powerful interest in silencing the prostitute. Our thirst to know *about* her seems unquenchable next to our grudging willingness to hear what she is actually saying. We have often alleged that prostitutes do not – and have never – spoken or written about themselves. But this is only a partial truth. Céleste Mogador is one of a handful of venal women to have written about their experiences first before moving on to fiction writing – where her point of view is unique.

Prostitution has been a part of life since time immemorial. As an institution, its signification and function vary according to the particular history and civilization to which it belongs. One of my contentions in this book is that the venal woman can never be seen as divorced from society, however much that society might wish the separation. A more accurate account of her social role would be that of a negative validation of her culture's concept of respectability and legitimacy. As an ideological foil, she plays a crucial role as a reverse barometer of social acceptability.

As critical as that role might be, however, the prostitute exercises a symbolic fascination which is difficult to overstate. She is the fantasmatic site uniting politics, desire, domination in all its forms, and the exercise of power. In her fantasized body a whole range of discourses coalesce and conflate. Invested in her persona are both individual and collective erotic impulses including the fear/pleasure of transgressing taboos and of assuming – however evanescently – postures of authority or subjugation.

In the pages which follow, I explore nineteenth-century France's obsession with the figure of the prostitute to the extent that it allows me to be attentive to the question of voice. In the pamphlets, scientific tracts, journal articles, and literary works which abound during this period, who is speaking about the prostitute? Rarely herself. Nearly always she is positioned as the object of discourse. But this human phenomenon – the sex worker – which has for centuries been the subject of description, prescription, inscription, proscription; of philosophizing, medicalizing, hypothesizing, and stigmatizing: this human phenomenon can speak! In this book, I propose to listen.

Among other things, *Writing with a Vengeance* scrutinizes the many ways through which the prostitute was rendered inaudible. Stereotypes crystallized around her with astonishing rapidity, leaving her little discursive space of her own. Poverty and illiteracy precluded her from occupying such space as there was. Moreover, nineteenth-century France's segregation of respectable women from their dishonoured sisters tended to isolate the latter from potentially compassionate listeners.

And if these obstacles to self-expression were not enough, the male-authored literature about prostitution which abounded in France of this period positioned the venal woman exclusively as an object through lenses distorted by a justifiable fear of syphilis, conflicted desire, newly evolving theories of genetic criminality, class-consciousness, or a host of other biases and anxieties which could only cloud observation. Indeed, imposed silence and denial of her subjectivity were essential to maintaining certain myths and scientific discourses credible and intact. However, arguably the most important of all the reasons behind her silence was the fact that the prostitute was simply an inconvenient witness.

In his *Confessions d'un journaliste*, Maxime Rude reports on how the young Baudelaire had decorated his room in the Hôtel Pimodan by hanging 'stuffed crocodiles and serpents brought back from the Tropics, which seemed to writhe about under the ceiling. There was a black velvet divan where Mogador, with her supple, snake-like body, was paid to sit – on condition that she did not speak' (cited by Richardson, *The Bohemians* 63–4).

But what about today's silences? If the nineteenth-century voice of middle-class morality and the institutional discourse enforcing it precluded Céleste Vénard from occupying a space of respectability, surely today, with the benefit of distance and the luxury of research tools, we can rethink her status. In contemporary scholarship there has been a reticence to break this silence that can only be qualified as bizarre.

To all appearances, recent historians of the subject and literary scholars appear determined *not* to hear the few voices which do cry out. It is understandable that a spokesperson for nineteenth-century bourgeois respectability might wish to deny the prostitute a voice on the grounds that the voice might be that of a siren: alluring, corrupting ... or all too revealing. But to what can we ascribe the systematic refusal to consider the evidence which does exist? The most prominent scholars in the field persist in maintaining the myth of the prostitute's muteness.

Laure Adler's otherwise excellent study of prostitution in France, *La vie quotidienne dans les maisons closes: 1830–1930*, claims that little or no direct testimony from prostitutes exists: 'Hélas,' she laments:

> les prostituées sont restées sans voix. Ce sont toujours les hommes qui ont voulu les raconter. J'ai pu miraculeusement, et à travers de rares reprises, trouver trace de leurs vies dans des archives mais pour les doléances particulières et de façon parcellaire. Rien ou si peu sur leur intimité, leur vie quotidienne, leurs émotions, leurs passions. C'est donc à partir du vacarme et de la rumeur de la littérature prostitutionnelle masculine que je vais tenter de restituer partiellement des fragments de leur histoire. (19–20)

> Alas, prostitutes have remained voiceless. It has always been men who have recounted them. Miraculously and on rare occasions, I have been able to find traces of their lives in archives but [only] for specific grievances and in partial fashion. It is thus through the sound and fury of masculine prostitutional literature that I am going to attempt partially to restore the fragments of their story.[5]

While the copious male-authored fiction and documentation treating the subject does certainly offer insights into the lot of the prostitute, these representations are nonetheless coloured by complex cultural and individual baggage, to say nothing of the arrogance of anyone attempting to speak the truth on behalf of women whose situation he could never be in a position to experience first-hand. Repeating Adler's omission is Jann Matlock's 1994 study, *Scenes of Seduction: Prostitution,*

Hysteria, and Reading Difference in Nineteenth-Century France. Once again, in an otherwise elegant analysis, she makes the rather categorical assertion that '[the prostitute] has left us few traces, little writing, certainly no novels of her own' (21).[6] She then goes on to affirm: 'Even the few texts in which the prostitutes supposedly recounted their stories [...] smack of a sensationalism that casts doubt on their authenticity. We will not find memoirs of women who escaped the tolerance system and lived to tell its tale' (21–2).[7]

In point of fact, Mogador's *Mémoires* (both the 1858 and the 1877 sets) are anything *but* sensationalist. As noted earlier, they remain chaste at all times, no doubt a disappointment to her contemporary reading public (though perhaps a relief to her erstwhile swains). Names of 'respectable' individuals are rarely if ever mentioned: even her husband Lionel's name is disguised as 'Robert' in the 1854 and 1858 editions, and only much later, following his death, does Mogador give him his real name. As angry as she was about her lot in life, Céleste remained remarkably discreet. What of the nature of the stories she chose to recount? Her accounts are peppered with the 'small,' daily tragedies of the underprivileged and the downtrodden, accounts never tinged with sentimentality. Her stories are straightforward and down to earth and, as such, speak volumes about the culture in which she lived. In short, nothing is further from sensationalism.

We are fortunate in that Chabrillan's memoirs – both series – have been translated into English recently and are readily available.[8] Likewise, her first novel, *The Gold Robbers*, is available. Furthermore, in 2007 Harmattan Press issued her second novel, *La Sapho* (in French). Two full-length biographies of Chabrillan exist in French: Françoise Moser's *Vie et aventures de Céleste Mogador* (1935) and Pierre-Robert Leclerq's *Céleste Mogador: une reine de Paris* (1996). Of the two, Moser's is the most factually reliable, whereas the strength of Leclerq's study lies in the evocation of the context in which Mogador lived. Most of Moser's account has been summarized in English by Joanna Richardson in a chapter of her book *The Demi-monde in Nineteenth-Century France*, reprinted in 2000. A condensed version of this chapter is also available on the internet. Richardson is an expert in nineteenth-century French bohemia, and her chapter is well worth reading.

Within the last decade or so, the topic of the courtesan has generated an extraordinary number of books. Several have appeared on geishas, from Arthur Golden's inspired 'faux memoir' *Memoirs of a Geisha* (1997) to its apparent rebuttal by Miseko Iwasaki in her *Geisha: A Life* (2002).

Two spirited works celebrating eighteenth-century British courtesans have recently appeared: Paula Byrne's *Perdita: The Literary, Theatrical, Scandalous Life of Mary Robinson* (2004) and Jo Manning's *My Lady Scandalous: The Amazing Life and Outrageous Times of Grace Dalrymple Elliott, Royal Courtesan* (2005).

On a lighter note, *The Book of the Courtesans: A Catalogue of Their Virtues* by Susan Griffin selects various qualities which the author feels a courtesan must possess (for example, 'a sense of timing') and interweaves the lives of various notorious women, including Mogador, through these categories. She includes modern sex stars and one male courtesan. Published in 2003, Virginia Rounding's *Grandes horizontales*, a carefully researched book, tells the stories of Apolline Sabatier, Cora Pearl, Marie Duplessis, and La Païva. Rounding's treatment is one of the most modern because it emphasizes the direct and active role these women had in constructing and promoting their own images.

On the scholarly side, two studies on the subject of venal women in classical Athens need to be recognized: James Davidson's lively and informative *Courtesans and Fishcakes* (1997) and Debra Hamel's *Trying Neaira* (2003), the account of a trial of a public woman whose claims to wifely legitimacy challenged the city of Athens's rigid and exclusionary definitions of citizenship.

In 2006, the secret archives of the Paris vice squad (dating from 1861 to 1876) were published by historian Gabrielle Houbre under the title *Le livre des courtisanes*, while just released, also from France, is *Un joli monde: romans de courtisanes* (2008). As usual, the novels *of* courtesans evoked in the title should be read as 'novels *about* courtesans,' and we are thus returned, even today, to the well-trod paths of works framing the prostitute as an object.

Indeed, only two published studies deal with that rare commodity: venal women who became writers. Margaret Rosenthal's *The Honest Courtesan: Veronica Franco, Citizen and Writer in Sixteenth-Century Venice* (1992) examines the life and work of the remarkable courtesan Franco against the social backdrop of Renaissance Venice, which practised rigid claustration of 'virtuous' women as opposed to the public-ness of a venal woman, and further one who had the audacity to render herself even more public through acts of publication. Then, the biography of Neel Doff (1858–1942) by Evelyne Wilwerth (1997) is the first dedicated to this Belgian novelist who, like Mogador, grew up in impoverished circumstances but managed to write despite all odds.[9] Doff was a couple of generations younger than Mogador and born into an era which was considerably more forgiving of these women; her work was hailed as an example of social realism.

Although prostitution is hardly a career to which one aspires today, it nonetheless carries nothing like the social stigma which adhered to it a century and a half ago. In order to situate her life as a venal woman within the mentality and mores of her time, the first three chapters comprising part 1 of this book offer contemporary commentary which speaks volumes as to how Mogador and her sisters were viewed in the nineteenth-century public eye. This testimony will contribute to an understanding of the depths of her shame regarding her past and the desperation with which she sought to erase it.

Did other women in her cohort experience the same levels of self-hatred, or did Céleste de Chabrillan have a sense of degradation greater than that of the majority? Cora Pearl recounts her life quite gaily, merely saying that she is documenting her life because it may be of interest.[10] Marguerite Bellanger, mistress of Emperor Napoleon, begins her auto-biography on a bitter note and in a somewhat defiant tone, but she does not seem to harbour regrets of a moral nature. Famous dancer Jane Avril (not a prostitute) is quite candid and unabashed about her life as a dancer and kept woman during the belle époque. She refuses blame of any sort. It is significant, however, that the memoirs of these three women were all written from twenty-five to eighty years after Chabrillan's. Times and values were changing. More important still is the fact that the three memoirs just alluded to were composed from the mellow perspective which can be the gift of old age. The recollections of Pearl, Bellanger, and Avril all relate to a bygone era. Mogador's memories, on the other hand, are recorded almost in the midst of the events they describe. Her account is untempered by the work of time. It possesses a rawness and spontaneity that set it apart.

Chapter 1 of *Writing with a Vengeance* sketches the broad outline of Céleste de Chabrillan's life based on her memoirs and such additional evidence as has been possible to find. I do not enter into details, but enough information is provided to acquaint the reader with the principal events and personalities in her life. (For a more ample account, I refer the reader to the previously mentioned translations of her memoirs.) Chapter 2 discusses the system by which the French police 'managed' prostitution as well as the medical theories and public health policies which formed the theoretical justification of that management. The subject of prostitution in nineteenth-century France has drawn an unusual amount of scholarly attention, and a number of books studying different aspects of the topic exist. Perhaps the high level of interest corresponds to the fact that many other nations adopted the 'French method' later in the century: the French solution to the health issues posed by prostitution was seen internationally as exemplary.[11] What I have aimed to do in chapter 2 is to intertwine Chabrillan's observations on the regulatory system to which she was subject with the official discourse on prostitution: its causes, the 'nature' of its practitioners, its effective management, and so on. By confronting the voice of authority with the voice of one woman who was forced to comply with the dictates of that authority, I open up a new space which can accommodate the testimony of those who have always been considered as mute objects, or, more to the point, objects to be muted.

Because the Countess de Chabrillan learns to write, and then proceeds to write play after play and novel after novel, it is essential to consider the unusual subjective position she occupies as a writer, but a writer whose past has already straitjacketed her into an object of contempt. Finally, chapter 2 also proposes a theorization of the existence of the demi-monde, a social space which has consistently been taken for granted by historians and other scholars. I contend that this semi-licit shadow world arose in direct response to historical and legal changes unique and specific to France.

Chapter 3 conducts a thematic overview of the extensive male-authored works of fiction dedicated to the figure of ill-repute, to use Charles Bernheimer's excellent phrase. The intense scrutiny-through-fiction typical of nineteenth-century French literature can only be qualified as a cultural obsession: there is no other word for it. The readings I present are not meant to be detailed textual analyses, but rather broad-brush attempts to capture overall literary trends as well as to observe the process of myth making which takes place over the course of the century.

The three final chapters comprising part 2 of *Writing with a Vengeance* are entirely given over to the novelistic production of this extraordinary and unstoppable woman. This is my other narrative about Céleste de Chabrillan, and it is one whose aim is to explore the power of the process of writing. The overarching question I shall be posing about her work is the following: what happens when the very person who embodies all the stereotypes of the prostitute actually takes up the pen and decides to write a rebuttal? Chapter 4 treats Céleste de Chabrillan's early novel, *La Sapho* (1858), which does just that. It is her only work to address the question of the courtesan's place frontally (as it were), but it is clearly a necessary stop on her literary and emotional itinerary. Chapters 5 and 6 examine Chabrillan's novelistic oeuvre as it evolves from naive – albeit fascinating – melodrama to a more complex and textured writing characterized by multiple points of view, irony, and humour.

Over the span of her fiction, a number of themes recur with considerable persistence. The articulation of these issues, however, can assume a wide range of forms. My reading of her work attends to the metamorphosis which these themes undergo from one novel to the next. As I sift through the subtle changes in the way these recurring topics are expressed, I shall be asking: is some kind of new and perhaps overarching narrative being constructed through these permutations? If so, why, and where does it seem to be leading? Because the discussions take major themes and their variations over time as their basis, the reader of this book need not have prior knowledge of Chabrillan's oeuvre in order to follow them. It is, in fact, one of the central goals of this project on the Countess de Chabrillan to introduce her and her work to a reading public who may not suspect that such a remarkable woman existed.

PART ONE

Chabrillan's Contexts:
Biographical, Historical, Literary

1 The Wages of Shame

From the standpoint of the twenty-first century, it is difficult to imagine the level of social opprobrium which adhered to the fallen woman of nineteenth-century France. Despite the shame, however, few personal transactions were as common as those of venal love. Clients, then as now, spanned the social spectrum and could purchase love legally in *maisons closes*, illegally on the street, and alfresco in some of the *bals publics* (public dance halls) which often boasted gardens. In his 1864 'treatise,' *Les cythères parisiennes: histoire anecdotique des bals de Paris*, Alfred Delvau, bard of *bohème*, fondly recalls his mating seasons of yesteryear. Especially dear to his heart was an establishment known as 'Number 13,' located strategically close to the bal de la Chaumière on Paris's Left Bank:

> Ah! le Numéro 13! il était bordé d'une foule de petits cabinets particuliers, d'où partaient des pétillements de gaieté et de champagne, des éclats de voix, des éclats de rire et des glouglous de bouteilles. On y entrait timidement, avec la beauté qu'on avait cueillie entre deux quadrilles dans le parterre d'en bas, avec Jeanne ou avec Louise, avec la blonde ou avec la brune, et on en ressortait fièrement, comme Alexandre après la conquête de l'Asie ou comme Napoléon après la conquête de l'Europe, – et cependant, convenez-en, vos Europe et vos Asie, souvent, ne valaient pas les vingt sous de pourboire que vous aviez généreusement donnés au garçon, en soldant l'addition, qui alors s'appelait la carte. La carte d'Europe! la carte d'Asie! Ah! les ignorants géographes que vous étiez, que nous étions alors! Si vous aviez, si nous avions su! si l'on savait! ... Imbécile! si l'on savait que les poupées sont faites de son au lieu de sang, on ne les adorerait pas, – et on aurait tort, parce qu'il faut toujours adorer les poupées, quitte à leur casser la tête après, d'un coup de pistolet ou d'un coup de canne. (6)

Ah! Number 13! Along its edges were a host of small private rooms whence came sounds of sparkling gaiety and champagne, bursts of voices and laughter, and bottles gurgling. One would enter timidly with the beauty one had picked up between two quadrilles on the dance floor down below, with Jeanne or Louise, with the blond or the brunette, and one emerged full of pride like Alexander after the conquest of Asia or like Napoleon after the conquest of Europe. And yet, you must agree, your Europes and your Asias were often not worth the twenty sous tip which you had generously given to the waiter in paying the bill, which was then called the menu [pun: *carte* is also map]. The map/menu of Europe! The map/menu of Asia! Ah! Ignorant geographers that you were – that we were then! If you had – if we had known! If one had known! ... Imbecile! If one had known that dolls are made of stuffing instead of blood, one would not adore them, – and that would be a mistake because dolls must always be adored, though one must be prepared to blow their heads apart afterwards, either with a pistol shot or a cane.

Delvau beckons to the former youth in the nostalgic mode, binding together those erstwhile male frequenters of bohemian night spots before erupting in an act of rhetorical violence vociferated around what the period commonly referred to as 'ces créatures' (these creatures): the many ladies of the evening available in these nocturnal haunts. The maps of Europe and Asia – no doubt a nod at two of Balzac's more corrupt women characters of *Splendeurs et misères des courtisanes* – also designate the wide range of ethnic choices available to the clientele of the Parisian bordello in the nineteenth century.

More celebrated than the Grande Chaumièrě was le bal Mabille. Mabille was located on the Right Bank not far from the Champs-Élysées, which, at the time, was a somewhat unpopulated district and anything but the glamourous commercial area it is today. Mabille drew men from all nations and ranks of society. The women who frequented this hotspot, however, were drawn strictly from the ranks of the demi-monde. Mabille's dancing and music – with an orchestra sometimes conducted by Jacques Offenbach – were second to none in Paris.

For men, of a summer evening, it was the place to be; for respectable women, it was a place not to be. Nonetheless, its notoriety could not fail to arouse curiosity, and thus, 'Des dames du monde,' writes one journalist, 'ont eu l'idée de traverser ce faux Eden [...]. On a organisé une escorte, ce sont les amis de la maison qui la fournissent [...]. On ne prendrait pas plus de précautions s'il s'agissait de traverser en caravane le désert de Sahara' (Arsenal 4 RO 12953). (Some society ladies had the idea of crossing this false Eden [...]. An escort was organized with friends of the owners arranging it [...]. One would not take more precautions if one were crossing the Sahara desert in a caravan.)

One of the 'creatures' who made her reputation at the Mabille dance hall in the 1840s was Céleste Vénard. It was here at the bal Mabille, dazzling in its modern gas-lit splendour, that she was dubbed 'la Mogador' in honour of the Moroccan town recently conquered by the French. Her life story was as remarkable as anyone's.

Céleste Vénard was born in 1824, the illegitimate daughter of hat makers, in a working-class district of Paris. Her father died when she was six, and shortly thereafter, her mother, Anne-Victoire, took a new companion, 'Monsieur G.,' who paid off his old debts with the couple's money and regularly beat them both. One night, following a particularly brutal bout of violence, Anne-Victoire was carried on a stretcher to file a complaint with the Paris police. The inspector of police, sympathetic to her cause, reminded her that by law, she had no recourse. He agreed to detain her companion in jail for as long as possible and recommended that mother and daughter flee the city: '[S]i j'ai un conseil à vous donner [...] quittez Paris, allez-vous-en le plus loin possible [...]' ([I]f I have one piece of advice to give you [...] leave Paris; go as far away as possible! [*Mémoires de Céleste Mogador* 1: 9]).[1]

So the two set off immediately for Lyons ... on foot. Fearing pursuit by Monsieur G., mother and daughter were employed incognito in one of the city's many famous silk factories by an owner who agreed to house them in secrecy. Alas, however, the irate companion managed to track them down, reclaim them, and set up a household which they shared with criminals plotting to rob a local castle. It so happened that these familial events converged with the 1832 insurrection of the Lyons textile workers (the *canuts*), a proletarian uprising considered by many as prefiguring the 1848 Revolution. By sheer luck, Monsieur G. was killed in the attempted robbery. Liberated, mother and daughter returned to Paris. Céleste was eight years old at this time, and with all the hardships and lack of domestic continuity which she had already endured, she had formed an extremely close bond with her mother.

Back in Paris, at age eleven, it was time for Céleste to learn a trade. Like so many other girls of the proletariat, she found employment in the textile industry. After apprenticing to a seamstress, she became an 'ouvrière à la journée' (day worker), earning 20 sous per day. By the age of fourteen, she was professionally considered to be a woman and was promoted to the more technically demanding job of embroiderer.

On the domestic front, however, the intense mother/daughter relationship so important to Céleste had been eroding. At the heart of this emotional deterioration – aside from Céleste's entry into adolescence – was her mother's new lover, Monsieur Vincent. Portrayed as a freeloader, a drunkard, and a womanizer, Vincent completely dominated Anne-Victoire, at least in the eyes of the daughter who felt spurned by her mother: 'Ma mère était moins tendre pour moi' (My mother was less tender with me), she laments (1: 99). At this juncture, Céleste experienced levels of rage and a sense of betrayal which she was to carry with her for her entire life. Céleste's description of the escalating hostility between her mother's lover and herself, the daughter, as well as the honesty with which she avowed her own jealousy and meanness of spirit create a subtle and credible portrait of unbearable domestic tension.

The rivalry between Céleste and Vincent reached its peak when Anne-Victoire was called away to care for her ailing father. Vincent first attempted to seduce Céleste and then, having failed in that, to rape her. Céleste escaped through a window and was forced to spend several nights out of doors. It was on one of these evenings, as she was sitting on the steps of the Saint-Paul church in Paris's fourth arrondissement, that a nice lady, on hearing her misfortune, offered to house the miserable girl until her mother could be found. Her benefactress, named Thérèse, cryptically murmured that she was running the risk of being arrested for corruption of minors. Whereupon Céleste understood the nature of her profession.

The result of this act of kindness was that the worst *did* come to pass. Céleste and Thérèse, caught in a police raid, were carted off to the dread Saint-Lazare, the prison for female criminals, prostitutes, and wayward young girls. While Céleste was not booked on charges of prostitution in this arrest, she was held in Saint-Lazare until her mother, at long last, came to claim her. The chapters of the *Mémoires* which describe her internment provide a frank view of what she observed in prison, including the strong lesbian relationships she witnessed and, indeed, in which she participated. She also reports that the prison provided a fertile recruiting ground for future prostitutes.

When her mother finally did come to claim her, Céleste related the tale of Vincent's attempted seduction and rape. Anne-Victoire refused to believe her daughter and instead allied herself with her companion. At this moment Céleste declares: 'Tout lien affectueux entre ma mère et moi se rompit' (1: 212) (All emotional bonds between my mother and me broke). Céleste experienced this as an abandonment, the final betrayal in the already-strained mother/daughter relationship, and informed her mother soon thereafter of her desire to register as a prostitute. A friend she had met in Saint-Lazare, Denise, was already employed in a brothel; Céleste knew the address; all that was required now that she was sixteen was her mother's consent. Her mother, after attempting to dissuade her daughter, consented to give the written parental permission required for minors. It was with this decisive episode that the breach of trust between mother and daughter became absolute, and it was a wound which Céleste would attempt to heal all her life.

In 1840 Céleste Vénard registered herself with the Parisian police as a prostitute in accordance with the regulations: 'J'étais inscrite sur ce livre infernal d'où rien ne vous efface, pas même la mort!' (1: 226) (I was registered in that infernal book from which nothing erases you, not even death!). She rejoined Denise in one of the more elegant brothels in the rue du Temple: 'Le lendemain du jour dont je parle,' she reports in her narrative, 'j'ai compris que j'étais morte, morte sans retour au monde, dans lequel j'avais vécu jusqu'alors' (1: 212) (The day following the day I am speaking of, I understood that I was dead, dead with no return to the world in which I'd lived until then). Little had she realized before registering with the police that for the rest of her long life, Céleste Vénard would have to live with the irreparable consequences of a decision made at age sixteen, never knowing how to assign blame or assess responsibility, but always attempting, both in action and in word, to arrive at a resolution.

In her memoirs Céleste relates the work conditions and the internal economy of these brothels where the madams exacted such high prices for clothes and the necessities of life that their *pensionnaires* ('boarders,' as they were euphemistically termed), unable to leave the house, became more indebted with each passing day. In regard to her activities in this house of ill-repute, it is worth mentioning perhaps that at no point do Céleste's *Mémoires* indulge in any form of prurient description. No scabrous details are evoked even by way of illustration. At all times, she remains true to her originally stated intent to recount 'as chastely as possible' her life as a public woman. Finally, having suffered repeated humiliation and abuse at the hands of a famous literary personality (who remained unnamed by her but whose identity was later to be acknowledged), Céleste determined to leave the public harem at all costs. At last, good fortune struck in the form of a wealthy patron who bought her out of this indentured sexual servitude.

Following her liberation from the brothel, Céleste would earn her living with another Saint-Lazare friend on the streets. This was a far riskier existence since she was no longer 'legal': which is to say that she no longer submitted to the routine, forced sanitary visits to the doctor, or the public invisibility required by the elaborate regulatory system of the Paris police. Women who worked outside the pale of 'tolerance,' as it was known, were subject to being arrested and incarcerated at any time and in any place.

It was several years later, in 1844 at the tender age of twenty, that Céleste earned her nom de guerre at the famous Mabille dance hall where she and her comrade-in-arms, Lise Sergent, so excelled at dancing the latest fad, the polka, that they were dubbed 'la Mogador' and 'Queen Pomaré,' names referring to recent French colonial exploits in Morocco and Tahiti respectively. Such sobriquets could make a girl's career, as Balzac had clearly understood in naming Esther, the courtesan of *Splendeurs et misères des courtisanes*, la Torpède. La Mogador's career as a celebrity in the erotic arts was launched.

Céleste had a figure which was legendary, and her admirers fêted her in prose and in poetry. Poet Barthélémy penned the following stanza in alexandrines:

L'astre déjà fameux au temps de Pomaré
La fière Mogador étale avec luxure
Sa taille dont Minerve envierait la cambrure
The star already famous in Pomaré's time
Proud Mogador bawdily displays
Her body whose curves would be the envy of Minerva

From obscurity to the beginnings of notoriety, Céleste was now poised for ascent within the demi-monde, a shadow culture of 'moral' society every bit as hierarchical as *le monde*. Of course, in this subterranean culture, many were called to glory, but few were chosen. For example, the much-fêted Queen Pomaré (who lived for a time with poet Charles Baudelaire), contracted tuberculosis and, like so many of her sisters, died in the blossom of her youth. With the exception of a small number of established actresses and courtesans, life in the demi-monde was a life on the brink. And while escaping the demi-monde was technically possible for a woman who had become a 'public' woman, the doors to respectability remained firmly closed, at least in the 1840s, 1850s, and 1860s.

As the nineteenth century moved toward its close, however, women who led public existences were increasingly accepted by mainstream

1. Céleste Mogador. Daguerréotype, Mayer frères. Source: Département d'Estampes et photographie, Bibliothèque nationale de France (Rés EG4-162, probable date: 1844).

society. In literature, it is Marcel Proust who best captures this societal opening up in the figure of Odette de Crécy, suspected by her lover Swann of having worked in a brothel and who, in the final tableau of time recovered, has become the titular mistress of the Duke de Guermantes, the quintessential representative of the French landed nobility whose origins hark back to some dim Merovingian past.

It was sometime around 1846 that Mogador met Count Lionel de Moreton de Chabrillan, scion of a noble family from the Isère region, who was rapidly dilapidating his considerable fortune through gambling, playing the horses, and supporting expensive mistresses: in short, the pastimes of the wealthy youth of his generation. Chabrillan and Mogador began a tempestuous relationship which would last, off and on, for many years. During this time, the Count was shopping around to 'marry a dowry' (to use the cynical expression of the day). Also at this time, Mogador found herself thrust upward into a more worldly sphere of the demi-monde. During this period, Mogador was kept by a number of wealthy men. Now at the pinnacle of her career, she could be seen in a handsome blue coupé driven by domestics in livery participating in the fashionable Parisian ritual of the promenade down the Champs-Élysées to the Bois de Boulogne.

Still, when fortune was fickle, as it often was, and she was down on her luck, the versatile and adaptable Mogador found other sources of income. Occasionally she took minor acting roles in one of the many Parisian theatres. She also trained and became an accomplished equestrienne for the Hippodrome, an enormously popular entertainment in Paris, and one which showed her legendary figure and suppleness to good advantage. Indeed, it was in the Hippodrome that Lionel de Chabrillan caught his first glimpse of her: 'Tout ce qu'il y avait de plus élégant à Paris était là' (2: 27) (All the elegant people of Paris were there).

But this was dangerous employment, and during one performance of the staged Roman chariot race, she was trampled by the horses and badly injured. The accident put an end to this chapter of her career, although later, in Australia, she would break a rebellious horse when it was unfit for others to ride. From this and other experiences, it is clear that Céleste Vénard/Mogador was gifted with an indomitable spirit, one which could rise to meet the most challenging of circumstances. Her energy and strength of willpower go a long way toward explaining how this uneducated woman of the working classes could endure the myriad hardships she recounts in her *Mémoires*, ultimately launching a literary career with all the odds against her.

All the while that she was performing at the Hippodrome, she remained technically outside the regulations. As a registered prostitute who was not in compliance with public health obligations, she was always at risk of being picked up by police or denounced at any time. In spite of her obvious vitality, Mogador attempted suicide on more than one occasion. To see the human misery around her is to understand why. Her unpredictable life was criss-crossed by many of the ill-fated whom she often attempted to aid. There was the young woman who complied with her husband's request to serve as a front for an illegal gambling operation and who could not seem to elude his grasp: Céleste helped her to escape his clutches. There was her own maid, who contracted cholera and bequeathed her daughter to Céleste to raise, which in fact she faithfully did. The reader of the *Mémoires* is constantly brought up short by these tragedies of ordinary people which form the backdrop of Céleste's own dramatic – and oft-times desperate – activities.

More trouble was on the horizon, however. At long last, her lover Lionel de Chabrillan had so indebted himself that even his noble name no longer sufficed to keep his creditors at bay. They invaded Céleste's residence on the presumption that what was hers must have been his, little imagining, apparently, that she could be a wealthy woman in her own right. Public woman that she was, the judicial assumption seemed to be that all she owned was also public domain, or in other words, that, as Mogador, she could have no private civil status. The truth of the matter seems to be, however, that for some time Mogador had been lending money to the Count. She decided to assert her claim to her own money by enlisting the aid of her lawyer-friend, Desmarest, who filed a suit in her behalf.

This was a critical juncture for Céleste Mogador because it was under these circumstances that she taught herself to write. She composed her memoirs beginning in 1851 as an act of self-defence and she is pleased to see that 'à force de répondre aux attaques dirigées contre moi par mes adversaires, de faire des notes pour ma vie, notes indispensables à mes procès, je finis par prendre goût à ce griffonage. Je me défendais mieux en écrivant qu'en parlant' (4: 175) (By dint of responding to the attacks directed against me by my adversaries, by taking notes on my life, notes which were indispensable to my case, I ended up developing a taste for this scribbling. I defended myself better in writing than by speaking). Thus, as will be the case during much of her life, the activity of writing emerged from the need to defend, explain, and exonerate herself, often in situations where others would not be called upon to do so. It is out of this gesture of exculpation that the four-volume *Mémoires* were composed.

Some clarification about her writing skills is required here. In her *Mémoires*, Céleste notes that prior to 1851–3 – that is, the period of the composition of her memoirs – she was unable to write. This is a claim which needs to be nuanced, for it is clear to any reader of the memoirs that she did write the occasional letter before this date. What should probably be understood by her assertion is that she wrote with an un-steady and unschooled hand, learning how to trace out letters of the alphabet solely based on her exposure to reading, and possessed virtu-ally no knowledge of spelling. This understanding of her semi-literacy is borne out by the many characters in her novels which display similar limitations and are deeply ashamed of them.[2]

Once her autobiography was completed, her friend, lawyer Desmarest, took the liberty of circulating the manuscript among his lit-erary acquaintances for their opinions: even the wealthy and cultivated Delphine de Girardin, who, as a high-society woman might have been shocked by their content, advised in favour of publishing them. It was based on this encouragement that Mogador signed a contract to pub-lish *Adieux au monde: mémoires de Céleste Mogador* with Locard-Davi et de Vresse. The 1854 edition of her memoirs begins almost apologetic-ally thus: 'Ces Mémoires sont la vie d'une femme que tout le monde connaît' (These Memoirs are the life of a woman whom everyone knows). The 'whom everyone knows' might easily have been read in the biblical sense with no distortion of meaning, particularly since the caricaturist Gavarni had already famously defined the whore as a woman who 'stood to gain by being known.' With the benefit of hind-sight, it was in fact the publication of her memoirs – that is, the render-ing public of her already-too-public life – which would define her entire subsequent life and career. If ever she had wished to retreat into the shelter of private life (as later she fervently wished to do), with the pub-lication of her memoirs that door was now definitively closed. Thus it was that, in terms of her immediate future, the signing of this contract soon appeared to her to be an enormous blunder.

For the events of her life then took an unexpected turn. Lionel de Chabrillan had so disgraced himself in the eyes of the *monde* that it was clear he would never land the dowry for which he had been shopping for over a decade. Hoping to redeem himself while striking it rich, he set off in 1852 on a ship to Australia, then in the full fever of its gold rush. He was hardly the only one to do so, and Mogador's entourage included more than one broke young man going off to California or Australia in search of wealth. As for the Count's prospects, Mogador remains sanguine. In spite of the level of dishonour to which Lionel de Chabrillan had sunk because of his gambling debts and bohemian lifestyle, there is always a reprieve, notes Mogador, for those with connections. A person like the Count, she comments wryly, 'retrouvera l'expiation du passé, des influences, des protections, des amis qui vous tendront la main pour vous aider à remonter, surtout quand on a un des beaux noms de France et qu'on possède des parents puissants et riches. Mais pour une pauvre créature comme moi [...] la ruine, quand elle arrive, est définitive,' (4: 81) (will find expiation for the past, influence, protection, friends who hold out their hands to help you to recover, above all when one has one of the grandest names of France and when one possesses rich and powerful relatives. But for a poor creature like me [...] ruin, when it comes, is definitive).

As Mogador continued to live the high life in Paris, Lionel quite literally dug himself deeper and deeper into misery in this land where greed and lawlessness prevailed. Far from home (and no richer), he wrote letters that became more tender with each passing day. Céleste would in fact incorporate these letters into her memoirs, where they form, together with some of her own autobiographical pages, some of the earliest eyewitness testimony on the colonization of Australia.

It was thus completely unexpected that he arrived back in Paris, interrupting a dinner party which Céleste was hosting and, a latter-day Odysseus, causing the many suitors in attendance to disperse. However, Mogador had not been – nor indeed had she ever claimed to be – a Penelope, and over the next several months, vicious domestic scenes ensued. At length, recognizing that he always seemed to come back to her, Lionel proposed marriage and she accepted.

When news of the engagement became known, the rage of the Chabrillan family knew no bounds. Nor, it seems, did its influence. On more than one occasion, they attempted to bribe Céleste not to marry Lionel. All efforts failed: Lionel and Céleste took the necessary precautions against the Chabrillan family and fled to London, where their marriage was celebrated at the French embassy on 3 January 1854 just a few days after her thirtieth birthday.[3] Céleste poignantly recounts her fear and shame as she enters the confessional to ask for pardon before taking the vows of matrimony. And it is said of this flight to England that Queen Victoria herself made arrangements to catch a glimpse of the notorious French courtesan.

But to return to the journey to the end of the world (as the 1877 sequel to these memoirs would style it), the newlyweds set off for Australia, while *le Tout-Paris* seethed over their marriage. They set sail aboard the *Croesus*, a ship whose name speaks volumes of the aspirations of the emigrants on board. Australia: land of opportunity and collective penance. Australia, where one in three of the population was a convict or an ex-convict, the Countess will later note with some acrimony. While on board ship, Céleste made a secret vow never to allow her husband to dominate her, while Lionel spotted other couples who, like themselves, were heading off to Australia to hide their love.

It would emerge, however, that Céleste was hiding more than her love: she had also failed to disclose to Lionel that her painstaking efforts at teaching herself to write had culminated in the composition of her autobiography. She imagined that now, from the safe embrace of wedlock, she would be able to annul the publication contract. Prior to leaving Paris in 1854, and despite the fact that fifty copies of the *Mémoires* had been printed and sold, she and her friend Alexandre Dumas attempted to persuade Prince Napoleon to put a forcible halt to the publication. The Prince, Emperor Napoleon III's cousin, would later become a minister and he already enjoyed considerable power.[4] Mogador knew him well since he was an ardent frequenter of the demi-monde. For a time at least, he was able to block further publication. So this immense favour had been granted, but unbeknown to her, word was already out. Whereas the Countess de Chabrillan believed that she would be embarking on her new life with a clean slate, the Australian newspapers had already featured a review of her memoirs and even pointed out a local bookstore which carried them. She was branded on arrival in Melbourne and would subsequently be excluded from any official invitation which Lionel (who had managed to secure a minor consular position) would receive. Once again, her dreams of forging a new identity of respectability were shattered.[5]

With no friends, in a pestilential climate and a frontier culture in which violence and dishonesty were the rule, Céleste de Chabrillan sought solace in her newest companion: writing. Perhaps she could write herself into rehabilitation? She began composing a narrative based on an account of a bloody robbery-*cum*-love story which Lionel had witnessed during his first sojourn in Australia. And she took that time-honoured precaution so often practised by women of hiding her writing activities from her husband. She reported that such was her shame at her levels of ignorance, she spent her nights in reading and self-instruction. Her later accounts of this period are quite fascinating: she predicts, for instance, the extermination of the aboriginal population and describes the kind of war being waged between the colonizers and the indigenous peoples.

By 1856, however, climate and hardships having taken their toll on her, she returned to France, partly with a view to re-establishing her health and partly to seek of the government an extended leave for Lionel. And, in her luggage, she carried back the manuscript of her first novel, *Les voleurs d'or*. But another of the major motivations for her return was to defend herself in the lawsuit which the publisher of the *Mémoires* had brought against her for breach of contract. Her publisher was suing the Countess so it could resume publication of her memoirs halted earlier through the intervention of Prince Napoleon.

In Paris, her various projects met with mixed success. She did manage to secure the leave for her husband, and he eventually returned to Paris. Her health was on the mend in spite of her now frenetic writing and studying. But she suffered one major setback: on 7 March 1858, she lost her trial to halt publication of her memoirs, and, shortly thereafter, the volumes rolled inexorably off the press and into the bookstores to create a sensation. This edition quickly sold out. (The *Mémoires* were republished in 1876, by which time she had become reconciled to their 'publicness,' going on in fact to publish their sequel, *Suite des mémoires de Céleste Mogador par la comtesse de Chabrillan* in the following year.) Finally, with the support of her good friend and mentor, the prodigious writer Alexandre Dumas père, she negotiated a contract with Michel Lévy to publish her first novel, *Les voleurs d'or*. By some irony of literary destiny, *Les voleurs* appeared in 1857, that is, at roughly the same time as Gustave Flaubert's *Madame Bovary*, and Dumas's review of both novels appeared, side by side, in his journal *The Montecristo*.[6]

The Countess says little about her writing activities in the memoirs, so it is difficult to tell exactly when and where she composed her second novel, *La Sapho*, published in 1858 and reissued in 1876 as *Un amour terrible (Sapho)* and again in 1897. Dumas's review of *Les voleurs* had praised that novel and mentioned that she had returned from Australia with several others in her suitcases, so this would suggest that her second novel was also composed in Australia.

Meanwhile, Lionel had returned to Paris, having obtained and read copies of her two novels. Unexpectedly for her, he was proud of her achievement and reproached himself for not having participated in her efforts at self-education: 'J'ai regretté de ne pas t'avoir aidée dans tes études, mais j'étais loin de m'attendre à une si grande transformation de ton esprit' (*Un deuil* 238) (I regret not having helped you in your studies, but I was far from imagining such a great transformation of your mind). It was time for him to return to his duties in Australia, the plan being that she would join him shortly thereafter. The Countess received letters from him mailed at various ports of call. He had become ill during the long sea voyage, and each letter sees his health deteriorating further. When, at last, he reached Australia, he was cared for by their mutual friend Antoine Fauchery, a Parisian poet who had also emigrated to the Antipodes. In late 1858, Count Lionel de Moreton de Chabrillan, age forty, finally succumbed to his malady, and the Countess learned of his death in a letter written by Fauchery. She was devastated and found some solace commiserating with Judith Félix, the sister of the great actress Rachel who had also just died.

The Count's death put an end to this phase of Céleste's life, a life which had never been an easy one, except for the occasional periods of opulence. Now it would seem that the issue of whether or not she retained her title of countess was to become an *affaire d'état*. One day Théodore de Lesseps, an official of the Foreign Affairs Ministry and brother of the future developer of the Suez Canal, called her into his office and attempted to persuade her to drop her title and married name. When he proposed a sum of money in exchange, the Countess understood that the influence of the Chabrillans was at work behind the scenes. She refused the proposition, and thereafter the Chabrillan family would impede her every effort to earn an honest living, whether in the domain of publishing, theatre production, or acting.

It is true that Céleste still had an entire circle of influential male friends, because it was their prerogative to pass from *le monde* into the demi-monde and back with impunity. Now, with the death of Lionel, she found herself at an impasse. Her male friends did not desert her, but at the same time, they could hardly help her to cross the invisible but ever-so-impermeable barrier separating her from respectability. It is the case, as Berlanstein has demonstrated for the world of actresses and as Anne Martin-Fugier has shown for the upper crust of nineteenth-century French society vis-à-vis the bourgeoisie, that between 1830 and 1848 many social distinctions were eroding, and that definitions of respectability – and even its social relevance – were slowly being transformed as the century progressed. But the Countess de Chabrillan, who had stooped so low as to be registered with the police and then had dared to tell the tale, would never be pardoned. Perhaps her sin lay less in the doing, and more in the telling.

2. Céleste Mogador. Par Nadar. Source: Département d'Estampes et photographie, Bibliothèque nationale de France (87C 130958)

Thus far this account has summarized, in highly condensed form, the four volumes comprising the first set of memoirs (1854/58) and the second single-volume instalment (1877) entitled *Suite des mémoires de Céleste Mogador* signed, significantly, the Countess de Chabrillan. Whereas her first series is signed by a *demi-mondaine*, the author of the later instalment, the Countess de Chabrillan, has taken distance from her prostitutional identity by situating herself on the 'right' side of respectability, almost as if she were writing about her earlier self from the position of an alter-ego of sorts. The Countess de Chabrillan also wrote a third and final set of memoirs which has never been published and which covered her life between 1877 and 1907, before her death in 1909 at the age of eighty-five. The unpublished manuscript, which reportedly consists of sixteen notebooks and 1200 pages and carries the revealing title of 'Les deux noms' (The Two Names), was brought to light by her biographer, Françoise Moser in the mid-1930s.

Nothing is more murky than the whereabouts and history of the transmission of these manuscript memoirs which were in a small chest accompanied by correspondence to the Countess from Prince Napoleon. Georges Montorgueil, a prominent figure of the belle époque who had befriended the elderly Countess in 1902, claimed that she had promised him these documents following her death. In his belated obituary of her published in the 2 March 1909 issue of *Chroniques parisiennes*, Montorgueil complains: 'Elle m'avait dit "Quand je serai sur le point de m'en aller, accourez vite. Il y a, là-dedans, un petit coffret que je vous léguerai [...]"' (When I am about to depart, come over here quickly. Inside there is a small chest which I will bequeathe to you [...]). When at last Montorgueil comes to stake his claim (he had been ill when she died), the small case had vanished! It was, in fact, his peer Jules Claretie who somehow had come into possession of these memoirs. Subsequently they passed into the hands of antiquarian book dealer Charavay. In her biography, Moser thanks Georges Andrieux for alerting her to the existence and whereabouts of this final set of memoirs, which she purchased.

Moser used these unpublished memoirs in the final part of her biography, which appeared in 1935 under the title of *La vie et aventures de Céleste Mogador: fille publique, femme de lettres, et comtesse (1824–1909)*. Although it was evidently her intention to publish the final instalment, Moser never did so, and after a sighting of them at a 1938 Paris opera exhibition devoted to Georges Bizet (one of the Countess's friends), they have disappeared from view.[7] Are they lying in some dusty attic or buried in a long-forgotten private collection, or were they perhaps destroyed during the Second World War? For now, these questions must remain unanswered. Moser does report that when Guy de Maupassant, Alexandre Dumas fils, and others were asked whether Chabrillan should publish the final part, they had advised her against it.

In any case, the following summary of the Countess's final years relies heavily on Moser's account, with occasional complementary information culled from newspaper articles, reviews, and, in one instance, an open letter from the Countess herself which forms a preface to one of her final literary works. For, although the Countess would write eight more novels between 1859 and 1885 (excluding three second editions and her memoirs), she turned her attention increasingly to that more lucrative literary arena, the theatre.

At a time when her star was shining brightly, Céleste de Chabrillan had purchased a country property in the new real estate development of Le Vésinet, then highly desirable because it had become accessible by train from Paris. It was, in fact, on the train that she met the much younger Georges Bizet, who subsequently came often to her country residence to practise on her grand piano. It appears that she was supported during this period by lawyer Desmarest, who established her in a chic Paris address near the Tuileries in exchange for daily luncheons with her (an arrangement reported by Moser with considerable innuendo). During the 1860s, the Countess also hosted a salon which drew, among other political personalities, Léon Gambetta and Garibaldi.

Little documentation exists about her playwriting career, but we do know that not only did she write these dramas and comedies (twenty-six in all), she was also heavily involved in producing them, occasionally acting in them and even, when it appeared that the Chabrillan family was persuading theatre directors not to accept her plays, managing a theatre. Since women were not permitted to manage theatres, once again, Prince Napoleon intervened on her behalf, and in the mid-1860s, she took over the direction of the Folies-Marigny, behind, of course, a front man. In the 1860s, the Countess's plays enjoyed some success. However, the Franco-Prussian war of 1870 put a halt to what appeared to be her burgeoning theatrical reputation and ultimately to the Second Empire itself. During the war, the intensely patriotic Countess founded a women's paramedical organization baptized by press mogul Émile de Girardin Les Soeurs de France (The Sisters of France). Les Soeurs went into action on 21 September 1870, two days after the Prussians laid siege to Paris. These women conveyed the wounded to hospital and administered what relief they could on site. A number of theatre women were sprucing up their reputations by similar acts of public service including the much younger Sarah Bernhardt, who used the Odeon Theatre as her base of operations (*Ma double vie* 167–96).

When, at length, it was clear that the Prussians would be the victors of this conflict, and the spectre of civil war – the Commune – loomed large, Chabrillan left the city. Already a witness to the 1832 Canut revolt in Lyons and having remained in Paris during the bloody February Days of the 1848 Revolution, she did not have the heart to witness yet another political upheaval. So it was that she returned on foot to her Vésinet property, only to find it had been looted and pillaged by the Prussians.

By now, the world of the Countess's youth was disappearing. It was around this time that her dear friend and mentor Alexandre Dumas père died. Following the disastrous defeat of the French in the Franco-Prussian war, her erstwhile benefactor Prince Napoleon was now in exile. And, most significantly of all, the year 1874 saw the death of her mother with whom her relationship had remained conflicted to the very end, largely due her mother's continued loyalty to Céleste's 'stepfather,' Vincent. Gone now was the Paris of yesteryear. She had grown up near the boulevard du Crime, which had teemed with small theatres offering a broad range of entertainment to all classes and owed its name to the melodramatic nature of its offerings. Much of the old Paris depicted by Balzac and Hugo was being swept away in the 'Haussmanization' of the city with its enlarged avenues no longer easy to barricade during social unrest and its displacement of the working population toward the suburbs. The political landscape had also altered dramatically. The fits and starts which characterized post-revolutionary France as it slowly lurched toward democracy had finally given way to the Third Republic. Now men of all classes could vote, and women's causes, too, were making substantial social progress.

In terms of literary production, the 1870s and the first half of the 1880s were a fertile period for Céleste de Chabrillan. Between 1881 and 1885 alone, she published four lengthy novels. Her final novel, *Un drame sur le Tage*, was published in 1885, and her last play, *Pierre Pascal*, was also completed in 1885. With the exception of one brief monologue, no works appear later than this. Part 2 of this book will propose an explanation for this definitive silence, which might be considered premature since Céleste would live in good health for another twenty-five years.

Besides the legacy of her considerable literary production, the Countess de Chabrillan also wished to be of some practical help to uneducated girls who found themselves in the predicament of her youth. She therefore donated her Vésinet property and, with financial aid from Monsieur de Naurois (a friend of Lionel's whose relationship to her at this time is unclear), established it as an institution to house, educate, and train young women who had no means of supporting themselves. This charitable establishment opened in 1875 and was run by the Sisters of Saint-Charles under the patronage of a number of dignitaries and academicians: the Counts d'Haussonville, de Greffulhe and de Chambord, the Duke de Périgord, Princess Amédée de Broglie, and others. However, these worthy sponsors imposed one condition upon its existence: namely that its founding mother, Céleste de Chabrillan, not be linked to it in any official way. Thus it was that the social norms of the day conspired on every level to refuse this fallen woman admittance to respectable society. What ex-Mogador craved the most – social redemption within her lifetime – was denied to her consistently, systematically, and tenaciously.

The final twenty-five years of the Countess's life were difficult ones during which she attempted to cobble together the financial wherewithal to live. During some of this period, she lived at 17 passage de l'Opéra, where she maintained a small reading room. Although some accounts suggest a shadier traffic, such does not seem to have been the case (Moser 285). As she aged, her attempts to obtain pensions were repeatedly thwarted. René de Pont-Jest reported in an 1894 untitled newspaper article that her request for a pension from the government as the widow of a civil servant was turned down. Then, when backed by Dumas fils, Camille Doucet, the influential director of Paris theatre, and the Calmann-Lévy press, she applied for retirement support from the Société des auteurs dramatiques, her request was greeted thus: 'Toutes vos références, vos certificats, attestent que, depuis quarante ans, vous êtes femme de lettres. Il n'y a eu ni plainte, ni procédure contre vous, mais, ajouta-t-il en l'examinant sans indulgence, il y a votre passé' (Moser 298) (All your references, your certificates, attest to the fact that you have been a woman of letters for forty years. There has been neither complaint nor suit filed against you, but, he added examining her without indulgence, there is your past).

It was at this time, in the 1880s, that her principal publisher, Calmann-Lévy, purchased her rights to eight of her novels published by them for 1200 francs. This was probably not an exploitative gesture but rather a way for the publisher to help its author as she sank into poverty, much as they did for her contemporary, Gyp, as described by Willa Silverman in *The Notorious Life of Gyp*.

By 1900, a new literary generation had sprung up, among which were literary critics whose interest in *bohème* and the demi-monde was historical rather than nostalgic. This group, which included Jules Claretie and Georges Montorgueil, was interested in preserving the vestiges of the reign of Louis-Philippe (1830–48), the Second Republic (1848–51), and the Second Empire (1851–70). With the help of these new friends, Chabrillan was able to receive a pension from the Société des gens de lettres as well as one from the Société des compositeurs de musique (she had written some operetta libretti). With these modest but guaranteed resources, she was able to secure a room at the Providence retirement home in the rue des Martyrs (a religious establishment ironically situated in one of Montmartre's most bohemian streets adjacent to the Divan Japonais of Jane Avril and Toulouse-Lautrec fame). Sadly, financial difficulties continued to plague her. A manuscript letter to Dumas fils contained in the Bibliothèque nationale's collection depicts the elderly woman struggling to pay her rent with barely enough money left over for firewood. Moser reports that the Countess continued to write her memoirs, which became, after 1900, increasingly incoherent and embittered in tone. Her final journal entry dates from 1907, and on 18 February 1909, Céleste Vénard – aka Mogador, and ultimately the Countess of Chabrillan – died.

This hardly seems a happy ending to a long and remarkable life. However, what Chabrillan was denied during her life, she was able to achieve – at least to some extent – through her writing. Moreover, if the publication of her memoirs in 1854/58 shocked a reading public, the male half of which, in any case, participated with impunity in the very life she describes, other memoirs of notorious women would follow. The *grande horizontale*, Liane de Pougy, composed her *Blue Notebooks* from 1919 to 1937, Cora Pearl's memoirs appeared in 1886, and Sarah Bernhardt's fascinating but expurgated *Ma double vie* was written with considerable retrospective distance in 1907.

Since Chabrillan's last novel, *Un drame sur le Tage*, will be analysed in some detail later, this biographical sketch will end with her open letter to Monsieur Ulysse Bessac, published and attached to her final play (actually a musical drama written in 1885), *Pierre Pascal*. Because the manuscript of the third and final instalment of her memoirs is lost, this letter constitutes, to my knowledge, one of the last available autobiographical testimonials of the Countess de Chabrillan.[8] This letter begins on a defiant note by pointing out that the production of *Pierre Pascal*, in spite of its rocky beginning, netted good profits and brought in some 35,000 spectators. 'J'ai toujours soutenu,' remarks the Countess, que *vouloir c'était pouvoir* [...]. C'est tout ce que je puis opposer au sujet de cette éternelle scie de la reprise de Mogador. Le public est resté froid à tous ces rabâchements qui consistent à vouloir soulever le masque d'une femme qui n'en a jamais porté! Il va au théâtre pour voir jouer *une pièce*.

En fait, s'il reste à l'avoir du passé [...] trépassé, de Céleste Mogador, les chansons et les vers de Nadaud, Murger, Méry, Lachanbaudie, des articles élogieux signés par d'anciens fanatiques du plaisir devenus des puritains aujourd'hui, il reste à celui de madame Lionel de Chabrillan, bon nombre de brevets de *capacité littéraire* qui lui ont été décernés par ces maîtres de l'art et de la critique qui avaient noms: Alexandre Dumas *père*, Jules Janin, Fiorentino, Nestor Roqueplan, de Girardin, Théodore de Banville, de Villemessant, Rousseau, Hostein, Jules Claretie qui a écrit que si l'une de mes pièces, *L'Américaine*, qui l'avait profondément ému, était signée d'un autre nom que *le mien, cette piece suffirait à elle seule à faire la fortune de l'auteur.*

On m'a souvent dit que mon grand tort était de m'obstiner à porter le nom que mon mari m'a donné. Mais si j'avais signé mes oeuvres de celui de Mogador, on aurait mis en regard celui de Chabrillan. Si j'avais pris un pseudonyme, on l'aurait certainement souligné entre mon nom de guerre et de femme [...]. Il y a trente ans que j'ai l'honneur de pouvoir faire éditer mes romans par la maison Calmann-Lévy, de faire partie de la *La Société des Auteurs Dramatiques*. Mais cela m'a encore suscité des jalousies de métier [...]. [I]l me semblait qu'il était inutiles [*sic*] que mes [...] collègues exhumassent de gaieté de coeur les cendres de Céleste Mogador pour les faire recomparaître aussi impitoyablement devant l'opinion publique, puisqu'il ne s'agissait, en réalité, que de juger l'oeuvre nouvelle de madame Lionel de Chabrillan. Et je crois qu'ils auraient dû méditer, un peu avant, cette belle pensée qui dit aux travailleurs, aux émigrants, et même aux filles repenties: '*I ask you what you are and not what you were* [...].' Les bravos du public m'ont affirmé ma confiance en la valeur de mon *travail* et m'ont rendu toutes mes espérances pour l'avenir [...].

I have always maintained that *where there's a will, there's a way* [...]. That is all that I can say to oppose that eternal refrain of the taking of [the city of] Mogador. The public has remained cold to all the rehashing about taking off the mask of a woman who has never worn one! It goes to the theatre to *see a play*.

In fact, if anything remains of the dead past of Céleste Mogador – the songs and verses of Nadaud, Murger, Méry, Lachanbaudie, the elogious articles signed by former fanatics of pleasure now become puritans – Madame Lionel de Chabrillan can claim a good many certificates of *literary quality* which have been granted by those masters of art and criticism with names like: Alexandre Dumas père, Jules Janin, Fiorentino, Nestor Roqueplan, de Girardin, Théodore de Banville, de Villemessant, Rousseau, Hostein, Jules Claretie who wrote that if one of my plays, *The American*, which had moved him profoundly, had been signed with a name other than *mine, this play alone would have sufficed to make the author's fortune.*

I've often been told that my big mistake was to insist on bearing the name my husband gave me. But if I had signed my works with the name of Mogador, then the name of Chabrillan would have been brought up. If I had taken a pseudonym, then both my nom de guerre and the family name would have been raised [...]. For twenty years Calmann-Lévy has been publishing me and I have belonged to La Société des auteurs dramatiques. But this continues to evoke jealousy in the trade [...]. [I]t seemed futile for my colleagues to gaily exhume the ashes of Céleste Mogador in order to display them mercilessly before public opinion when in fact it was a matter of judging the new work of Madame Lionel de Chabrillan. And I think they should have contemplated a little earlier this lovely thought which tells workers, emigrants, and even repentant prostitutes: '*I ask you what you are and not what you were* [...].' The bravos of the public have confirmed my confidence in the value of my *work* and have revived all my hopes for the future [...].

Csse Lionel de Chabrillan, 31 August 1885

In the end, when put before that great popular tribunal which is the theatre, Céleste de Chabrillan has been judged worthy. Such is her claim in this open letter of 1885, her last available autobiographical statement. And it is a claim which her final novel, also dating from 1885, will second in the more profound ways that only fiction can.

2 Worlds Apart: Mapping Prostitution and the Demi-monde

Si l'on veut réellement détruire cette puissance des femmes galantes, qui touche à tout, qui commence dans les plus hautes sphères pour finir dans les derniers rangs de la société, le meilleur moyen c'est d'étudier les faits. L'histoire vraie des femmes qui ont vécu de cette vie infernale serait plus éloquente, pour en détourner les jeunes filles, que les idylles attendrissantes ou les contrastes forcés, dont le public parisien s'amuse tour-à-tour à pleurer et à rire.

(*Mémoires de Céleste Mogador* 2: 4)

If one really wishes to destroy this power of loose women, which affects everything and which begins in the highest spheres to finish in the lowest ranks of society, the best method is to study the facts. The true history of women who have lived this infernal life would be more eloquent in deterring girls from it than the moving idylls or forced comparisons which the Parisian public finds alternately amusing to cry or laugh at.

To this day we delight in narratives like Zola's *Nana* and revel in the operatic beauties of Verdi's *La traviata* or Puccini's *La bohème*. We are, to be sure, aware that the reality presented in these stories is a distorted one but remain enthralled by the sumptuous mantle which the music casts over them. However haunting these narratives may be, authentic they are not. In her memoirs, Mogador vehemently insisted on providing authentic depictions of the prostitute because she realized that the straitjacketing of these women into the stereotypical roles they occupied in music and literature was, in fact, tantamount to silencing them as real women.

In order to better understand Mogador's experience as recounted in her *Mémoires*, this chapter will place them in historical context by discussing the policies according to which prostitution in Paris was managed at this time. Prostitution, in turn, is better understood within the encompassing framework of the demi-monde. And because the demi-monde as a construct has always been taken for granted and has not yet received the critical attention it deserves, I propose to begin to close that gap here. This chapter then concludes with a tour of various of the *bals publics* which were springing up all over Paris of the 1840s. These *bals* represent the beginning of an opening up of public spaces to women at a time when the chasm separating the private and the public sphere was unbridgeable.

The rise of urbanization experienced in France and in most of Europe during the nineteenth century and the doubling of Paris's population between 1800 and the 1840s from 500,000 to one million was accompanied by a concomitant increase in prostitution.[1] The social dislocation which was a by-product of industrialization – coupled with abysmally low wages for working women and a near-total absence of social protection for working men, women, and children – gave rise to living conditions in which mere sustenance could be a challenge. If, as the Countess had claimed, a man might occasionally sink to some indignity in order to make ends meet, he was never beyond social recuperation. However, a woman who made ends meet through the occasional recourse to prostitution stood little or no chance of rehabilitation if her activities became known. Moreover, if a woman chanced to become pregnant out of wedlock, the 1803–4 Code Napoléon explicitly forbade paternity claims. Forced to support herself and her offspring, a woman faced a narrow range of choices.

Most of the many outcast women who populate Céleste Mogador's pages have met with some mishap which tipped them over the edge of respectability into social perdition. Thérèse, the prostitute who, at her own peril, housed the fifteen-year-old Céleste, reported having been raped two weeks earlier and had since resigned herself to working as a *fille en carte*, a registered streetwalker. Denise, whom Céleste met in Saint-Lazare prison and who later helped to 'place' Céleste in her first *maison close*, died as a result of childbirth. Her long-time lover had refused to marry her because she was *une fille inscrite*, and in fact, he had just landed a 'dowry' as she was dying.

Then there is the story of Lise Sergent, later to become la reine Pomaré, the Mabille ball's other reigning queen opposite la reine Mogador. Pomaré had come from a respectable family, her father having owned one of the theatres on the boulevard du Temple. She was literate and was also a gifted musician. Then, catastrophe struck. Her father's theatre burned to the ground and she, it turned out, was pregnant by one of his clients. After giving birth to a still-born son, Lise Sergent found no other recourse but to enlist herself on the registers of the Parisian police. She met a disastrous fate of the type much idealized in theatre and in opera. She returned from Nice with an advanced case of tuberculosis. Her protector abandoned her, and Céleste Mogador witnessed the creditors emptying Pomaré's house in the hours preceding her death. Like Balzac's Rastignac of *Le père Goriot*, the lone person in Goriot's funeral cortège, Mogador was the sole mourner to accompany her friend to the grave on 8 December 1846. Queen Pomaré was twenty-one years old.

Within the context of Europe, French science had its own particular philosophy of the sociological function of prostitution. Its policies of containment and regulation were meticulously articulated in Dr Alexandre Parent-Duchâtelet's influential 1836 treatise *De la prostitution dans la ville de Paris*, although the policy of tolerance within a framework of regulation initially dated from the Consulate (1795). Over the course of the next several decades – including both the July Monarchy (1830–48) and intensifying during the Second Empire (1851–70) – the apparently urgent need to isolate and contain 'vice' was translated into increasingly restrictive laws. Containment was far from being a simple moral issue. Since the beginning of the century, syphilis had been on the rise, and by century's end fear and dread of it had evolved into a veritable hysteria.

In 1829, the practice of prostitution was forbidden outside a *maison close*. Women wishing to leave one such house could do so only if they moved on to a second one. (This rule was later relaxed.) In one of the most influential studies of the subject, Alain Corbin reports that in the mid- to late 1840s (when Mogador was practising), the prefect of the Parisian police forbade whores to be seen at windows or doors of their establishments (58).

Both Corbin's and Adler's studies describe an entire economy which revolved around the traffic of women. At its most 'local' – that is, at the level of the brothel itself – prostitution gave all the appearances of being a women's business. The madam managed the commerce, was responsible for keeping accurate records of each 'boarder's' medical visits, and exacted respect and obedience from the women under her tutelage. She was often aided by a *sous-tenancière*, also a woman.

Where the *real* profits were reaped, however, was precisely where the economic superstructure was at its most invisible: namely, at the level of the acquisition and sale of the properties housing the brothel. The commercial worth of a brothel could be enormous, including its inventory of women, its often rich furnishings and acquired clientele, and, above all, the bribes to police to maintain its 'tolerated' status. These properties, as Corbin reports, were only within the reach of the wealthy, who would lease them out for extravagant sums (102). Thus the fortunes of respectable men might well repose, in circuitous and mediated ways, on the trafficked bodies of women.

Within the broader context, a considerable mobility characterized the trade in women, perhaps due to the clientele's continual demands for novelty. Placement bureaus and national networks helped to circulate the supply. Corbin's study reports well-established trade routes connecting Paris and the provinces (64), and in the port cities of Bordeaux and Marseille there were agents specializing in the traffic of creoles, women of colour, and mulattoes (67).

In the medical and administrative views of the period, the prostitute was considered a necessary evil, part of the collective dynamics of desire and its evacuation inherent to city life. Adler cites Dr Saint-Paul as summarizing her civic function thus: 'La prostituée est indispensable à la cité comme la poubelle à la famille' (15) (The prostitute is as indispensable to the city as the garbage can is to the family). The analogy is a telling one for even as the middle-class woman becomes increasingly domesticated (the so-called 'angel of the home'), it is understood that the needs of the male body required being met: elsewhere. This elsewhere – be it the garbage can or the sewer of society, another oft-used analogy – was carefully regulated and administered by the municipality in the assumption – or hope – that vice, syphilis, and the dregs of society could be isolated and contained.

Corbin describes the underlying philosophy of tolerance as a system by which desire was managed, compartmentalized, and then projected and performed in the margins of society with the broader goal of keeping the family intact and respectable women respectable. 'Endiguer, contenir, canaliser les excès d'une manière efficace par l'arbitraire administratif, en dehors de toute intervention judiciaire, tel est le projet réglementariste exposé par Parent-Duchâtelet' (Corbin 35–6) (To block, contain, and channel excesses efficiently through administrative arbitration outside any judiciary intervention: such is the regulatory plan presented by Parent-Duchâtelet). Bearing in mind this urgent need to contain, we can reflect back on the organized tours of the *bal Mabille* with a better understanding of the social stakes involved for 'decent' women in the transgressing of public spaces considered taboo.

Containment of vice thus took place through the designation of tolerated areas of prostitution and the careful management of these urban erogenous zones (to use Berlanstein's term) through police intimidation of women, regular raids, obligatory sanitary measures, punitive incarceration, and forced prison labour directly benefiting the state. As suggested by Delvau's remarks regarding the girls Asia and Europe, a brothel would often propose an ethnic array of women: 'Une quinzaine de filles s'y mélangent dont une Négresse, ornement obligatoire de ces temples d'amour, en compagnie d'une Algérienne, d'une Grecque, d'une Chinoise, d'une Allemande et des Françaises de régions différentes' (Adler 73) (About fifteen women would make up this mix including a Negress, an obligatory ornament of these temples of love, in company of an Algerian woman, a Greek, a Chinese, a German, and French women from various regions). For the client, a visit to the brothel could thus become a form of vicarious tourism.

Municipal regulations insisted on maximum invisibility of these hot spots. The windows of the brothel had to remain draped, the 'boarders' themselves could not go out in the light of day, although they were allowed the occasional Sunday off. Only a number on the house would reveal its function. To render invisible was to isolate: a woman employed in a brothel became a virtual slave. Thérèse of Mogador's *Mémoires* had described her life as a prostitute thus:

> Je ne suis plus une femme, je suis un numéro; je ne suis plus ma volonté, mais le règlement d'une carte.
>
> Si je veux aller tête nue, le règlement me commande de mettre un bonnet. Si je veux sortir le jour, le règlement me le défend […]. Je ne dois jamais me mettre aux fenêtres, et surtout je ne dois jamais sortir avec une honnête femme. (1: 131)

> I am no longer a woman; I am a number; I no longer follow my will, but the rules of a document.
>
> If I want to go bare-headed, the regulations order me to put on a bonnet. If I want to go out during the day, the rules forbid it […]. I can never stand at the windows, and above all, I can never go out with a respectable woman.

As we shall see, one of nineteenth-century France's most persistent and pervasive nightmares was the possibility that the demi-monde just might become confused with *le monde*.

In the provinces, the occupants of the brothels never saw the money they earned, although they were allowed to keep tips (Adler 115). In

Paris, however, notes Adler, 'les filles touchent généralement directe-
ment le prix des passes mais toute l'habileté de la tenancière consiste à
leur faire dépenser leurs gains à l'intérieur de la maison [...]' (Adler
116; see also Corbin 119) (the girls generally keep the money from their
tricks but the Madam's skill consists of making them spend their profits
inside the house). Mogador's account from within confirms the financial nature of the bondage: 'Le grand moyen de gouvernement des
femmes qui dirigent ces sortes de maisons, est le poids de la dette sous
laquelle elles écrasent leurs malheureuses victimes' (*Mémoires* 1: 229)
(The real method of governing used by the women who manage these
kinds of houses is the weight of the debt beneath which they crush their
unfortunate victims). In this strange, closed economy, the *pensionnaires*,
unable to leave the brothel, would nonetheless have to purchase their
wardrobe and all the necessities of life, which the madam conveniently
made available to them – for a price. Indeed, as earlier noted, Céleste
Vénard, not yet Mogador, only escaped by being bought out by a male
admirer. In *La Sapho*, her only novel dealing with prostitution, the
Countess de Chabrillan has one of her characters purchase the freedom
of one of her sister brothel inmates.

In her memoirs, Céleste Mogador honours her promise to furnish the
least salacious account possible. Few grisly details are given, and we do
not know, for instance, if she was trained by an 'essayeur,' a man employed by brothels to initiate the prostitute-to-be into the arcana of lust
which would form the required repertory for jaded clients already well
versed in erotics (Adler 123). Nonetheless, Céleste does give an account
of her multiple, humiliating encounters with one of the 'plus grands lit-
térateurs du siècle' (*Mémoires* 1: 234), 'une ruine prématurée' (1: 233) (one
of the century's greatest writers, a premature ruin) by the age of thirty:
violent, authoritarian and given to excessive absinthe consumption.

Her description is that of a client who is obsessed with degrading and
'taming' her and who returns two or three times daily in the attempt to
force her to drink: 'À toi, maintenant, bois ou je te bats' (*Mémoires* 1: 235)
(Now it's your turn; drink or I'll beat you). Their encounters evolve into
a contest of wills as she repeatedly throws the contents of the glass into
the fire. When she voices to the madam her desire to be spared this
particular client, however, 'on me fit sentir brutalement que je ne
m'appartenais pas' (1: 237) (I was brutally made to understand that I did
not belong to myself). Although Céleste Mogador never goes so far as to
name this customer in writing, he was widely believed to be Alfred de
Musset. And, though she always remained discreet in print, her friend

and confidant in later life, Georges Montorgueil, reveals in his 1909 obituary article of her a clear mutual understanding of the identity of this difficult client:

> Ce fut à cette époque de sa vie qu'elle rencontra Alfred de Musset. L'ivresse du poète, certain soir plus que de coutume cruelle, martyrisa la jeune déchue dans le cabinet du restaurant où il avait l'autorisation d'emmener, pour s'égayer, cette esclave du sérail public. Et, soixante ans plus tard, le souvenir de ce tête-à-tête lui restait encore comme le pire de toute sa jeunesse. (*Chroniques parisiennes*, 2 March, 12–13)

> It was at this period of her life that she encountered Alfred de Musset. The poet's drunkenness, crueller than usual that evening, tortured the young fallen woman. [It was] in a private room of the restaurant where for his pleasure he had been authorized to take this slave of the public harem. And sixty years later, the memory of this tête-à-tête remained with her as the worst of her youth.

It was common knowledge that Musset heavily frequented the demi-monde.[2] In his *Confessions*, Arsène Houssaye, the director of the Comédie française during the Second Empire, who seems to have known everyone in Paris between 1830 and 1870, remarks that the verb 's'absinther' was coined for Musset, who would, indeed, often 's'absenter' due to excessive alcohol consumption (2: 363). And one finds what can only be a pointed and catty allusion to the broad 'range' of Musset's fréquentations in the Goncourt brothers' successful 1853 book, *La lorette*, when they discuss the attractions, for the call girl, of being kept by an elderly man: 'Il apporte à la Lorette de l'or tout neuf [...]. Il a eu, pour la Lorette, des billets le jour où M. de Musset a été reçu de l'Académie' (50) (He brings the Whore new gold [...]. He has procured, for the Whore, tickets for the day M. de Musset was admitted to the Academy). Years after her painful encounters with this client, reports Mogador, she was petrified when he entered a more respectable salon where she was with some literati lest he disclose to the group her registration with the police. But to her great relief, he seemed not to recognize her.

A system which required police registration of all prostitutes as well as periodic mandatory medical examinations clearly needed elaborate and consistent enforcement mechanisms. In Paris, surveillance and punishment were the province of the *police des moeurs*, the vice squad of the police prefecture. Women practising prostitution without being registered (known as 'insoumises') were forcibly registered if caught and obligated to serve time in Saint-Lazare. Women who plied their trade outside the walls of a brothel, the so-called filles en carte like Thérèse, were required to present themselves for the medical examinations, which took place, according to Adler, at the rate of fifty-two per hour (229). Moreover, officers of the squad had particular incentive to arrest girls known as disparues: that is, those who, once registered, then abandoned their public health obligations but were suspected of practising their art anyway. For this type of catch, an agent would receive a bonus.

After her liberation from the rue du Temple brothel, Céleste – now become Mogador – worked for herself and chose not to comply with the regulations. Prostitutional venues in Paris were innumerable. Notwithstanding municipal attempts to isolate prostitution within brothels, the arcades of the Palais Royal were teeming with such life. Remunerated sex flourished even in the most unexpected places. Maupassant's story Les tombales revolves around the venal women – les pierreuses, as they were known – whose professional haunts were cemeteries, a sinister conflation of love and death. And the modern Right Bank shopping districts, the covered arcades, and the newly fashionable boulevards with their famous cafes such as the Café de Paris and Tortoni's were places of particular prostitutional predilection. It was in fact in the celebrated Café de Paris with its myriad private rooms that Mogador got her first taste of the glamourous lifestyle of the aristocracy:

> En sortant du théâtre, nous allions presque toutes les nuits souper au café de Paris […]. Le repas, préparé d'avance, ressemblait à une féerie. Les convives étaient jeunes, riches et élégants. Leurs noms étaient les plus beaux noms de France; mais leur vie était frivole, leurs caractères étaient capricieux et changeants. Ce monde ne ressemblait en rien à celui que j'avais vu pendant que j'étais à l'Hippodrome. (Mémoires 2: 305–6)

> On leaving the theatre in the evenings, we would almost always go sup at the Café de Paris […]. The repast, prepared in advance, was something out of a fairy tale. The guests were young, rich, and elegant. Their names were among the grandest of France; but their life was frivolous; their personalities were capricious and fickle. This monde in no way resembled that which I had seen while I was at the Hippodrome.

To live a life of prostitution outside the regulations was to live the life of a hunted animal, susceptible of being arrested anytime, anywhere.

Cl. B.N.

« ses grandes pattes simiesques et son parler criard et baveux. »
Facéties de M. Mayeux par Traviès

3. Le Cabinet particulier. Traviès. Source: Département d'Estampes et photographie, Bibliothèque nationale de France (AA 79B82875 SNF Traviès)

And even the registered women were forced to comply with so many strict and arbitrary rules that they too were often arrested.[3] 'À Paris,' reports Corbin, 'chaque fille soumise est, en moyenne, arrêtée et détenue plusieurs fois par an. Le Dépôt et la prison de Saint-Lazare, qu'elles ont surnommée leur "campagne," font partie de l'univers quotidien des prostituées inscrites' (158) (In Paris, each *fille soumise* is arrested and detained several times a year on average. The lock-up facility and Saint-Lazare prison, which they nickname their 'country residence,' are part of the daily universe of registered prostitutes). And yet the police requirements were so onerous and the enforcement procedures so humiliating that large numbers of women chose not to conform to the policies.

After her liberation from the brothel, it was this risky life which Mogador chose to lead, always glancing over one shoulder lest she be recognized and incarcerated in Saint-Lazare. 'Je n'avais pu me résigner à retourner à la Préfecture, avec ces femmes qui sont tenues de s'y présenter toutes les quinzaines sous peine d'être punies,' she reports. 'J'étais en contravention: on aurait eu le droit de m'arrêter partout où l'on m'aurait trouvée ... Je ne passais jamais sur les boulevards; le quartier Montmartre étant rempli de femmes, la surveillance y était plus active qu'ailleurs' (*Mémoires* 2: 14) (I could not resign myself to return to the prefecture, with those women who have to present themselves there every fortnight on pain of being punished. I was outside the regulations and could have been arrested anywhere I was found. I never ventured out on the boulevards; the area being filled with women; surveillance was more active there than elsewhere). At one point in their tempestuous love–hate relationship, Lionel gives her a magnificent carriage with the insult: 'une fille comme vous ne peut sortir à pied, la police pourrait l'arrêter; je vais vous faire cadeau d'une voiture' (3: 160) (a whore like you cannot go out on foot: the police might arrest her; I will give you a carriage).

Mogador's memoirs are full of accounts of women running from the law. When Lise Sergent (Queen Pomaré) was in just such trouble, Céleste regrets that she could not come to the aid of her friend, 'car j'étais moi-même sous une surveillance qui me désespérait' (2: 11) (for I myself was under a surveillance, which made me despair). Another young prostitute, Angéline, jumps out of a window and breaks her legs rather than be caught by the police (2: 13). And once at a masked ball, a 'respectable' woman rips off Céleste's mask, revealing the notorious visage of Mogador: 'on vint me prier de passer au bureau de la police' (3: 216) (I was asked to stop by the police station).

Everything about the regulatory system of prostitution conspired to keep registered women inside it. When, for instance, Céleste attempts to open a fashion shop ('je voulais quitter cette servitude des autres' (2: 160) [I wanted to leave this servitude of others]), police agents immediately descend to check her papers: once again she is forced into hiding. In reality, few women ever eluded the long and vigilant reach of the police. Adler estimates the number of escapees to have been in the 5 to 6 per cent range, and of these, most succeeded 'pour cause de vieillesse, d'infirmité ou parce qu'elles deviennent tout simplement à leur tour – tenancières' (140) (because of old age, infirmity, or simply because they in their turn have become madams).[4] One of the only ways to be removed from the infernal register was for a 'protector' to guarantee the woman a permanent income sufficient to live on, and in this case, his credentials and finances were meticulously scrutinized by the authorities (Adler 88). In the end, this is how Mogador's police registration was erased in 1852: the Count de Chabrillan, in anticipation of their marriage, purchased her removal from the rosters of shame. She was one of the lucky few.

Like the *grand monde*, the demi-monde had its clear hierarchy, and the fact of her police registration meant that Mogador occupied one of the lowest rungs. As a registered prostitute, nothing but disdain would await her in her ascent into what she would later term the 'aristocracy' of bohemia. Marguerite Bellanger, one of the mistresses of Emperor Napoleon, takes great pains to measure the social distances within the demi-monde. In her *Confessions de Marguerite Bellanger*, she declares her position at the outset: 'Je n'entreprends pas mon apologie [...] je n'entends pas dire que je fus la plus chaste des femmes, mais entre la prostituée qu'on a voulu faire de moi [...] et la courtisane que j'ai véritablement été, la distance est grande' (3) (I am not seeking to justify myself [...] I'm not claiming I was the most chaste of women, but between the prostitute I've been made out to be [...] and the courtesan which I really was, the distance is great).

Thus, even within the demi-monde, Mogador's trajectory was a remarkable one. Gradually, as her male affiliations become more select (or at least more aristocratic), Mogador would find herself in more refined company. While 'on display' as an equestrian at the Hippodrome, she was also being kept by a Spanish duke. In this context, she ascended into a new social sphere: 'J'écoutais; mon intelligence se développait à ce contact: j'en avais bien besoin, car j'étais tellement ignorante que souvent je m'arrêtais court au milieu d'un mot que je n'osais finir dans la crainte de dire quelque sottise' (*Mémoires* 2: 85) (I listened; my intelligence was developing through this contact: I really needed it because I was so ignorant that I would stop short in the middle of a phrase which I dared not finish for fear of saying something dumb). And, although it is not mentioned in her memoirs, Moser notes that Mogador would 'rise' to be one of two women who frequented a kind of weekly masculine 'salon' presided over by Prince Napoleon at the fashionable Café Voisin (178).

Eventually Mogador began to be assimilated into the upper echelons of the demi-monde, although her entry into those august circles was painful. Invited to accompany a count to a private ball, she notes: 'N'y allait pas, en fait de femmes, qui voulait. On n'invitait que des actrices, des femmes entretenues' (*Mémoires* 2: 247) (Not every woman who wanted to went. Only actresses, kept women were invited). Contempt and ostracism are hardly the exclusive province of respectability: her very presence elicited reactions of outrage from the other women: 'Mogador! une écuyère de l'Hippodrome! une femme qui a dansé dans un bal public!' (2: 248) (Mogador! A rider at the Hippodrome! A woman who dances in public dance halls!). Mogador, humiliated, finds comfort in the explanations of Chouchou, 'moins aristocrate que les autres' (less of an aristocrat than the others), who takes pleasure in reciting the modest origins – laundresses or maids – of each of these women. Adds Céleste: 'Il en est de cette classe comme de l'autre; les prix seuls diffèrent' (2: 247) (This class is the same as the other one; only the prices differ).

In one humorous episode, Mogador recounts a dinner conversation she has with three actresses. She refers to them as 'number 1, 2' and so forth, in her portrait: 'On se donnait des airs de grandes dames,' she notes dryly, 'pour se venger d'avoir mangé des pommes de terre dans sa jeunesse' (3: 273) (They put on airs to avenge themselves for having eaten potatoes in their youth). The conversation could not be more frank and revealing in its details of the lifestyle. The ladies report on their earnings. One requires two thousand francs per month plus presents from just one of her lovers: these women were often kept by several men in an arrangement resembling time-sharing in real estate. A lady confides that she gives birth once a year, while another retorts that unless she took 'measures,' 'j'en aurais sept' (I would have seven). Still new to this caste of the demi-monde, Céleste listens 'looking stupid' (3: 277) while one courtesan recounts how one of her men lent her his wife's diamond buttons to put on a dress. When she replaces the wife's buttons with costume jewellery and keeps the gems for herself, the man dares say nothing, fearing scandal.

By this time, Céleste had been engaged for small roles at the Folies-Dramatiques theatre. A similar scandalized outcry awaited her there, as other actresses rebelled at having to play next to 'une Mogador.' At last, she managed to be invited to a party given by Alice Ozy, noted courtesan and successful actress. It is here that she first glimpsed the enchanting actress Adèle Page:

> Parmi toutes les femmes qui étaient dans ce salon, une me plaisait plus que toutes les autres. Elle était jolie comme les amours, et elle avait l'air fort aimable.
>
> Je la suivais des yeux, je sentis que je l'aimais beaucoup, elle avait un charme irrésistible; c'était la petite Page. Je n'osais lui parler. Ozy refusa de me la présenter. (*Mémoires* 3: 155)

Among all the women in this salon, one pleased me more than all the others. She was as pretty as a cupid, and she seemed very nice.

I watched her; I felt that I liked her very much. She had an irresistible charm. It was the little Page. I did not dare talk to her. Ozy refused to introduce her to me.

It is difficult *not* to read this attraction as a homoerotic one. However, Moser – Mogador's most serious biographer – does everything she can to dispel this possibility, even though she does acknowledge that others qualified Mogador's friendship with Adèle Page as 'particulière.' 'Particulière' was (and still is) a code word for homosexual.

Moser's biography of Mogador contains invaluable information available nowhere else: her study is indispensable because it is based on documents which are now lost. As essential as her account is, however, Moser is dismissive of certain of Céleste Mogador's claims which are, apparently, distasteful to her. Here is another concrete example of a dismissive stance adopted with respect to Mogador's testimony. At the age of fifteen, when her mother was caring for her ill father, Céleste Vénard reports that her stepfather attempted to rape her. As a result of his advances, Céleste had fled, taking refuge in empty buildings while awaiting her mother's return, and so began the incident which would land her in Saint-Lazare prison, where a whole new underworld was revealed to her.

One of the aspects of life in Saint-Lazare according to Céleste was an abundance of same-sex amorous relationships. 'Ce qui faisait le plus de ravages dans cette maison,' reports Céleste of Saint-Lazare in both the

1854 and 1858 editions of the *Mémoires*, 'c'étaient ces affections [aux-quelles je n'ose donner un nom] entre des filles de douze et de quinze ans et des femmes de trente et de quarante ans. Elles parviennent à tromper la surveillance la plus active' (*Mémoires*, 1854 edition, 2: 41–2; bracketed portion purged from 1858 edition, 1: 183) (What caused the greatest ravages in this place were those affections [to which I dare not give a name] between twelve- and fifteen-year-old girls and thirty- and forty-year-old women. They manage to deceive the most active surveillance).

In the 1854 edition, whose publication had been halted, Céleste had gone so far as to depict one such relationship which she herself had entertained with Denise, a woman whose life trajectory would intersect again with hers later as we have already seen: 'C'était un vrai garçon que cette Denise. Elle avait les cheveux coupés et faisait sa raie de côté. [...] Elle me mangeait de caresses. Je m'étais attachée à elle, et au lieu d'éviter les occasions de la voir je les cherchais' (1854 edition, 2: 17–18) (This Denise was a real boy. She had short hair and parted it on the side. [...] She devoured me with caresses. I had become attached to her, and instead of avoiding occasions of seeing her, I sought them out).

In her biography, Moser – who usually takes Céleste at her word – chooses to cast doubt on Mogador's testimony in this particular instance: 'Dans ces tragiques conjonctures,' she muses of Céleste's stay in Saint-Lazare, 'quelle est la part du roman-feuilleton? Quelle est la part de la vérité?' (35) (In this tragic situation, how much is fiction? How much is the truth?). And, referring to the chapter on Denise, she continues: 'La même question se pose pour ce qui va suivre [...]' (35) (The same question can be asked of what follows). Even in the 1858 edition, with its erasure of such code expressions as the 'love that dare not speak its name,' the issue of lesbian relationships is fairly obvious. In this way, censorship of the existence of Mogador's lesbian story operates both institutionally and biographically: to begin with, Céleste was acting on Father Mullois's advice when she deleted 'a certain confession' about herself in preparing the 1854 text for its 1858 publication. Then, some seventy years later, Modagor's first biographer, Moser, calls the veracity of the already watered-down 1858 version into question. Failing to ask herself why Céleste Mogador would have lied about this issue, Moser nonetheless goes on to acknowledge that Céleste Mogador's later friendship with actress Adèle Page 'fut qualifiée de "particulière"' (128) (was considered 'special').

What, then, are the potential implications of this particular instance of censorship? First, it reduces a rich and complex set of life data to a narrow and culturally normative story line. And second, in so doing, it renders the homoerotic readings of at least two of the Countess de Chabrillan's novels less credible and more difficult to support. The question of lesbian relationships will be revisited later in the discussion of the Countess's novels.

To return to the *Mémoires*, however, Mogador never ceased to denounce a system in which men and women indulging in identical behaviours and lifestyles could have such different social roles as a result of these same lifestyles. 'C'est une injustice,' she complains, 'Ce qui porte le nom de la femme entretenue est la sangsue du coeur, l'usurière de l'âme. Les hommes, qui ont créé cette milice de l'enfer, sont fiers de leur ouvrage et mettent ces démons sur un piédestal' (3: 285) (It's an injustice. Those who go by the name of kept woman are leeches of the heart and usurers of the soul. Men, who have created this hellish militia, are proud of their handiwork and put these demons on a pedestal). Rare indeed were Mogador's contemporaries who understood the alleged power of the 'dangerous' demi-mondaine to be part of a systemic disorder. In fact, time after time in her novels, the Countess de Chabrillan insisted on the responsibility of her androcentric culture in the creation and, indeed, maintenance of this 'infernal militia,' as she was wont to call it.

For all her understanding of the fundamentally social underpinnings of prostitution, however, one cannot say that Céleste de Chabrillan possessed a feminist awareness of how women's oppression operated in the society of which she was a part. In this regard, George Sand, Olympe Audouard, and other of the latter's saint-simonian sisters were more far-sighted. This failure of vision might seem surprising until one realizes that social perspective was only available to those who were actually inhabitants of the respectable world: Mogador having no access to that world, how could she have grasped its particular oppressions? Her consciousness of how the system worked was instead forged through repeated acts of personal humiliation.

A final, striking aspect of the *Mémoires de Mogador* is the many illustrations they offer of poor women working together in community. When Céleste and her mother were in Lyons working for the silk weaver, Monsieur G.'s ploy to force his companion Anne-Victoire to capitulate to him was to kidnap Céleste and take her to the brothel where he was staying. But when her mother showed up at the brothel to claim her, she spelled out the real situation: 'Ma mère leur avait en quelques mots expliqué sa position […]. La vérité a une force qui éclate d'elle-même' (1: 33)

(In a few words, my mother explained her situation to them [...]. The truth has a force which bursts out by itself.) Then, when Monsieur G. attempted to beat wife and child, 'toutes les femmes nous firent un rempart de leurs corps' (1: 33) (all the women made a rampart of their bodies for us). The group of women then threatened to beat him up and chased him away.

Thus, if the world of the proletariat was a tough one, affording working women few protections, the *Mémoires* sketch a portrait of considerable solidarity among women who shared similar lots. This kind of community is rarely invoked in the fiction of the period, where women's relations with each other are often presented as jealous and combative. The famous fight in Zola's *L'assommoir* between two women in the laundry (over a man) comes to mind immediately as does a similar scene taking place in a cigar factory in both the novella *Carmen* and Georges Bizet's operatic elaboration of Mérimée's novella.

Céleste Mogador was only one in a vast population of women available for short-term purchase or long-term maintenance in Paris. Throughout the nineteenth century, the city of Paris was the pleasure capital of the Western world, not the least because it featured this remarkable shadow culture – known as the demi-monde – which was readily accessible to men of all stations and nations. So accessible was it, in fact, that in 1881 the Paris police actually published a guidebook in English called 'The Pretty Women of Paris,' wherein, sadly enough, the illustrious Cora Pearl was recommended for her value as a relic.

Many factors contributed to making the demi-monde highly visible at this time. Historian Berlanstein rightly contends that ostentatious mistress-keeping by middle-class males represented an attempt to rival nobiliary prestige by adopting its values. Too, as of 1851, the financial moment was right: the Second Empire, with its large-scale capital investment policies, ushered in – for some, in any case – a period of unparalleled prosperity. The rich and the privileged put their wealth and power on display in a lavish social pageant which featured, among their other acquisitions, extravagantly kept courtesans. Accounts of this aspect of the demi-monde – its notoriety and scandals – are legion. Sensationalism always sells.

But what, in fact, lies beneath the appearances, below the slick surfaces, the gaudy and bawdy layers which form the typical accounts of the bohemian life? So far we have been using the terms *bohème* and demi-monde fairly loosely. This is partly because, even at their most precise, they are indeterminate concepts whose meanings shift constantly according to who is using them, when, and for what purposes. As alternative social spaces, moreover, their definitions directly relate to the notion of the respectable *monde*, itself an unstable concept. Adding to the confusion is the indisputable fact that there is overlap between the two social spaces, both as they are defined today and as they were lived at the time.

The phenomenon known as 'bohemia' began with the idealistic Romantic generation of the 1830s and persisted through numerous iterations well into the twentieth century.[5] Though it has been well studied, it is currently undergoing a welcome critical reappraisal through the lens of gender. For, like the twentieth-century modernist movement, accounts of it are heavily male-centred; indeed, one of bohemia's finest historians, Jerrold Seigel, has little to say about women's participation in this significant movement.

The terms 'bohemia' and 'demi-monde' were both named post facto. Although 'Bohemia' had already been in casual use for two decades, it was not until 1849 through Henry Murger's blockbuster musical play *La vie de bohème* that the word itself crystallized into a construct and began to take on a life of its own. Murger made his name solely thanks to this play, which enjoyed several revivals during the course of the century. Fascination with the notion turned into ossification when Puccini's opera *La bohème* hit the world's stages in the fin de siècle. Our modern concept of the bohemian life – youth striving in poverty to create art (sanitized of its original valence of socio-political resistance) – owes itself to Puccini's representation, constantly performed and re-performed to this very day.

If Murger was a (not-always-willing) inhabitant of bohemia, the women around him – and they included his good friend Mogador and her lover Adèle Page (who, incidentally, was cast as the first Musette in his play) – resided permanently in the demi-monde. But what exactly is this half-world? For all its ubiquity, the demi-monde, as a construct, has always been taken for granted. The term itself was coined in 1855 by another good friend of Mogador, Alexandre Dumas fils. He intended it to designate specifically women who had fallen from a respectable station in life into the arena of purchasable sex.[6] Almost immediately, however, the understanding was broadened to denote simply the universe inhabited by women of easy virtue and particularly those who sold their favours. Because of the date of its coining, the term is most accurately applied in conjunction with the Second Empire, but it is clear that a demi-monde was already emerging in the early 1840s.

In her recent book *Courtesans*, Katie Hickman tries to make the case for the existence of a similar such 'half-world' in England from 1830 to 1880 but defeats herself in trying as she wonders why England had 'no chronicles of "la grande bicherie." Englishmen, I suspect,' she says, replying to her own question, 'did not care to remember their misspent youth with quite the same affection as their Continental brothers were inclined to do' (24). As we have already seen in the reminiscences of Alfred Delvau (one memoirist among hundreds), not only did the French 'brothers' not consider their analogous youth as misspent, they seemed to revel in its retelling – to such a degree that their retrospections practically constitute a genre. In this respect at least, the English Channel is a gulf.

The term appears to be specific to both gender and French culture of this period. As a nebulous space defined solely in terms of social exclusion, it could not produce artists and thinkers, even if many of the latter were its regular visitors. One might best characterize the demi-monde as a space of social repression and a category defined in contradistinction to other social territories: a kind of Hades forever intent on reclaiming its Persephones.

Of course, the functional equivalents of the demi-monde have existed always and everywhere. Indeed, the very definition of social structures and practices as licit and existing within norms automatically implies an extra-normal and an illicit. Nonetheless, the lavish demi-monde as it existed in France between roughly 1840 and 1900 was a unique phenomenon which arose, I contend, as a very specific response to historical circumstances particular to France, circumstances which had their origins in the 1789 Revolution. In a manner completely distinct from other cultures of the same period, the French demi-monde became a structural necessity occasioned by the dominant culture's need to invent and maintain distinctions and social hierarchies at a time when centuries-old values and their attendant distinctions and exclusions had been shattered by revolution.

It is almost impossible to overstate the scope and magnitude of the upheaval wrought by the French Revolution. In the wake of the Revolution and during much of the nineteenth century, France remained politically turbulent because it was faced with the redefinition and renegotiation of virtually all its traditionally held values and institutions. This was hardly a task to be accomplished overnight since all its former norms and hierarchies – legal, political, social, and religious – had been dislocated. Schematically put, the 'work' of the century would consist of nothing short of the complete reconstruction of a viable socio-political order, one which would take into account philosophies emergent from the Revolution. If, over time, the implementation of these Enlightenment philosophies would entail bringing communities together under the equalizing canopy of democracy, new differences and distinctions were also being forged, marking the formation of new systems of rights, privileges, and – equally important – exclusions.

In her recent book *Husbands, Wives, and Lovers*, Patricia Mainardi has demonstrated that one of the central preoccupations of the Gallic cultural imagination between the late eighteenth century and the end of the Restoration (1830) was the subject of marriage. During this period, social values underwent a radical shift, reflecting a new emotional sensibility, an emergent political philosophy underscoring the importance of the individual and citizen, and a new legal configuration of the family. The new body of laws, known as the Napoleonic Code or Civil Code (1803–4), was in fact an amalgamation of pre-existent customary and written legal systems, and ethical concepts issuing from the Enlightenment. It reflected the existence of a public sphere which for some time had been evolving to feature democratic political participation of the citizen/individual as well as the concomitant creation of a private sphere, a social space of domesticity.

The Napoleonic Code did nothing to advance the status of women: on the contrary. In its intention to dismantle the Ancien Régime's hereditary system based on primogeniture, the code now attributed all authority to the paterfamilias. In the new nuclear family, the wife had no legal status, few rights over her own children, and no say in the management of family money – even if she had brought that money to the marriage in the form of a dowry. Nor could she enter into contracts. Her disenfranchisement was total.

It was Article 340 of the code which forbade paternity searches. This article stipulated that a single woman who found herself pregnant had no recourse before the law: she was forced to bear the entire financial burden of raising her child herself. No doubt this provision was conceived to spare philandering husbands the inconvenient consequences of their acts as well as to keep the holy nuclear family hermetic and intact. But the disallowing of paternity searches does have an interesting – and probably unintended – corollary: namely, that a child born of an unfaithful wife was legally part of that family regardless of who had fathered it. And so it is that the spectre of a tainted and counterfeit – but legally legitimate – paternal lineage raises its ugly head. Balzac's short

story 'Gobseck' recounts just this 'nightmare' and how the angry cuckolded husband, the Count de Restaud, 'corrects' this failing in the law
by disinheriting his two youngest children, the products of his wife's
adulterous liaison. Strictly speaking, this is precisely the kind of exclusion prohibited by Article 340, but in his fiction, Balzac often found
ways to counter laws which offended his ideological commitments.[7]

Since paternity searches were now illegal, the only real means of guaranteeing the purity of the paternal line was by enforcing wifely virtue.
So, although in Catholic France fidelity of the female spouse had of course
always been a value, it became far more essential under the code since a
black lamb could no longer be ostracized from the flock. Illegitimacy was
thus poised to insinuate itself into the very bosom of the family, and this
with the sanction of the law! The stakes involved in ensuring a female
spouse's virtue suddenly skyrocketed. This fact was not lost on law-
makers of the time. In a paper presented to the Corps législatif in 1810,
Louis Joseph Faure notes that adultery is a far greater crime when committed by the wife 'because it leads to greater consequences and could
bring a child into a legitimate family who is not in any way the offspring
of the man who is its legal father' (cited in Mainardi, 16).

Thus, in the case of the wife, the less she was exposed to public per-
usal, the better, although in France, sequestration of women was hardly
an option, given the well-established tradition of salon culture associated with the feminine dating back to medieval *amour courtois*. It is
worth interjecting that two other cultures in which courtesans played
major public roles – sixteenth-century Venice and classical Athens –
were cultures which practised extreme claustration of 'respectable'
women. For Venice, it was a matter of family (that is, masculine) honour.[8] In Athens, citizen/progeny could only issue from the union of an
Athenian citizen and his respectable Athenian wife, who was also required to be of impeccable parentage. Courtesans, barbarians (that is,
any non-Athenian), and slaves could not mother citizens.[9] For reputable women, chastity was thus an affair of the state.

Despite the obvious historical differences between these cultures,
all three seem to couple an obsession with a patriarchal form of repro-
ductive legitimacy requiring wifely fidelity on the one hand, with a
flourishing demi-monde on the other. Whether or not it was due to an
established tradition of libertinage, French men had long enjoyed sexual freedom across a broad range of classes while remaining within the
parameters of social acceptability.[10] The Civil Code's new provision on
paternity searches whose effect was to render wifely fidelity primordial

to legitimacy within the family required a corollary shift in male sexual behaviour to the extent that respectably married wives were, more than ever, off limits. The 'overflow' space – that is, the world of erotic entertainment, already available in any case – took on greater prominence because it had been rendered more necessary. In this sense, then, it is possible to say that the *extreme* preoccupation with legitimacy which emerged in part as a result of the new paternity laws actually resulted in the creation of a more capacious demi-monde.

What is being suggested here is that the rise of the demi-monde in France at this particular historical juncture had everything to do with the seismic shift effected by the instituting of the Napoleonic Code and with the sense of urgency which the new polity brought to questions of familial and political legitimacy. What this in turn implies is that the feminine demi-monde and the highly contained world of female respectability are two sides of the same coin.

The interdependence of two social worlds supposedly miles apart is strikingly echoed in literature. To take one example, Léo, the young protagonist of Huysmans's novel *Marthe*, admits that it is precisely the demi-mondaine's vice which legitimizes the respectable woman. Referring to his erstwhile mistress, he declares: 'quant à Marthe [...] je lui pardonne toutes ses vilenies, toutes ses traîtrises; les filles ont cela de bon qu'elles font aimer celles qui ne leur ressemblent pas; *elles servent de repoussoir à l'honnêteté*' (166, emphasis added) (as for Marthe [...] I forgive her all her dirty deeds, all her betrayals; what is good about sluts is that they make one love those who do not resemble them; *they serve as foils to decency*).

Clearly, then, the close connection of feminine respectability to disrepute was recognized. Since the stakes in keeping these worlds apart amounted to nothing short of guaranteeing genealogical legitimacy, respectable women were relegated to the private sphere: the public domain was the realm of women who, like Mogador, 'knew everyone' – meaning, really, 'knew every man.' It was only at considerable peril to her reputation that any woman might appear in a space considered public.

This segregation remained the rule throughout the nineteenth century. Martin-Fugier reports that at a grand private charity ball given in 1830, *le bal des indigents*, even the likes of fashion boutique owners were invited, whereas the great actress Mademoiselle Mars was not: 'une comédienne reste une femme *publique* et on ne la reçoit pas dans une manifestation que l'on veut considerer comme *privée*' (19–20) (an actress remains a *public* woman and she is not received at an event which is deemed *private*). Martin-Fugier goes on to report the surprise which the Duchesse de Maille felt about this: 'ce qui me parut le plus singulier, ce furent les hommes qui s'y opposèrent' (19–20) (what seemed to me the most odd was [that it was] the men who were opposed to it). The fact that this exclusion arose from masculine ranks is less astonishing when one reflects that it was perhaps more in men's best interests to keep the private segregated from the public. After all, they freely attended Mademoiselle Mars's lavish parties at her splendid mansion, so it was hardly a preoccupation with virtue which was at the origin of their outrage.

And when, some forty years later, Paris Opera Director Halanzier-Dufrenoy decided to admit women to the orchestra section of the opera house, it caused a furore (Lacombe 41). Any woman associated with the public sphere, whether that be as a result of publication, artistic renown, or political visibility – with rare exceptions – risked being branded as a public woman, that is to say, a whore. (Given this ideological backdrop, one can only admire George Sand the more as a woman who successfully negotiated the public/private divide.) This absolute conflation of 'public,' 'woman,' and promiscuity is made explicit in the *Grande Larousse du XIXe siècle*'s definition of 'public':

[D]u Latin publicus, pour populaire, poplus – peuple, qui appartient a l'universalité des citoyens, qui concerne tout le peuple: autorité publique, morale publique, chose publique, services publics, trésor public, ministère public, charges publiques, droit public, femme publique. [...] Femme publique, fille publique, femme qui fait un métier de la prostitution, ex; 'Il vous faut cent mille femmes publiques pour abriter la vertu des femmes honnêtes.' E. Barrault.

[F]rom the Latin, publicus, for 'of the people,' poplus – people, that which belongs to the universality of citizens, which concerns all the people: public authority, public morality, public entity, public services, public treasury, public ministry, public taxes, public law, public woman. [...] Public woman, public prostitute, woman whose trade is prostitution, ex: 'You need one hundred thousand public women to shelter the virtue of respectable women.' E. Barrault.

Not only does the most authoritative dictionary of the period proclaim the direct linkage of respectability to disrepute, but the necessary pool of demi-mondaines must be truly vast if womanly virtue is to be protected! Two spheres which might seem worlds apart – the public and private – cleave together as one. Small wonder, then, that the level of anxiety associated with any possible permeability of the two worlds was so high.

However, the more visible and commodious the social netherworld became, the greater the fear it inspired among the denizens of respectability. According to most accounts, police efforts to contain prostitution, however diligently pursued and financially rewarded, resulted largely in failure. Public women continued to flood the cityscape. Furthermore, the upper castes of the demi-monde were essentially untouchable because often they enjoyed the patronage of important men and were thus unlikely to be hounded by the police.

As the century progressed, fear surrounding the figure of the venal woman developed into real paranoia as syphilis continued its ravages unchecked and new (erroneous) medical theories held that the disease could be passed on down the generations. What indeed could be scarier? The dread of the venal woman was founded in undeniably legitimate and pressing public health concerns. And it did not help that there were no effective treatments for syphilis and that the one most often used – mercury – was itself often fatal.[11]

Still, medical epidemiology of the time coincided strikingly with social topography. Notes Jill Harsin in *Policing Prostitution in Nineteenth-Century Paris*: 'The virtual hysteria that surrounded clandestinity [of prostitutes] and venereal disease cast suspicion on working-class women in general, since contemporaries seemed willing to believe that all those who were not *soumise* [had not submitted to the regulations] must be *insoumise*' (279). The connection between public sanitation and contamination was easily reformulated in the bourgeois mind as well as in health policy as a contagion among social classes. In this respect as well, the demi-monde was a political category, a space promoting social contagion.

If the dread of illegitimacy within the family haunted the male imagination in this period so crucial in the cementing of the nuclear family, the spectre of class illegitimacy and hybridity, as a fear, was not far behind. Whereas in the Ancien Régime, contends Berlanstein in his cultural history of actresses, thespians qua public women could share the same space as women of the *monde*, this ceased to be the case in the nineteenth century (86). Simply put, the rigidity of class hierarchy previous to the Revolution was so great that even in close proximity there was no danger of a confusion of worlds. The distinctions were absolute. So it is not coincidental that extreme preoccupation with the public woman goes hand in hand with the beginnings of class mobility and the creation of a private sphere encompassing respectable women. The new *Tout-Paris* referred to by Martin-Fugier as a melding of notables, artists, some aristocrats, and other prominent persons had everything to fear from public women – and even more from a demi-monde already frequented by a widely circulating male population. Never was the perceived need to police social borders and the concern to maintain distinctions between private and public greater. This, then, is the juncture at which the figure of the prostitute came to haunt the collective imagination, for she represented contamination in all its forms. The alarm occasioned by these women of dubious origins who might be able to pass for respectable is repeated like a refrain throughout the literature of the period.

One of the spaces of potential social contamination was precisely the public dance hall of the type which had rendered Mogador illustrious. The role of the *bal public* as a place of negotiation between public and private has not been adequately recognized. These venues functioned as liminal spaces given over entirely to the pursuit of physical and social pleasure, unlike the theatre, which might make intellectual demands of its audience. Because of the unabashedly hedonistic nature of this type of entertainment (and no doubt, the mixing of classes), a police agent was always present to uphold the standards of public decency.[12] Furthermore, the existence of these dance halls was not without its social justification since one-eighth of their proceeds were dedicated to aid of the poor (Rozier 191).

The earliest *bals publics* such as the Ranelagh and the Grande Chaumière in fact date back to the late eighteenth century, but it was in the 1840s that this new form of public entertainment gained its real popularity with numbers of dance halls opening during that decade. Those establishments well known to us today through Toulouse-Lautrec paintings – le Moulin rouge and le Moulin de la Galette – were only two of the many which graced Paris's cityscape, and they were latecomers.[13]

Every quartier had its *bal*, and each *bal* catered to a different public. Some even attracted a different clientele according to the day of the week. For instance, on Sundays the Château des fleurs dance hall became a place for family entertainment: 'un bal où la famille distinguée ne craint pas d'aller se délasser [...]. On comprend que ces dames se contentent de se promener ou de s'asseoir, et qu'elles ne danseraient sous aucun prétexte' (Rozier 37) (a dance hall where the distinguished family can go to relax without fear [...]. One understands that the ladies will be content to stroll about or sit, and that under no circumstances would they dance). Under no circumstances, thus, would 'ces dames' – decent middle-class women – make a public spectacle of themselves by dancing.

Other *bals* were less tame, however. Numerous of these establishments were located within Paris itself: the young Eugène de Rastignac of Balzac's *Père Goriot* was given to frequenting le Prado in the Cité and the *bals* near the student district of the Odéon (73). The very low-class 'filles à soldats' (soldiers' whores) depicted in Goncourt's *La fille Elisa* had made their debuts as dancers at the Prado. Mogador's trajectory could have been the same as theirs, if she had not had luck and talent on her side. Most *bals* were situated just outside the customs walls which encircled the city and where alcoholic beverages were far cheaper. The Montmartre area in particular featured a heavy concentration of these pleasure palaces: two of the most (in)famous were l'Ermitage and l'Élysée-Montmartre. The latter featured gardens landscaped with small rivers, groves of trees, and even a shooting gallery. Writes Maurice Artus, a latter-day chronicler of the Paris *bal* scene: 'Céleste Mogador, la future comtesse Lionel de Chabrillan […] ne dédaignait pas l'été, lorsque les grands bals d'hiver avaient fermé leurs portes, de venir, sous les ombres de l'Élysée, émerveiller les habitués en dansant la Polka' (11) (Céleste Mogador, the future Countess Lionel de Chabrillan […] did not feel it beneath her to amaze the regulars by dancing the polka in the summertime here, in the shade, when the big winter dance halls had closed their doors).

Across the Seine, on the south side of town stood la Closerie des lilas (formerly le Bullier) and la Grande Chaumière. The latter venue drew largely from the student and *grisette* population as Flaubert certainly knew, for it was there that Emma Bovary's second lover, Léon, had completed his 'education' in the company of *grisettes*. As a younger man, he had been timid with Emma, but when he returns to her town, he is versed in the art of seduction. And seduce her he does. Then there was l'Astic, which attracted artists and female models, often Jewish according to Delvau (24–5) and the bal du Mont-Blanc, which, contrary to the elevation its name suggests, specialized in chambermaids and cooks.

Still, it is the bal Mabille which is most often described in the literature on the subject, perhaps because it was the harbinger of modernity both from the technological point of view and for the advertisement posters its owners used to considerable advantage. Situated on the Right Bank on what is now the avenue Montaigne, it must have been a

LE BAL VALENTINO.

Ainsi dénommé par ce qu'il est situé rue St Honoré dans une salle construite par
Mr Chabrant.

Croquis d'expression, pris au moment où Mogador, prononcez Mogad, se livre à un balancé
plein de caractère vis à vis d'un danseur qui ne manque pas d'élévation.

4. Le bal Valentino. Source: Département d'Estampes et photographie, Bibliothèque nationale de France (80B89573, probable date 1844). [Translation: 'Thus
named because it is situated on the rue St Honoré in a ballroom constructed by
Mr Chabrant. Expressive sketch drawn as Mogador – pronounced Mogad –
executes a step full of character facing a dancer not lacking in elevation.']

breathtakingly magical place. In the 1840s, the old oil lamps were replaced by some three thousand gas lights, which sparkled in the gardens. Multicoloured lanterns swayed in the summer breeze accompanied by one of the best dance orchestras in town. This is the *bal* which ladies of *le monde* had visited, outfitted as if they were on a caravan in the Sahara and protected from the natives by male guides. This is the *bal* which drew scores of foreign men – English, Russian, and American. It was even said that here a 'Mohamedan' took leave of his senses at the mere sight of so many beautiful (and available) women (Rozier 33)!

If the feminine constituency of the bal Mabille were women of easy virtue who required remuneration, the male public could come from any social strata, although in practice the entrance fee excluded the poor. It was rumoured that Louis-Philippe's sons, the Dukes d'Aumale and de Montpensier, were among those who enjoyed this pleasure garden: one of the salient features of the demi-monde is that while its women inhabitants were always excluded from other sectors of society, its male visitors could circulate freely in both worlds, although doubtless the male elite were careful of their reputations when visiting a public dance hall.

With all these dance facilities available, what did one dance? Since the late eighteenth century, dancing was shifting away from the stylized ritual promenades performed collectively toward more spontaneous dancing performed in couples, an evolution analogous to the movement away from the highly codified socio-political behaviours of the Ancien Régime toward a more individualistic social persona emergent with the Revolution and made manifest in Romanticism's cult of the individual.

The political parallels were not lost on the various observers of *bal* culture. One more left-leaning commentator has nothing but praise for the bal Mabille for the various 'liberties' it afforded:

Ce bal me plaît encore, et fait honte à la société bourgeoise [...]. On est libre à Mabille, à la Chaumière [...]. Là, chacun danse comme il l'entend: il peut marcher, comme dans le grand monde, il peut aussi tricoter des entrechats et faire la roue dans les solos de pastourelle; les dames sont libres de boire et de fumer.

Tout cela, direz-vous, c'est de l'orgie. La liberté des bals publics touche à la licence orgiaque, je l'avoue. (*Paris dansant* 10)

This dance hall pleases me as well, and it puts bourgeois society to shame[...]. One is free at Mabille, at the Chaumière [...]. There everyone dances as he wishes: he can walk, as in high society; he can cut a caper and strut about in the pastourelle solos; the ladies are free to drink and smoke.

All that, you'll say, is an orgy. The freedom of the public dance halls borders on orgiastic licentiousness, I admit.

Our anonymous, progressive author implies that rhythm varies according to class, with the upper classes still stuck in sedate promenades. Nonetheless, the waltz, introduced after 1815 to a scandalized Paris society, had proven popular across the classes. If it was possible to hear such murmurings as 'she has her virginity minus the waltz,' the dance was soon adopted, and one imagines the many public and private dance parties swaying and tilting to the tune of Chopin's waltzes.

The next dance to cause a furore was the polka, an eastern European import. It was Mogador's skill at dancing the polka that earned her celebrity at the bal Mabille in 1844 and Paris looked forward in anticipation to her exploits the following summer. The 21 May 1845 issue of the *Corsaire-Satan* newspaper announced: 'Le jardin Mabille va être témoin, cette année, d'une lutte homérique entre les célébrités de la polka [...] Mlle Céleste Mogador, Mlle Maria [...] se livrent déjà une bataille acharnée' (The Mabille Garden will be witness this year to a Homeric struggle among the celebrities of polka [...] Mlle Céleste Mogador, Mlle Maria [...] are already engaged in relentless battle).

So adept was Mogador at this new dance that composer Jacques Offenbach would even compose a 'Chabrillan Polka' in her honour.[14] But polka disease had in fact contaminated all of Paris, not only the demi-monde. Martin-Fugier reports that doctors 'soignèrent une épidemie de ce "polka morbus," enflure des pieds et ligaments douloureux' (132) (treated an epidemic of this 'polka morbus,' swelling of the feet and painful ligaments). For even if the women of respectable society and their fallen sisters were not kicking up their heels in the same places, in some cases, at least, they were performing the same dances.

Still, as a general rule, even if the women of the demi-monde were looking more and more like ladies of high society, their paths would rarely cross – unless they chanced to attend the bal de l'Opéra. Since 1716, the Opéra had been authorized by the state to hold public masked balls as fundraisers because it received lower royal subsidies than the Comédie française (Hemmings 20). These masked balls were very lucrative and they continued throughout most of the nineteenth century (20).

In fact, 'masked' ball is something of a misnomer since the only persons to wear masks were the ladies. Except for the Carnival season, it was actually illegal for men to wear masks (Benjamin, *The Arcades Project* 492–3). If disguise served to protect the identity and reputation of respectable women, by the same token it allowed for the infiltration of undesirables. Whether or not social transgressions occurred there with regularity, the bal de l'Opéra, because of its unique status, served as a focal point for the expression of fear and even paranoia revolving around the potential incursion of the *monde* by the demi-monde. It is no accident that in two of the novels we shall explore in the next chapter, Balzac's *Splendeurs et misères des courtisanes* and Sand's *Isidora*, the significant encounters take place at the bal de l'Opéra.

3 Fictions of Prostitution

This chapter will demonstrate the extent to which the persona of the prostitute and the institutions defining and confining her stand at the heart of the literary imagination of post-Revolutionary France. Whether it be as the structural foil to feminine respectability, as the quintessence of the Body feminine in contrast to the Mind consistently coded as masculine or, finally, as the incarnation of the dangers of cross-class contamination, the prostitute anchors several binary systems which constitute the ideological underpinnings of the new order. Small wonder, then, that the cultural production of the period between 1840 and 1900 should be obsessed with her.

The high level of angst surrounding the figure of the prostitute would find expression in myriad ways by individual authors. The discussion which follows constitutes a review of nineteenth-century French fiction involving the demi-monde from the 1840s. While this thematic summary is indebted to Peter Brooks's *Reading for the Plot* and Bernheimer's *Figures of Ill-Repute*, both of which stand as classics on the topic,[1] the ultimate goal here is to demonstrate what Céleste de Chabrillan – the former Mogador – was up against when she decided to embark on her own writing itinerary.

During the nineteenth century, depictions of the prostitute in literature ranged from sordid to sympathetic; from hard-hearted to generous; conniving to innocent; inherently vicious to societally deformed; from desiccated hags haunting deserted cityscapes to plump and succulent young women primping in moist, opulent boudoirs; from the peripatetic to the carriage-borne; from unstoppable and omnivorous to the devoured; from all-consuming to consumed by all including consumption. In short, the venal woman was represented as a being who was protean to a degree which was alarming to her contemporaries, and it was this mutability along with the sheer numbers of her 'depraved' cohort of demi-mondaines which demanded taming through naming.

Accordingly a whole nomenclature was invented as part of the collective cultural project to neutralize the danger posed by women in the sex market. First, there was the *grisette*. The *grisette* was not greedy and sometimes even managed to hold on to her virtue in the face of poverty. Usually a hardworking seamstress or embroiderer who enjoyed a good time, she might accept modest remuneration for favours in order to make ends meet. Depictions of her occur in Murger's *Scènes de la vie de bohème*, Musset's *Mimi Pinson*, and Mérimée's *Arsène Guillot*. A heavily idealized figure, this pretty, light-hearted lady corresponded to a Romantic sensibility and she chiefly graced works written prior to 1848.[2] She was also, not coincidentally, a woman who knew her place and who would not seek to rise above her station. Perhaps this is what best explains why representations of her 'type' tended to be sympathetic.

As the mood of romantic idealism of the century's earlier decades began to darken into cynicism in the face of the many ills engendered by urban industrialization, and the 'bourgeois' monarchy of Louis Philippe – the king who played the stock market – moved into a later phase, there is a remarkable upsurge in writing about the venal woman. Around 1840, a new breed known as the *lorette* began to replace the *grisette* both in literature and in the many pseudo-savant tracts devoted to women who market their charms. Whereas the *grisette* tended to fraternize with the students of the Latin Quarter, the *lorette* preferred the Right Bank, where the nascent banking industry and stock market were established, and where the newly fashionable boulevards and famous restaurants attracted dandies and men of influence, indolence, and money.

A hardened professional working the boulevards and arcades of Paris, the *lorette* was depicted as lazy and given to sensual excess, often to the point of depravity. As a shrewd businesswoman, never did she give it away. At her most dangerous (so went the myth), the *lorette* could strip a man of his wealth, divert him away from legitimate marriage, and move on to the next prey, leaving behind an abject wreck of masculinity and moral and financial ruin. *Lorettes* people the literature of realism, a mid-century trend which claims to capture the 'real' (as compared to Romanticism's ideal), rendering life in all its true grittiness. As of 1840, then, and well into the 1850s, the figure of the *lorette*

5. Man writing at a desk with a woman looking over his shoulder. Source: Gavarni, 'Les lorettes'; author's private collection [translation: 'Paris, 26 October 1841. On next January first, I shall pay to the order of Mademoiselle Beaupertuis the sum of three hundred two francs and seventy-five centimes, in exchange for … (what? Affection? Tender interest? Devotion?)' 'Don't be silly!' 'Merchandise.']

became the object of obsessive examination in novels, plays, and in the many tracts or 'physiologies' so popular in this period. These women were analysed, classified, and taxonomized not only by the entire panoply of the period's now-canonical writers but also by many more who have not left a permanent mark on literary history.

With the 1840s and the 1850s began a regular and frequent production of essays devoted to the prostitute across the full spectrum of her incarnations: from brothel women, to streetwalkers, to kept women, extending to theatre women (as opposed to actresses) and on up the hierarchy. Some examples of these learned tracts include *Physiologie de la lorette* (Alhoy, 1841), *Filles, lorettes et courtisanes* (Dumas, 1843), and *La lorette* (Goncourt brothers, 1853), which sold out in one week. Dumas fils's famous *La dame aux camélias* appeared first in novel form in 1848 and was redesigned for a highly successful theatre run in 1852. And few works were as successful as Murger's 1849 *Scènes de la vie de bohème*.

There was also an abundance of fiction which, although not necessarily explicitly devoted to the topic, nonetheless heavily featured prostitution or the demi-monde. Balzac's magnificent *Splendeurs et misères des courtisanes* (1838–47) remains, in this reader's eyes at least, *the* masterpiece on the subject.

Perhaps the most fascinating work, however, from a social standpoint, was Eugène Sue's 'blockbuster' novel, serialized in daily episodes from 1842 to 1843, entitled *Les mystères de Paris*. From men of state right 'down' to chambermaids, every Parisian devoured the daily instalment of this novel. Théophile Gautier, poet and contributor to all the major literary movements of his time, remembers the extraordinary appeal of the novel:

> Tout le monde a dévoré *Les mystères de Paris*, même les gens qui ne savent pas lire: ceux-là se les font réciter par quelque portier érudit et de bonne volonté [...]. Toute la France s'est occupée pendant plus d'un an des aventures du prince Rodolphe, avant de s'occuper de ses propres affaires. Des malades ont attendu pour mourir la fin des *Mystères de Paris*; le magique 'suite à demain' les entraînaient de jour en jour, et la mort comprenait qu'ils ne seraient pas tranquilles dans l'autre monde s'ils ne connaissaient le dénouement de cette bizarre épopée.[3]

> Everyone devoured *Les mystères de Paris*, even people who did not know how to read. The latter have some erudite and accommodating porter read it to them [...]. For over a year, all France occupied itself with the adventures

of Prince Rodolphe before taking care of its own business. Patients waited
for the end of *Les mystères de Paris* to die; the magical 'to be continued tomor-
row' dragged them along day by day, and death understood that they would
not rest tranquil in the other world if they did not know the end of this bizarre epic.

The novel's cast of characters features a *grisette* who holds on to her
virtue; various hardened criminals and evildoers from the lowest to the
highest classes of society; a prince disguised as a commoner who an-
onymously rights wrongs and punishes the truly wicked; hapless and
vulnerable widows and orphans; unhappy husbands; and – one of the
novel's central characters – Fleur-de-Marie, a fallen woman and prostitute who renounces her vile profession to embrace righteousness.

Rehabilitation and punishment: such is the overarching moral scaf-
folding of this seemingly never-ending narrative. The universe constructed through the characters as they move through what is at times
a gothic and lugubrious Paris is one of terrible symmetries. There is
no place for the arbitrary or the ambiguous in this world built upon
an ethical structure limited to two valences: good and evil. The world
of melodrama cannot accommodate the figure of the repentant whore.
The central character Fleur-de-Marie – she of angelic face and ser-
aphic voice – has been rescued from the very heartland of evil, la
Cité. Because her profession is too unspeakable to describe, allusions
to it are spare and sparse, to say the least. Nonetheless, in spite of this
relative silence, and even once firmly on the path to rehabilitation,
she is weighed down with a remorse and shame which do not even
need to be spoken, so thoroughly has she internalized them. She is
one of the many rehabilitated loose women whose presence remained,
when all is said and done, intolerable to respectable society. Her
death is a necessity.

Around 1853 – that is, two years after Napoleon III had seized power
and the short-lived Second Republic was dissolved – the writings surrounding prostitution seem to taper off, temporarily at least. This is an
odd phenomenon given the Second Empire's notoriously public pursuit of pleasure, supported by those at the highest levels of power and
financed by new fortunes built through speculation on the railroads, on
colonial industries, and, in one ill-fated case, the failed construction of
the Panama Canal. Indeed, the Second Empire ushered in a veritable
reign of the courtesan. Never had so many notorious women been so
lavishly – and publicly – kept.

6. Le Guide de la Cocotte. Source: Département d'Estampes et Photographie, Bibliothèque nationale de France (Oa22 M141241)

As of the 1870s, literary interest in the subject seems to have picked up again. By now the intriguing subject of the whore has been appropriated by the naturalist school. The new literary trend is to create a prostitute and examine her 'scientifically' through a fictional trajectory allegedly determined by her genetic heritage and class provenance. Huysmans's *Marthe* and Edmond de Goncourt's *La fille Elisa* must be two of the most depressing stories on the subject. At least the earlier literature had treated the reader/spectator to a vision of whorely happiness or wealth – however brief or undeserved – before the final plunge into the circle of hell reserved for her ilk. Huysmans and Goncourt begin with women or girls of modest origin and troubling predispositions: life is all downhill from there. Rarely do these women meet anything other than a tragic fate.

Things have completely changed by 1904. In *La maison Philibert*, Jean Lorrain displays the *maison close* – even the comfy provincial bordellos which Maupassant loved to depict – as an outdated institution. The action is now on the streets, increasingly controlled by pimps. Furthermore, prostitution is now functioning within an abolitionist context.[4] Though the actual system of tolerance would not be dismantled until 1946 thanks to the militant advocacy of ex-prostitute Marthe Richard, it is clear that by the turn of the century, conditions have radically altered, and the literature on the subject reflects that.

As previously seen, one of the century's major concerns was the contamination of *le monde* by elements of the demi-monde. Time and again, fiction of the period visits the interrelationship of these two using linkages which are articulated in the stylistic register, on the level of content, or, most often, both. One stylistic strategy exploited by both Flaubert in *The Sentimental Education* (1869) and Zola in *Nana* (1880) is the simple juxtaposition in successive chapters of bourgeois salon scenes with bohemian gatherings. Often, the male participants remain the same: only the milieu changes.

This narrative tactic can work in at least two ways. By insisting upon the similarities of dress, furniture, and wealth of the two the insinuation is that they are, at heart, indistinguishable: here it is the collapse of social difference which is being stressed. If the twinning of salon scenes displays, instead, the difference between the world of social respectability as opposed to the orgiastic events of, say, a demi-mondain dinner (where the hostess may stage herself as dessert, uncovered in nude repose on a silver platter), what is being evoked is the hypocrisy of a society in which the same men frequent both worlds. In both scenarios, however, the conflation of class and values occurring through these fictional juxtapositions is meant to be read as a symptom of societal dysfunction.

In *The Sentimental Education*, the rapprochement of the two worlds takes place through women characters. Rosanette is a woman kept, at different times, and occasionally (it is hinted) at the same time, by members of the same circle of men. In fact, as Evelyn Woestelandt has pointed out, this young woman, a former worker in the textile industry like so many of her sisters, is the one person 'qui a connu tout le monde masculin du roman' (123) (who knew the novel's entire masculine world). She 'sert aussi à l'établissement de relations entre tous ces hommes, qu'elles soient de rivalité ou de complicité' (123) (also serves to establish relationships among all these men, whether these be relationships of rivalry or complicity).

Her narrative function, therefore, is to promote male bonding: in this respect, she is a mere vehicle for the highly important activity of the consolidation of male power. But Rosanette is more than a simple catalyst: she is one of the few venal women in the literature to succeed in integrating herself into respectable society (through marriage) and to survive the narrative's ending. Most of the literature about prostitution ends by killing off the harlot. The methods of dispatch vary. In the case of Nana, for example, she remained rotten to the core, and in consequence her beautiful body is made to putrefy before the reader's very eyes into an amorphous mass of seething pustules, a death commensurate with her life and a sneak, if more dire, preview of Dorian Gray's 'transfiguration.'

Many, however, are the wanton women who, like Sue's Fleur-de-Marie, at last espouse virtue but meet nonetheless a tragic – if exemplary – death. For these redeemed prostitutes, death is not as gruelling as Nana's. Their numbers include Balzac's Esther of *Splendeur et misères* and Marguerite of the *Lady of the Camellias* (in its play version), a whore with a heart of gold and a social conscience.[5] And let us not forget the coughing opera *grisette* Mimi, who, amazingly, belts out her swan song, bringing Puccini's *La bohème* to its bathetic close.

In short, for these women who have come to see the light, it is as if true redemption can only be achieved in death. Their souls may indeed have been purified, but the body retains its stigma. Yet it is essential in this type of literature that the reader or viewer feel that the newly purified lives of these deserving women *can*, in fact, begin anew, that their sordid pasts have been put behind them, and that a rosy horizon might rise up to greet them. Within this framework of expectation, how much greater the tragic irony, how terrible the sting when these worthy women perish at the very dawn of their new existence! In a word, all the narrative paths *seem* to point to hope for the repentant Magdalene character.

And yet the sheer numbers of the rehabilitated-but-alas-deceased should give us pause for thought. For the death which is made to feel to the reader like a catastrophic mistake, a fluke of fortune, a mischance, when replayed so many times, should be understood, at some level, as really an inevitability. If it is an affront to human compassion, to the then prevailing Christian value of forgiveness, and to simple logic to deny the truly repentant access to normal life, we can only surmise that the veritable cemetery of Magdalenes have died a death by ideology. Here it may be useful to invoke the model of the public versus the private sphere according to which the feminine virtue characteristic of the private *itself depends* on the existence of a world of non-virtue (the demimonde). The prospect that a demi-mondaine, redeemed though she might be, might slip into the ranks of bourgeois (virtuous) respectability threatens to undermine the stability of an entire model based on upholding this distinction.

The nightmare of the intermingling of *mondes* is a central theme running through all of Balzac's *Human Comedy*. And nowhere does this intermingling coupled with prostitution find more effective expression than in *Splendeurs et misères des courtisanes*. The novel opens in 1824 on the notorious Opera Ball, notorious, it will be recalled, because it is the only public *bal* in Paris in which the wearing of masks is legally permitted. The anonymity thus afforded makes this particular dance hall an ideal arena for intrigue, amorous or political: a space where class distinctions become invisible, and where women of the *monde* and the demimonde mix freely.

What this means, of course, is that vice can circulate without being recognized for what it is. It is hardly accidental that this is the equivocal scene with which Balzac opens his *Splendeurs*. A group of 'lions,' as elegant young men of the day were known, are speculating as to the identity of the masked female walking arm in arm with one of the novel's protagonists, Lucien de Rubempré. Eugène de Rastignac, a young noble from the provinces whose gruelling ascent into Paris's highest circles formed the subject of the earlier *Père Goriot*, tells the group that he is betting that the mask hides the identity of the Countess de Serisy. Other aristocrats present agree. But the journalist Bixiou wagers a dinner that beneath the mask is, in fact, La Torpille (Esther), a well-known courtesan. The group is stumped: 'En ce moment, journal-istes, dandies, oisifs, tous examinaient, comme des maquignons exam-inent un cheval à vendre, le délicieux objet de leur pari' (65) (In this instant, journalists, dandies, idlers – all examined, like horse traders examining a horse for sale, the delectable object of their bet).

Comparisons of women, particularly venal women, with equines or bovines is common throughout the literature of prostitution. It implies the cool and expert appraising eye of the male judging an object whose function is, when it comes down to it, that of an animal. The only real question here is the *value* of the animal: hack or thoroughbred?[6]

What is shocking, of course, in this group speculation is not only the fact that a lady from *le grand monde* might be mistaken for the likes of a Torpille, but also the very notion that, under the equalizing cover of a mask, there might be no real way to assign distinctions. There is a sense in which the novel's opening scene encapsulates *Splendeur*'s central theme, which is that of post-Revolutionary society's interpenetration of worlds. Each of the three protagonists present at the *bal* harbours aspir-ations to move beyond his or her station. In courtesan Esther's case, it is simply by virtue of who she is that she represents a force potentially disruptive of middle-class values.

As for Lucien de Rubempré, the news which he brings to this mixed gathering is that he has just been ennobled by the King, who has offi-cially permitted him to use his mother's noble name (*de* Rubempré), thus shedding his embarrassing patronym 'Chardon,' whose reson-ances imply not only a plebeian origin but one associated with that most ignoble of plants: the common thistle. And he brazenly describes his new coat of arms to the bristling aristocrats present. Armed with his gracious new name, Lucien is poised for an obvious social ascent. What he now lacks – and what the ensuing narrative will labour to produce – is the fortune which will allow him to marry into one of France's bona fide noble families. This is where prostitution will come in handy.

Esther the courtesan has fallen *faithfully* in love with Lucien and is willing to comply – at least to a point – with a scheme to market her body to the Baron de Nucingen, who is besotted with her charms. Once he has gifted her with a lifetime annuity, the Baron will be granted ul-timate access to her. All of the monies generated out of her marketing, once properly laundered, are destined to constitute the 'dowry' which Lucien de Rubempré will need in order to contract the appropriately stratospheric marriage for which he longs.

However, no one had counted on Esther's newly acquired fidelity. Just minutes before capitulation to the enraptured Baron, she commits suicide, joining the ranks of the 'rehabilitated-but-alas-dead.' Still, she has served her purpose in this economy of prostitution and extortion, and Lucien now has at his disposal a fortune, however unclean.

Readers of the novel know that the plans so carefully laid out by Carlos Herrera (the self-appointed architect of Lucien's ascent) go wildly awry. Tragedy ensues followed by the grim irony of criminal Herrera's 'apotheosis' into the Chief of the Secret Police. What has gone less remarked, however, is the novel's other finishing touch, namely the fact that Herrera rewards his faithful accomplices and former servants Europe and her husband Paccard by purchasing for them – what else? – a whorehouse. Their future is thus secure, and with this final gift, the novel has come full circle, returning to the infinite money-generating possibilities of prostitution. No doubt, too, the brothel will serve as an ideal site of espionage. In Balzac's universe, few indeed are the authentic values and fortunes which subsist untainted by crime and social miscegenation. The body of the prostitute is a medium for transformation: a catalyst for the social alchemy so brilliantly described everywhere on Balzac's pages.

Around 1870, the literature about prostitution enters a new phase reflective of the evolution of scientific and medical theories of the mind as well as new theories about race, criminality, and sexual 'perversions.' Banished is the romantic concept of the repentant Magdalene, rehabilitated in memory if dead in the flesh. Outmoded, too, is the preoccupation with the *lorette* as a social type. Two novels which appeared at this time explore the 'actual' personalities of venal women, drawing heavily on the ambient medical discourse for their characterizations. Huysmans published his first novel, *Marthe, l'histoire d'une fille*, at roughly the same time that Edmond de Goncourt came out with *La fille Elisa* (1876 and 1877 respectively). The subject was not new to Goncourt, who, with his elder brother Jules, had given the world the best-selling *La lorette* over twenty years earlier.

Mentalities had changed fundamentally since the 1850s, however, and both these novels bear the imprint of a new ideology wherein science is king. In his early writing career, Huysmans had been a disciple of Émile Zola and his new theory of naturalism, expounded in the latter's 1880 manifesto, *Le roman expérimental*. Zola was well known to have documented his literary production with great care in the belief that, given the correct data about social milieu, genetics, and etiology of disease, a character's life course could be accurately – even scientific-ally – charted in literary form.

Huysmans is thus true to his (early) literary master Zola when he writes, in a footnote included in *Marthe*, that the prostitute is the 'chem-ical product of *Laziness and Neurosis*' (footnote 4, 172). Using this 'for-mula,' Huysmans's novel traces the path of unmitigated misery of a young woman from the working classes, whose personality and inher-ited traits determine her long and protracted descent into immorality and alcoholism. Originally able to keep well-paying lovers, Marthe sinks from one brothel to another, each one more sordid than the last, evading the police, and finally living with a drunkard who nearly beats her to death.

Given *Marthe*'s scientific premises, it comes as no surprise that the novel ends on the dissection slab with the intern Monsieur Charles discussing with artist Léo, a former lover of Marthe, where the bo-hemian life *really* leads. What are some of these traits which seem to predispose Marthe to so degrading a doom? She was, notes our narra-tor, a strange woman: 'Des ardeurs étranges, un dégoût de métier, une haine de misère, une aspiration maladive d'inconnu, une désespérance non résignée [...] une appétence de bien-être et d'éclat, un alanguisse-ment morbide, une disposition à la névrose qu'elle tenait de sa mère [...] fourmillaient et bouillonnaient furieusement en elle' (74) (Strange ardours, a disgust for work, a hatred of misery, a sick aspiration for the unknown, a hopelessness to which she had not resigned herself [...] an appetite for well-being and display, a morbid languor, a dis-position toward neurosis which she got from her mother [...] seethed and boiled furiously within her).

Unhappy with the misery into which she was born, evincing a desire for well-being, stubbornly unresigned to her lot: who indeed can blame her? The (not-so-) covert message here dressed up as science would seem to be that women of the proletariat should stay in their place lest they meet with a terrible destiny. This social message is peppered with pseudo-medical terms (neurosis, morbidity), yielding a composite por-trait of the lower-class young woman as volcano. So much for the dis-tance and allegedly objective stance of naturalist discourse.

Goncourt's Elisa fares no better. The reader of *La fille Elisa* is con-ducted into a courtroom where Elisa is being sentenced to death for having killed her soldier lover. The reader is then treated, in a long flashback, to an account of her youth and life of degradation, before be-ing introduced to the Noirlieu prison. We learn that Elisa's sentence has been reduced from death to life imprisonment and follow Elisa's excruciating descent into bestialization.

Her upbringing boded no good for her future. As the daughter of a midwife, she had been privy to all manner of corrupting information: 'Du milieu de la nuit de son cabinet, l'enfant alitée, assista aux aventures de déshonneur, aux drames de liaisons cachées, aux histoires de passions hors nature [...] à la divulgation quotidienne de toutes les impuretés salissantes, de tous les secrets dégoûtants de l'Amour coupable et de la Prostitution' (16) (In the middle of the night in her bedroom, the child, in bed, was able to hear all the dishonourable adventures, the dramas of hidden liaisons, the stories of unnatural passions [...] the daily divulging of all the sullying impurities, all the disgusting secrets of guilty Love and Prostitution). Worse still, her mother barely made the distinction between 'les femmes en carte et les autres [...] les femmes honnêtes' (31) (the registered women and the others [...] the honest women). Here again the spectre of virtue's contamination by vice looms.

Notwithstanding all these vicious influences, however, the narrator pins the blame for Elisa's fall into prostitution squarely on *her*: 'la vraie cause déterminante était la paresse, la paresse seule' (32) (the real determining cause was laziness, laziness alone). In what is emerging as a time-sanctified discourse on the prostitute, sloth is surely at the top of the list of characteristics attributed to her: indeed, this defect had already cropped up in the literature surrounding the *lorette* some twenty years earlier.

Elisa's downward trajectory is a predictable one and includes the usual 'stations of the cross,' as it were, especially the ever-popular lesbian dalliance, which is standard in this literature and becomes more overtly expressed over time. (Indeed, Parent-Duchâtelet had already cited this practice as the province of prostitution.) Once incarcerated, Elisa, as a character, finds herself within the kind of closed and heavily observed environment so dear to the naturalist school. She is stripped of an identity, and is now 'number 7999,' much as the dead drunkard Ginginet of *Marthe* was 'number 28 in Saint-Vincent room,' Mimi of the more cynical novelistic version of *Scènes de la vie de bohème* was tragically mistaken for 'number 8' (379), and, indeed, as Céleste Vénard was 'number 3748' in the rosters of the Paris police. As commentary on prison camps has amply demonstrated, the exchange of a name for a number is one of the first steps in the process of dehumanization.

Dehumanization is what happens to number 7999 in the course of her imprisonment. The forced labour and much of the prison life of

Noirlieu were conducted in silence, and the prison had the reputation of producing throat illness (147). Slowly, Elisa loses the faculty of speech and, then, of thought. Her only 'verbal' responses became 'un marmot-tage [...] un bruit de gorge et des lèvres qui ne disait rien' (186) (a mumble [...] a noise from the throat and the lips which meant nothing). She eats with 'animal-like voracity' (187), and toward the end her doctor finds that she no longer has a 'perception nette et rapide des choses, qu'elle avait perdu la concentration de l'attention, qu'elle était soumise à des impulsions étrangères à sa volonté' (200) (clear and rapid perception of things; that she had lost the ability to concentrate; that she was subject to impulses which were alien to her will).

Elisa shares with other inmates strange outbursts. Disorganized words would pour from her mouth only to melt into 'des gloussements craintifs' (205) (fearful clucking). Completely dehumanized, this harlot who never repented dies inarticulate, 'des lèvres enflées de paroles qui avaient à la fois comme envie et peur de sortir' (216) (lips swollen with words which both seemed to want and to fear coming out). Goncourt's novel appears to be ideologically torn between whether Elisa's inherently vicious personality is responsible for her bestializa-tion, or whether the penitentiary system bears some of the blame. Either way, however, the reader is witness to the slow and meticulous silencing of another prostitute.

As a form of determinism, the naturalist representation of the prosti-tute thus repudiated the very concept of redemption while following its practitioners of venal love grimly to the grave. Despite its pretensions of documentary realism and its allegedly objective narrative stances and distances, the depiction of the prostitute occurs through a discur-sive web of stereotypes, cultural anxieties, and the already-existent nar-rative on prostitution which has been developing over the previous several decades.

Although we have already briefly discussed Zola's 1880 novel *Nana* with respect to the anxiety and downright paranoia it expresses re-garding the prostitute as agent of social collapse, it will be useful to re-place the novel here in its chronological context. In a sense, Zola's novel sums up the collective angst around prostitution while also recapitulat-ing and reinforcing the societal and institutional discourse which has been under construction since the 1840s.

Nana is inherently lazy. A gourmand, she devours luxury foods with the same voracity and sensuality with which she will consume men. She is given to frivolous and arbitrary changes of mind, for if 'la donna è mobile,' the courtesan is doubly so. Nana is sexually 'depraved' in ways that her sisters-in-arms are reputed to be. In spite of the parade of male lovers, her real beloved is Satin. Their sapphic excesses make it clear that they can do without men, perhaps the most threatening aspect of lesbian liaisons. Nana is also a femme fatale, which is not necessarily the equivalent of a prostitute. As a dominatrix, she destroys the good, the bad, the ugly, and especially the rich. The ultimate expression of her mastery is the scene which portrays the paragon of virtue, Count Muffat, romping around her boudoir on all fours with Nana astride him. Clearly, the 'natural' gender hierarchy has been turned upside down! Fortunately, when things have gotten out of hand to this point, it is the prerogative of fiction to restore the natural order. Thus, as earlier mentioned, the novel concludes with the grisly meltdown of this former beauty.

Nana was enormously popular as a novel and, as with so much of the fiction of the period, at least one stage version of it existed. In fact, Georges Montorgueil reports having attended a revival of a play version of the novel with the Countess de Chabrillan in the 1890s. The novel's Satin character was widely understood to be based on Chabrillan's friend Lise Pomaré (although this would have been an anachronism in a novel depicting the Third Republic). The novel transforms Lise, who died young of consumption, into an aged strumpet, a drunkard and a ragpicker. Montorgueil claims that the outraged Céleste de Chabrillan stood up in the middle of the performance, yelling 'Dire que c'est ça, leur naturalisme […]. C'est ça leur exactitude dans le detail!' (So that's their naturalism […]. That's their precision of detail!)

This summary concludes with a brief consideration of Jean Lorrain's *La maison Philibert* written in 1904, five years before Chabrillan's death. Lorrain's novel portrays the institution of the brothel as one which has completely changed with the new century. And for good reason: time has brought drastic social reform in France. Slowly, over the course of the two previous decades, important laws protecting women had been enacted. The 1880 Camille Sée law, for example, instituted reforms which included the establishment of *lycées* for girls, and the Naquet Law of 1884 reinstated divorce (Moses 209). A year after the publication of *La maison Philibert*, the first woman was allowed to take the *agrégation* exam in philosophy. And eight years later in 1912, the law forbidding paternity searches was at last repealed. If the highly visible demi-monde had owed its existence in some measure to the Civil Code's prohibition of paternity searches enacted in the early part of the nineteenth century, a number of elements were conspiring to render it socially and structurally unnecessary in the new century.

In addition to the above reforms, by 1900 a new consciousness about the traffic in women had developed, and international conferences devoted to the 'traite des blanches' (white slave trade) were held in London in 1899 and in Paris in 1902. Even more significantly, perhaps, the labour market was slowly opening up for women. The rise of the *grand magasin* (department store) created, besides a new mass consumer market, new job opportunities for women.

La maison Philibert reflects all these societal shifts, often in the elegiac mode of 'where are the brothels of yesteryear?' Philibert, the jovial and paternal owner of a whorehouse, complains to the journalist/narrator that the police, formerly allies of brothel proprietors, now have the nerve to spy on them: 'On nous épie, on nous traque [...]'(4) (They're spying on us, they're tracking us down [...]). Clearly, compared with Mogador's testimony in her *Mémoires* according to which she was constantly in hiding for fear of arrest, a half-century later the shoe is on the other foot.

More disastrous still for Philibert is that *pensionnaires*' debts to the brothel, formerly the single most effective way of keeping 'the livestock' corralled within one establishment, are now being ignored by the law. Add to these 'disasters' the fact that many eligible women are now finding jobs as tour guides for Cook's Travel Agency (Lorrain 96), and the catastrophe is complete. Recruitment has become nearly impossible. Only five years earlier, laments Philibert, it had been possible to pick up a 'package' at any railroad station or any dance hall. Now one can go to 'tous les bals des Halles et des deux Moulins, rien. Finis aussi, Grenelle et Montparnasse' (6) (all the dance halls in les Halles and both Moulins, nothing. Finished also are Grenelle and Montparnasse).

Although *La maison Philibert*'s ostensible focus is on that particular provincial brothel with which Lorrain's work begins and ends, the novel's real activity takes place on Paris's seediest streets. Lorrain in fact presents the mixture of the *monde* and the demi-monde as a fait accompli. The narrator/journalist is hoping to see one of his friends, the divine Illyne Ys, 'la plus délicieuse créature peut-être de toute la galanterie cosmopolite' (88) (perhaps the most delectable creature in the entire world of cosmopolitan gallantry [i.e. remunerated love]). If courtesans are still thriving in Paris, this one is currently hosting a dinner where 'il n'y avait que des femmes du monde, huit femmes titrées et du meilleur faubourg présidées par un grand couturier de la rue de la Paix'

(90) (there were only women of the *monde;* eight titled women from the best area of the city presided over by a great couturier from the rue de la Paix).[7]

Somewhere toward the emergence of the twentieth century, the distinction separating respectable, virtuous women and their public counterparts has become less all-defining: at least, such is one of the messages of this novel. No doubt Lorrain's depiction of the social meltdown apparent in this example is still meant to be naughty – but only slightly so. The *real* naughtiness lies in other issues which surge to the fore in this novel: mere questions of feminine virtue are no longer of much concern.

What does this breakdown of borders between virtuous and disreputable imply for the public/private bifurcation so essential to social organization following the Revolution? Clearly the two formerly absolute divides (public/private and promiscuous/virtuous) are crumbling. In ever greater numbers, women are entering the market of legitimate labour, and thus they are moving into the public sphere, although they will not be fully vested as citizens until they are granted the citizenship implied in the right to vote in 1944. As of the early part of the new century, it began to be possible for a woman to retain her good reputation *and*, to an ever-growing extent, participate in the public arena. In fact, women, too, could write about their experiences in the demi-monde and were no longer excommunicated from the respectable world: Colette and Anaïs Nin are cases in point. In short, they were now able to write about their personal, bodied experiences without being excluded from the ethereal realms of the intellect. Alas for Céleste de Chabrillan, however, this shift in mores arrived too late.

It is, in the end, as a result of his Parisian recruiting explorations that poor Philibert meets his doom, savagely murdered by a pimp. Through this sad demise, the novel returns to the issue of the function and position of the whorehouse as an institution within the broader economy. For Philibert leaves behind him a faithful and religious wife, Madame Véronique, and no fewer than four children who are being educated at a convent school. How is the widow to support this brood, particularly when French law forbade her to manage her property without being, as the French legal expression has it, 'en puissance de mari'? In other words, again, in one of those institutional ironies according to which 'vice' can only be sanctioned by respectability, she must be properly married in order to run her house of ill-repute.

Since Madame Véronique is a hunchback and unlikely, the narrator reasons, to encounter any conjugal prospects, a *mariage blanc* is arranged with the brother of a fellow brothel owner and friend of the late Philibert. The novel ends with the brothel safely in the hands of a married couple, making an 'honest' living for themselves and their children. As in other novels, such as Balzac's *Splendeurs*, the whorehouse stands – politically, socially, and economically – at the very heart of the culture which it in turn supports in ways which are not immediately apparent.

However, the real revelation contained in Lorrain's *La maison Philibert* is that the demi-monde is by now such a hackneyed cliché that it may only exist as a reference to the homosexual world. Lorrain's friend Jane Avril chronicled precisely this transition: 'les moeurs spéciales, pratiquées jusque-là seulement "sous le manteau," commençaient à s'étaler' (71) (special mores, until that time practised only "under cover," were beginning to come out into the open).[8]

What the *ancien* demi-monde may have been screening all along is its own shadow world – a taboo space one degree further removed from respectability than itself. This shadow demi-monde is now free to 'come out.' The detective portion of this novel (for it is a mixed-genre work) centres on the murder of a female prostitute which takes place at an orgy involving, it is revealed, male aristocrats of the highest order consorting with young street Adonises purchased for the evening's entertainment. In a word, Lorrain has beaten Proust to the punch.

What was it about the figure of the venal woman which elicited such obsessional treatment for six decades? In Chapter Two we explored the heightened importance of the demi-monde and its representations in nineteenth-century France. As an individual component of this world, the prostitute herself provided a focal point for the abundant social anxiety surrounding semi-licit sexuality with all its ramifications. The obsession with the persona of the venal woman must be understood as a societal symptom, a metaphor which translates a profound cultural malaise regarding sexuality (obviously), gender roles (needless to say), but also some fundamental epistemological questions dealing with the traditional philosophical partitioning of the categories of mind and matter, and their gendering as male and female respectively. Note the Goncourt brothers in a February 1854 entry to their *Journal*: 'La femme reçoit plutôt des impressions qu'elle n'a des sentiments; les circonstances physiques sont beaucoup plus agissantes sur la femme que sur l'homme, beaucoup plus rivée à la matière que l'homme' (1: 92) (Woman receives impressions rather than having feelings. Physical circumstances act far more on woman than on man; [she is] far more attached to matter than man).

7. Le demi monde à l'envers. Source: Département d'Estampes et Photographie, Bibliothèque nationale de France (Oa22 M141265) [Translation: 'Not surprising that business is down! There's so much competition!']

The Goncourts, although notoriously misogynist, are hardly unique in espousing this dualism. Mardoche and Desgenais write about courtesan Blanche d'Antigny in one of her dance performances: 'Blanche d'Antigny, avec ses "fossettes de gros amour lascif," c'était une sorte de Clodion de chair représentant sous la lumière électrique et les lorgnettes braquées, l'apothéose de la Matière' (31–2) (Blanche d'Antigny, with her 'dimples of plump lascivious love,' was a kind of Clodion of the flesh representing, under the electric lights and the opera glasses trained on her, the apotheosis of Matter).

If Woman corresponds to receptive matter, the venal woman constitutes the ultimate anchor, as it were, of Woman to the Flesh. She 'bears out' and offers the stage on which the age-old gender attribution of active, creative spirit to masculinity, and passive, receptive matter to femininity can be daily and ceaselessly acted out.[9]

This is not to suggest that this ancient gender partition of mind versus matter has been operative at all times in France's history. One has only to think of the *précieuses* and their seventeenth-century feminist intellectual movement – apparently supported by many men of the court – to realize that Aristotle's categories have not always applied.[10] The eighteenth century also had its share of recognized female intelligentsia. What does seem to be the case, however, is that the mind/matter divide (always latent as part of Western philosophy's venerable traditions) was easily invoked in the passage from the Ancien Régime to the limited democracy emergent from the French Revolution. The new socio-political organization based on public versus private readily accommodated this dualism.

In the post-Revolutionary order – so runs the account of much recent research – each citizen was construed to be the democratic equal of his fellow citizen. Each played his role in the public sphere, where the circulation of ideas presupposed the essence of the citizen to be rational, commutable, and indissociably linked to the mind, transcending particularity.[11] Berlanstein has noted that correspondingly men's fashion of the period veered away from the Ancien Régime's laces and silks – seen now as frivolous, feminine, and individualistic – to be replaced by uniformly dark suits suggestive of sober rationality and a certain interchangeability (88).

If the prostitute is the ultimate ideological anchor of woman to matter, she is also integral to a widely held scientific analogy: that of the prostitute-as-sewer. According to this dynamic (not to say digestive) view of things, erotic energy flows constantly through the body social, with the prostitute positioned at its point of evacuation. The assumption underwriting this circulatory model is that men required a level of sexual satisfaction that virtuous women could not (and perhaps *should not*) provide. For Parent-Duchâtelet and others who followed, the model of the prostitute as vessel of evacuation solves a host of problems and, as a paradigm, reflects a belief in a kind of collective social libido which Balzac, in his *La fille aux yeux d'or*, illustrates brilliantly. Having already referred to the perimeters of the city as the belt which the hussy Paris is constantly unfastening for the workers who visit her, the narrator goes on to equate this site of prostitution to a political space: 'Sans les cabarets, le gouvernement ne serait-il pas renversé tous les mardis?' (212) (Without the cabarets, would not the government be overthrown every Tuesday?).

Thus, whoring and drinking are the shock absorbers which staunch the flow of erotico-revolutionary energies. What Balzac has expressed in encapsulated form is a political model of the function of the prostitute: she is a privileged political conduit useful for purging social unrest, a channel for expressing aggression which cannot be articulated elsewhere, a site enabling the preservation of respectability in other places, a body/theatre upon which the dance of authority/subjection can be endlessly performed, an arena for the playing out of male competitiveness, or a forum capable of uniting men in the exercise of social bonding and consolidation of power.

The venal woman, as a fantasy construct, is thus an extraordinarily rich symbolic figure for psychic investment of almost any social persona in almost any permutation. Indeed, Mogador's very name – the city in Morocco which had proven so difficult for the French to conquer – suggests a vicarious imperial satisfaction which the possession of her body might procure for those passionately invested in nationalism. Erotics and nationalism may seem like odd bedfellows, but in a century and a country racked by revolution in which questions of political legitimacy were constantly and urgently being posed, the figure of the harlot offered allegorical possibilities too ironically rich not to exploit.

Depending on which conception of the prostitute supports any given world view, then, the venal woman can be depicted either as an exemplar of Womanhood, or – paradoxically – as a negative guarantor of legitimate Womanhood's defining feature: respectability. It is all a matter of philosophical convenience.

Before moving on to a discussion of Céleste de Chabrillan's fiction, it is critical to address the question of voice: Who is speaking about the prostitute (courtesan/kept woman/*grisette*/*lorette*)? With the prostitute positioned almost exclusively as the object of discussion, who is the subject making statements about her? Can the reader discern any of the narrator's agendas or any ideologies motivating his or her statements? And finally, what kind of satisfaction might the narrator derive from his – and more rarely her – vantage point?

To answer the last question, let us revisit the middle of the century. Maurice Alhoy's *Physiologie de la lorette* offers an example of an aggressive narratorial subjectivity. Written in 1841, this pamphlet is actually prophetic because it is written in *explicit anticipation* of writings by Balzac and others yet to come. First, the narrator/bard positions himself with respect to his subject matter (or really *object* matter): 'O Lorettes! je vais vous chanter' (8), he croons – before deciding to exchange his lyre for a fork and knife: '[O]u plutôt,' he revises, 'je vais vous croquer' (O Lorettes! I am going to sing of you [...] Or rather, I am going to chew you up ['croquer' also means 'to sketch']).

Thus, the narrator is going to crunch these dainty morsels described in the ensuing lines as 'meteors of unpredictable course and eagles with sharp talons.' Then he muses about the *lorette*'s future destiny under pens mightier than his own: 'O Lorettes, un jour Balzac vous saisira par corps, il vous fera une visite domiciliaire et instrumentera avec son inflexible plume' (9) (O Lorettes. One day Balzac will seize you by the body. He will make a house call and will operate on you with his inflexible pen). The equivalence between having sex with the *lorette* and writing about her could not be more flagrant. And lest the metaphor be lost on a naive reader, Alhoy revisits it with respect to writer/critic Jules Janin. Janin 'vous jettera sur la tête l'encre baptismal du feuilleton [...]. [I]l vous couchera sur sa phrase souple et moelleuse' (9) (will throw the baptismal ink of serialization on your heads [...]. He will lay you down upon his supple and mellow sentence). Verily the pen is mightier than the sword!

In answer to the question posed earlier, then, it seems that the satisfaction derived from writing about the prostitute can be in and of itself erotic in nature, and its motivation is one of mastery and domination. And so many of the post-Romantic generation of writers penned at least one book about a harlot that it is as if this subject matter (again, *object* matter) functioned as a kind of literary calling card among what can only be described as the 'brothelhood' of writers. To write about the prostitute (with one exception, as will be seen) is to situate oneself within a cultural community and to affirm the prevailing values of that culture.

To write about her is to *know* her, in the broadest sense of that term. Already in 1841, Alhoy notes about his object matter: 'On ne l'explique pas, on l'analyse, on la classe' (11) (One does not explain her: one analyses her; one classifies her). Hiding behind the falsely neutral '*on*,' here again our author reveals himself to be prescient of the scientific discourse of the future: the allegedly objective and unimplicated voice charged with impersonal observation. To observe is to dominate, master, and control. Sometimes, however, the objective narrative voice itself loses control. The conclusion of Zola's *Nana* is a case in point. Nana having wreaked havoc on the entire society, the narrator seems to take a sadistic pleasure in decomposing her beauty. And with this act of authorial sadism, we have come full circle to rejoin Delvau's reminiscences of his bohemian youth, in which a hooker too heartless could always be put back in her place with a good caning – or worse.

One realizes that one is in the presence of a subjectivity through the instances of stereotypes which abound in this literature and which often begin with the telltale 'The courtesan [*lorette, grisette*, prostitute] is …' Here are some of the many stereotypes which, taken together over time and appearing in different contexts (scientific, literary, journalistic), form a veritable discourse. The whore is lazy. She is often a lesbian. She delights in being treated cruelly. She is fickle and lacking in concentration. Such women are sterile – they are the very antithesis of motherhood. (Romantic) prostitutes are dying to sacrifice themselves for a good cause, especially if that cause is a man (Esther of *Splendeurs*; Marguerite of *La dame aux camélias*). Paradoxically, though, the prostitute is unknowable. She is essentially materialistic: indeed, she is the very embodiment of matter. Not infrequently she is an alcoholic.[12] Prostitutes are no better than animals: they are naturally depraved.

Each of the blanket characterizations conveniently calls up a corresponding reactive behaviour. If the lady of ill-repute enjoys being beaten, well then, it is appropriate to gratify her. If she is fickle, then pay her no heed. If she is sterile, then no sense of responsibility about pregnancy need be assumed. Since she is inherently slothful, there is no reason to create legitimate work opportunities for her. If she is a dominatrix, then she must be mastered. Her unknowability necessitates studies of her and authorizes medical dissections. Finally, if at heart she is an animal, there is no need to treat her as a human being.

It would be wrong (and depressing) to say that all the literature produced about prostitution subscribed to some or all of these beliefs. Indeed, many writers evince conflicted stances which seem to take into account the misery and poverty which, as Parent-Duchâtelet had noted, are prostitution's primary causes, while at the same time propagating some of the ambient mythologies on the subject. It should not be forgotten that many authors enjoyed personal relationships with these women and that their own particular experiences may often have clashed with the dominant discourse in which they are *also* participants. Mogador, for instance, was a good friend of Delvau, of Murger and of both Dumas père and fils.

The rehabilitated-but-alas-dead scenario typical of so many of these stories must be read as reflecting the ambivalence of both the male writers and their culture. Middle-class consciousness admits of the possibility of redemption on one level but shudders to contemplate the actual living aftermath of this social forgiveness on the other. The only resolution to this dilemma would seem to be to pardon the whore and then kill her off. In fiction, of course, this move is eminently feasible. But what if one is the whore in question – that is, Mogador? How can one face a society which would prefer one to be, if not dead, at least invisible and, above all, silent? Who can imagine telling the story of the ex-prostitute once she has become virtuous? Perhaps only a woman.

There is at least one novel involving a courtesan whose tone, stance, and narrative treatment differ fundamentally from those already mentioned. This is George Sand's *Isidora* (1846).[13] For the first time in this vast literary corpus, a courtesan – Isidora – militantly claims the right to successful expiation, by which is simply meant that she lives to tell the tale. This exoneration has been achieved through living an exemplary life characterized by good works. And significantly, it has been achieved through the agency of another woman.

Having already lived out her notorious life in Paris, Isidora is leading a reclusive existence in northern Italy, where each passing day spent with her adopted daughter Agathe brings her greater wisdom and tranquility: 'Il était donc dans ma destinée que les hommes me perdraient et que je ne pourrais être sauvée que par les femmes? Vous avez commencé ma conversion, chère Alice [...]. Agathe [...] l'achève' (226) (It was thus my destiny that men would be my downfall and that I could only be saved by women? You began my conversion, dear Alice [...]. Agathe [...] is completing it). Alice is Isidora's sister-in-law and, in a sense, her virtuous double. Sand's novels are full of such doubled feminine characters: one is generally gifted with a lofty, chaste, and spiritual nature, while the other is made to bear the heavy cultural weight of the female body.

In *Indiana* (1832), Aurore Dupin's first novel – and the first she signs with her nom de plume George Sand – Indiana has an almost consubstantial bond with her maid and milk-sister, Noun, who represents the body to Indiana's mind. Sand's next novel, *Lélia* (1833, with a revised edition in 1839), broaches the problem of the body frontally, as it were. The beautiful but overly cerebral Lélia has a sister, Pulchérie, who is a celebrated courtesan. Even if it is clear that Lélia finds her sister's trade morally abhorrent, at some level Pulchérie represents that body and its pleasures which Lélia has denied herself (the 'cher' rhymes with 'chair,' or flesh). In both of these stories, it is as if Sand's text were illustrating *the very process by which* the existence of the flesh is sublimated in favour of the mind.

Male writers of this period do not share this burden: Balzac, the Goncourts, Huysmans, Dumas, and company can comfortably examine a prostitute's body, probe its 'realities,' and dissect its mysteries, all the while remaining perfectly respectable as people. Neither Sand nor Mogador have this luxury. Even though the 1839 *Lélia* ends with its protagonist becoming an abbess, the mind/matter split continues to haunt the text.

It is in *Isidora*, a more mature work, that the question of the terrible divide is addressed and a kind of solution proffered. It is the generous Alice who takes the first step toward friendship with her sister-in-law, the ex-courtesan Isidora. Alice's aristocratic family is horrified, of course. Indeed, the only reason the family has decided *not* to try to deprive Isidora of her noble name is because of the scandal which the whole affair would provoke (evidently not opting to use its influence in the way that the Chabrillan family was to do in exactly the same circumstances a scant decade later).

It is either the two women's mutual misfortune or their salvation that Isidora in her past has had a brief relationship with Jacques Laurent, Alice's son's preceptor, with whom Alice is in love unbeknown to herself. Her feelings only become clear to her when she realizes that Jacques has spent the night with her new friend (and bearer of the body), Isidora.

Alice is crushed. She decides to retreat to her chamber and gives her maid instructions that she not be disturbed under any circumstances whatever might ensue. Thereupon, she goes into a kind of trance during which a mighty internal struggle takes place. Alice emerges victorious – that is, alive (for she had come perilously close to death) – but it is her love for Jacques which has expired. She has, in short, committed a kind of suicide of the body.

From this exalted (because disembodied) position, Alice can give her unrestricted friendship to Isidora and bless the relationship between Jacques and Isidora. Alas, the sad truth is that this couple has been unable to rekindle their erstwhile love. What a strange way for a novel to end! Even our narrator remarks upon this singular lack of closure.

But the novel has not in fact ended, and Part Three consists of Isidora's correspondence with Alice over at least another decade. The narrative is now written in the first person – that is, from Isidora's point of view. This is, I believe, the first (and perhaps only) novel in the century to take the risk of recounting from within the subjectivity of the courtesan.

Perhaps the risk Sand is taking is diminished because Isidora is no longer a courtesan, and she is slowly rehabilitating herself through the distant mediation of Alice. Jacques is no longer in the picture at all for this is really a novel about a friendship between two women. Isidora's self-rehabilitation is no doubt rendered possible by her defiance of the very attitude which led the beautiful Princess Amélie of *Les mystères de Paris* to her grave: 'Il me semble que j'ai assez expié, et que je mérite d'entrer dans le repos des justes' (215) (It seems to me that I have expiated enough, and that I merit entry to the repose of the just). In all the other works we have explored here, for those fallen women who *are* repentant, *there can never be enough expiation*. Absolution comes only with death. The novelty and uniqueness of *Isidora* lie in the way it allows the redeemed prostitute to live, and moreover, to live to tell her own tale! True, this has come at the expense of the body: both women now live semi-monastic lives of renunciation of the flesh. But this is the price to be paid if a woman is to write *and* remain respectable in France of the mid-nineteenth century.

Imagine, now, in this social context, what it might mean for a notorious prostitute, a public woman in the term's full extension, to pick up the pen (after teaching herself to write) and to embark upon the journey of becoming an author.

PART TWO

Chabrillan and the Uses of Fiction

4 *La Sapho*, or Staging Vengeance

[N]ul coeur honnête ne pourra savoir ce qu'il faut d'humilité à une courtisane, pour accepter sans mourir ou sans se venger les injures qu'elle reçoit.
(Mémoires 1: 231–2)

[N]o honest heart will ever know how much humility a courtesan must
have to accept the insults she receives without dying or without seeking
revenge.

Stifling the voice of the venal woman, declining to hear it when – against
all odds – it did break through the sound barrier, or, finally, discrediting
its message when the latter demanded social justice: all these silencing
strategies were at work in nineteenth-century French culture and literature. The time has now come to reverse the perspective: to view the
world from the point of view of the prostitute. By the end of her long life,
Céleste de Chabrillan had composed two series of memoirs, ten novels,
and twenty-six plays. Given the prevailing attitudes toward fallen
women, the fact that she wrote at all is remarkable. But when one takes
into account that she had to teach herself quite literally to form letters on
a page, then her achievement is nothing short of breathtaking.

Chabrillan is a writer who arises out of nowhere. So it is worth asking,
before exploring her work, what might have been the intellectual or cultural platform supporting someone who, while able to read, was unable
to write. We know from her memoirs that she undertook the task of self-
education in Australia, where she hid her reading/writing sessions from
the Count lest he attempt to discourage her. References to other writers
in her work are rare, the only names to appear consistently being George

Sand and Alexandre Dumas père. Céleste had probably read most of Sand's work, judging from her disappointment at not finding, in a trip to the Berry province, the world evoked by Sand in *La mare au diable*. Other references to Sand's writing appear sporadically throughout her work.

Her most likely source of literary acculturation would have been the theatre. Céleste Vénard was raised close to the boulevard du Temple, and she reports attending plays as a young girl on the so-called boulevard du Crime, a theatrical smorgasbord which attracted large numbers of spectators in search of nightly entertainment. On the celebrated boulevard, vaudeville and melodrama were standard fare: even the literati counted themselves lucky to have seen actor Frédéric Lemaître on stage. In 1770, the Italian author Goldoni wrote an eyewitness account evoking the atmosphere of this bustling quarter which was created around that time: 'crowds of people [...] ladies who simply want to be seen, cafés all spruced up, with orchestras and French and Italian singers [...] puppet shows, acrobats, barkers inviting you to come inside and see giants and dwarfs, wild animals and sea-monsters, waxwork figures, robots and ventriloquists' (cited by Hemmings, 27).

In his evocative description, Pierre-Robert Leclerq insists on the boulevard's demographic diversity: 'Au coeur d'un quartier populaire, le boulevard du Temple est un lieu de plaisirs comme il n'en est plus. Dès le crépuscule, s'y côtoient ouvriers et bourgeois, grisettes et militaires, artisans et dandies, grandes dames et pauvres étudiants, comédiens' (17) (In the heart of a working-class district, the boulevard du Temple is a place of pleasure the likes of which no longer exist. From dusk on, rubbing elbows are workers, and bourgeois, *grisettes* and military men, artisans and dandies, high-class ladies and poor students, actors).

Many were the works which, first published serially in journals, also found their way onto the stage. The story lines of what today we know as novels alone would thus have been accessible through a variety of forms including strictly oral elaborations for the illiterate. Thus, the scant access the Countess de Chabrillan had to literary culture would most likely have come via the stage. On the one hand, her intellectual clean slate meant that she was spared the anxiety of influence afflicting educated male writers doomed (in Harold Bloom's account) to define themselves *always with respect to* a pre-existent literary tradition. On the other hand, however, as a woman who was a pariah within the community of respectable, literate women, she benefited from few of the support structures which Virginia Woolf describes as critical to a writing woman's life. Very simply, it was against all sociocultural odds that Chabrillan was able to write any fiction whatsoever. The pages that follow will examine the reasons which compelled her to write, attempting to take the measure of the sheer force of her motivation given the many obstacles in her path. Henceforth, unless speaking of her in relation to her career as courtesan, her writing self will be referred to as Céleste de Chabrillan, the Countess de Chabrillan, or Chabrillan, in deference to the reality of her achievements, rather than as Mogador, her prostitutional sobriquet.

Although Chabrillan struggled against the limitations imposed by her artistic isolation, it is precisely because she was an autodidact that her literary images can have an unusual freshness. Her metaphors of feminine strength, for instance, remain distinctly untempered by any need to mollify a male readership. Her first novel, *Les voleurs d'or* (1857), features a character, Émeraude, who is 'impassible comme une statue de bronze' (56) (impassive like a bronze statue). And the titular character of her second novel, *La Sapho*, her 'work' accomplished by novel's end, 'se leva avec le mouvement de l'aigle qui s'envole' (306) (rose with the movement of an eagle taking flight). While caged birds commonly function as metaphors for women, the eagle – tough, strong, and free to attain the lofty ethereal reaches associated with the mind – has traditionally been a virile image, for those writing *from within* a tradition.

Her earlier novels are characterized by heavy use of dialogue, sometimes taking on a quasi-theatrical format, and so remain close to an oral representation of the world. Gradually, however, her work evolves toward increased use of narration as Chabrillan begins to master her trade. The situations and characters she creates move from melodramatic polarizations (with obvious heavy authorial investments) to a more plurivocal, distributed, and mediated world vision characterized by the kind of ambivalence and ambiguity which are reflective of more complex art. The creative itinerary of Chabrillan offers a remarkable insight into the writer's workshop.

Céleste de Chabrillan's life and writing criss-cross and reinforce each other in ways which, over time, will yield a strong new identity. With each step forward in her literary career, her sense of self-worth heightens. At the same time, her novels, while dealing ostensibly with situations different from hers (with the exception of *La Sapho*), visit and revisit a limited repertory of themes and motifs: the nature of guilt and innocence, the fate of the underprivileged, the indelibility of personal history, and troubled mother/daughter relationships. Over the considerable span of her writing career, these themes are constantly being stated in new ways, renegotiated and reconfigured.

Her sole novel which does feature a courtesan as the central character is the most important one in her writing itinerary for it is here that she sets up the conditions for a catharsis which is critical for her to achieve in order to move forward. Beginning with this novel, *La Sapho*, we shall watch as the constellation of motifs which first occur here are redeployed throughout her novelistic opus. We shall be asking if, through the multiple repetitions, the treatment of these obsessional ideas evolves, and if so, in what direction.

La Sapho opens with young aristocrat Richard Campbell, returning to Southampton from a voyage on the high seas, burdened with the news which he must convey to Madame Laurent, a widow, that her son Jacques has died on the trip. Richard, with an indecisiveness which will characterize him throughout the novel, cannot bring himself to break the news immediately, and he repairs to his family, dominated by his chilly mother, Lady Campbell. Lady Campbell is entertaining a rich shipping magnate, Monsieur Pallier, whose daughter, Léonie, is engaged to be married to the eldest Campbell son, Paul.

The next day, Richard sets out to tell widow Laurent his sad news, but he arrives at their home to discover that Madame Laurent and her daughter Marie, a young seamstress, have just sent the other son, Pierre, off on a long sea journey. Once again Richard cannot bring himself to relay the terrible news. He instead confides his dilemma to the other Pallier daughter, Henriette, a young woman whose intelligence and self-abnegation counterbalance the self-indulgent frivolity of her soon-to-be married sister Léonie. In a gesture of charity, the 'good' sister visits the Laurent household and places orders for embroidery and linen. On this occasion, the reader is afforded a glimpse of the conditions under which the working classes laboured. Marie Laurent is depicted as a hard-working young woman whose education is so limited that she is ashamed of her rudimentary and flawed writing capacities (a leitmotif in Chabrillan's work).

At last Richard Campbell finds the words to tell Marie – but not her mother – of her brother's demise. It is as she lies in a faint on the floor that Richard is struck by Marie's beauty. While Marie decides to withhold the tragic news from her mother, Richard becomes a regular visitor. One thing leads to another, and one evening they agree to marry, sealing the promise with more than a kiss: 'Elle venait de se donner tout entière; elle aimait!' (80) (She had just given herself completely; she was in love!).

Meanwhile, back at the Campbell homestead, the imperious Lady Campbell (who functions as the bad mother foil to Madame Laurent) has decided that Richard will marry Henriette Pallier, and Richard, whose honourable intentions vis-à-vis Marie are weakening, ('mais enfin c'est une ouvrière') (96) (but in the end, she's a working-class woman), accedes to his mother's wishes. It is only when Henriette visits Marie to change her linen order so that the initials to be embroidered will now read 'HC' that Marie understands the betrayal. Abject and furious, she discloses all her secrets to her mother: 'La même seconde apprit à madame Laurent la mort de son fils et le déshonneur de sa fille' (100) (in the same second Madame Laurent learned of the death of her son and the dishonour of her daughter), the two being equivalent for the ex-Mogador who always spoke of her own dishonour as a 'moral suicide.'

Madame Laurent, in a protective gesture which Céleste Vénard must have wished that her own mother had made, marches straight to Madame Campbell and demands that Richard marry her daughter. But the Campbells are people of privilege, accustomed to buying their way out of difficulty, and Richard proposes the disreputable solution of keeping Marie as a mistress on the side while marrying Henriette ('the dowry'). If the reader had any doubts as to where the narrator's investments and sympathies lie thus far, these vanish with the sad commentary, 'Même en amour, on compte moins avec les douleurs d'une pauvre fille' (114) (even in love, the sorrows of a poor girl count less).

The definitive and irreparable nature of a woman's 'fall' from virtue as well as the sheer injustice of the double standard which tolerates, even encourages, male sexual activity while condemning the female participant, is another refrain which resonates through Chabrillan's literary oeuvre. It is an angry refrain which calls into question the very meaning of guilt given the prevailing social conditions, and which protests and accuses society of victimizing the unprotected while protecting the privileged.

In *La Sapho*, the lamentation on the loss of innocence is articulated through the metaphor of the flower, but, instead of the suitor inviting his beloved to savour the rose of her youth, the seduction scene is told, remarkably enough, from the viewpoint of the rose. Declares a prostitute later in the novel:

Les fleurs vivent [...]. [E]lles s'aiment et sont capables de grands dévouements. Elles inspirent de petites ou grandes passions; un jour de printemps, je ne sais plus lequel, je vins au monde sur un rosier blanc, un fou passa, il brisa ma tige, me respira quelques heures et me jeta loin de lui. J'allais mourir lorsqu'un autre me ramassa. Quand je fus fanée, il m'abandonna pour une grosse marguerite sans parfum. Je pleurais. Les fleurs ont leurs larmes, vois-tu; les gouttes de rosée que le bon Dieu jette dans leur calice sont les pleurs tombées du ciel, et qu'elles rendent à la terre quand elles sont trop malheureuses. (254)

Flowers live [...]. They love and are capable of great devotion. They inspire small or great passions. One spring day, I don't know which one, I came into the world on a white rose bush. A crazy man passed by; he broke my stalk, inhaled me for several hours and threw me away far from him. I was going to die when another one picked me up. When I was wilted, he abandoned me for a big daisy with no scent. I cried. Flowers have their tears, you see. The dew drops which the good God throws into their cups are tears fallen from heaven, which they return to the earth when they are too unhappy.

By this time in the novel the melodramatic configuration has been set up: the moral dilemma has been unambiguously delineated, and the good and evil roles clearly attributed. The situation cries out for vengeance – or tragedy looms! Yet, bringing the melodramatic script to its anticipated cathartic closure would require the appearance, on the horizon, of a hero capable of protecting the widow and avenging the Laurent family's honour. No such hero presents himself. What are a mother and (dishonoured) daughter to do? The novel in fact rejects the melodramatic solution and undergoes, for the time being, a radical change of focus, introducing new characters, complete with flashbacks and, later, a change of venue.

Marie, having attempted to drown herself, is rescued by a sailor, although she will forever bear the stigmata of the hook he used to fish her out of the water. The sailor takes her, inert, to Monsieur Pallier, who, seeing her near-dead, refuses to succour her and instead fakes a suicide note from Marie to her mother. Marie is taken to a hospital and left there to die while Madame Laurent dies of grief. Meanwhile, Richard is shown the fake letter. As Monsieur Pallier had plotted, the contents of the letter free Richard to marry his daughter, Henriette. Richard, for his part, has no reason to doubt the letter's authenticity based on handwriting, for 'Marie ne lui avait jamais écrit, la pauvre fille avait donné tout son temps au travail; elle savait écrire, mais si mal qu'elle n'aurait jamais osé envoyer une ligne à Richard; il y a des femmes, qui ne savent pas que le mot: je t'aime, peut s'écrire de toutes les manières' (131–2) (Marie had never written him. The poor girl had given all her time to work. She knew how to write, but so badly that she never would have dared send a line to Richard. There are women who do not know that the phrase 'I love you' can be written in any way). There is a clear identification here of Céleste de Chabrillan, who would always require the services of a secretary to correct her phonetic spelling, with the unfortunate and unschooled Marie, ashamed of her ignorance.

Time passes, and Paul has already wed the frivolous Léonie, with whom he lives in London. Richard has married Henriette. However, a domestic has confided Monsieur Pallier's perfidy to his honourable daughter, Henriette, who, ashamed of her father, decides to live in chastity with her equally mortified husband in a mere simulacrum of marriage. Unbeknown to them all, Marie has recovered and has come to know of Monsieur Pallier's forged suicide note and of Richard and Henriette's marriage.

Suddenly, we are in London, where Léonie and Paul Pallier are living an extravagant existence. We are at the theatre, where that parable par excellence of good and bad daughters, *King Lear*, is about to begin. A woman in the audience has created a small sensation: 'Il y avait, dans cette riche coiffure, un certain désordre qui lui donnait une grâce parfaite [...]. Les plis de sa robe de dentelle noire, faite à la grecque, étaient retenus par des agrafes de rubis' (176) (There was, in this rich hairdo, a certain disorder that lent it perfect grace [...]. The folds of her dress of black lace, in grecian style, were held in place by ruby pins). The seasoned Londoner, Lucien, explains to his friends, the Palliers, that 'on l'appelle la Sapho, je ne sais pas pourquoi' (177) (she is called la Sapho: I do not know why).

No one, it would appear, really knows who she is: 'd'autres assurent qu'elle a été mariée, que son mari a été tué en duel par un de ses amants; tout cela, comme vous le dîtes, peut être plus ou moins vrai, mais ce qu'il y a de certain, c'est qu'il se passe chez elle des choses fort extraordinaires; si le passé laisse des doutes, le présent existe: on dirait qu'elle craint un danger: elle est toujours armée' (181) (others insist that she was married, that her husband was killed in a duel by one of her lovers. All this, as you say, may be more or less true. But what is certain is that most extraordinary things happen at her home. If doubts remain about the past, the present exists. You might almost say she is afraid of some danger: she is always armed). Intrigued and out of his wife's earshot, Paul Pallier asks Lucien to introduce him to Sapho. Lucien agrees, cautioning Paul: 'Prenez garde ... c'est une syrène [*sic*]' (182) (Watch out ... she's a siren). And so it is that Paul, already smitten, pays a visit to Sapho in her

palatial residence, where she declares to him and the other male admirers surrounding her that 'je suis un mystère pour moi-même' (192) (I am
a mystery to myself). However, Paul's visit is interrupted when the maid
rushes in to announce that while she was cleaning on the first floor, 'mademoiselle Lélia s'est sauvée' (204) (Mademoiselle Lélia has run away).
Sapho dons a veil and leaves her many suitors.

Who is Sapho, and who this mysterious Lélia who has evidently escaped from Sapho's residence? The plot thickens, and once again, the
novel shifts registers, moving rather suddenly into a flashback featuring a young woman bereft and roaming the London streets at night in
search of lodging. She is terror-stricken: every shadow looms large in a
nightmarish description which – through use of the 'vous' – forces the
reader, male and female alike, to experience a girl's fear of being stalked
in the streets. The quote is worth giving in its entirety:

> La ville ressemble un grand cimetière, chaque bec de gaz a l'air d'un feu
> follet, l'imagination fait mouvoir des ombres immenses, les rivières viennent
> à vous, les ponts s'éloignent, vous entendez des pas dans vos pas, il vous
> semble qu'une main se pose sur votre épaule. Votre respiration est un bruit
> de voix dans le lointain. Votre ombre grandit, vous dépasse de plusieurs
> pieds, vous la prenez pour celle d'un géant. Afin de fuir toutes ces visions,
> vous commencez une course insensée, vous arrivez dans un coin sombre,
> vous regardez en arrière: vous ne voyez rien, vous reprenez haleine; puis
> recommencent les hallucinations, les murs s'ébranlent, les portes s'ouvrent,
> les bornes marchent, on court encore …; il faut être bien forte, pour ne pas
> devenir folle en pareil cas. (207)

> The city resembles a great cemetery. Each gas light seems like a wild flame.
> The imagination makes immense shadows move. Streams come toward you;
> bridges move away; you hear footsteps behind yours; it seems to you that
> someone is putting a hand on your shoulder. Your breathing is the sound of
> a voice in the distance. Your shadow becomes larger; it looms several feet
> longer than you; you take it to be the shadow of a giant. In order to flee all
> these visions, you start on a wild race; you arrive in a dark corner; you look
> behind you; you see nothing; you catch your breath. Then the hallucinations
> begin again: walls shake; doors open; street markers walk; one begins to run
> again … one has to be very strong not to go mad in such situations.

If the urban gaslighting would herald for a Benjaminian flâneur of this
same period the advent of a modernity which he can savour from a place

of personal safety and detachment, the same landscape is fraught with danger for those in positions of vulnerability. One might even say that the expressionistic quality of the above description anticipates Joyce's 'Nighttown,' with the caveat that the nocturnal visions in that chapter of *Ulysses* are bacchanalia produced by intoxicants whereas the above London nocturne is the product of the stark reality of social conditions.

While the identity of the *flâneuse-malgré-elle* is not revealed, the reader does learn that an elderly man awakens her in a doorway where she is sleeping and promises to help her find employment: 'L'enfant le suivait sans méfiance, parce qu'il avait au front cette couronne blanche' (211) (The child followed him with no mistrust because his forehead had this white crown). The aged libertine, Monsieur Georges, takes her to a house, where the lady in charge, Mistress Bedell, 's'approcha de l'air d'un connaisseur qui va déguster un vin vieux' (213) (approached with the air of a connoisseur about to savour an old wine).

The appearance of a bevy of women and the evident stature of Monsieur Georges leave no doubt in the reader's mind as to the nature of the life which the young girl will espouse: 'Il dut se faire en son âme une révolution étrange. Elle se regarda avec tristesse dans un miroir, un sourire dédaigneux passa sur les lèvres pâles, elle était prête à subir son suicide moral' (217) (A strange revolution must have taken place in her soul. She looked at herself sadly in a mirror; a disdainful smile rose to her pale lips. She was ready to undergo her moral suicide). The reader then meets the 'boarders': there is Souzannah, the jealous queen whore; Reine, who will die soon of both gin consumption and consumption tout court; and Lélia, with whom the young woman seems to have an affinity: 'Ses compagnes semblaient lui inspirer un profond mépris, une exceptée, Lélia; on eût dit même qu'il y avait un secret entre elles' (221) (Her companions all seemed to inspire a profound contempt in her, all except Lélia. One might even have said that there was a secret between them).

The relationship between Lélia and Sapho is one enigma which will never be clarified, but the novel's title itself speaks fairly clearly. The waif-become-prostitute was originally dubbed 'Sapho' by two artist-flâneurs who frequented the brothel: ('ainsi posée, elle ressemble à la Sapho rêveuse de Pradier') (219) (posing like that, she resembles Pradier's dreamy Sapho). Souzannah, however, 'croyant lui dire une injure, l'appela Sapho. Tout le monde fit comme elle et ce nom lui resta' (220) (believing she was insulting her, called her Sapho. Everyone did the same, and the name remained with her). It is well known that references to Sapho have been differently intended and understood according to historical period. At the end of the eighteenth century, for example, Germaine de Staël's opera *Sapho* exalts the poetess as do comparisons in Staël's 1807 novel *Corinne*. However, by the end of the nineteenth century, 'Sapho' would refer to a poetess perhaps, but, above all, to a lesbian. In 1858, as Chabrillan's text itself makes clear, either understanding is possible, and there is little doubt that the novel is deliberately equivocal and provocative on this issue. Other of the Countess's novels feature relationships between women in which the women are called 'inséparables,' a code word for homosexuals (Adler 134), and often relationships in which one woman is the caretaker of the other.

These relationships do not preclude the same women entertaining relations with men, and indeed, in the 1883 novel *Marie Baude*, one such heroine espouses an all-inclusive approach to love thus: 'J'ai un rendez-vous à quatre heures chez un peintre et je dînerai avec lui; il veut me conduire au théâtre, mais c'est la première et ce sera la dernière fois, je te le jure [...]. Puis, tout à coup, prenant Jeanne dans ses bras nus, blancs, ronds et fermes comme du marbre, elle s'écria [...]. Mais c'est toi qui es la joie de la maison' (207) (At four o'clock I am meeting a painter and I'll dine with him. He wants to take me to the theatre, but this is the first and the last time, I swear [...]. Then, suddenly, taking Jeanne in her naked arms, white, round and as firm as marble, she cried [...]. But you are the joy of the household!).

A lesbian reading of Sapho's relationship with Lélia is supported by the existence of similar relationships in other works by Chabrillan, including the allusions which were censored out of her 1854 *Mémoires*. The fact that her publisher Michel Lévy chose to alter this novel's title to *Un amour terrible (La Sapho)* when reissuing it in 1876 and again in 1897 suggests that this particular content may have been deemed too racy for the period.

At length, the reader learns that Sapho has come by considerable wealth through a 'benefactor' who redeemed her – in the strict financial sense of the term – from Mistress Bedell's brothel. Subsequently Sapho herself was able to buy the freedom of Lélia, who, now living with her, vacillates between madness and lucidity. These 'buyouts' are reminiscent of the way Céleste Vénard was herself rescued from the brothel.

But where, one might ask, can the story go from here? All the emotional intensity and Manichaean polarization of melodrama are present, but the cast of characters has yet to yield the Redresser of Wrongs. And the heroine Sapho (if heroine she be) is far too ambiguous a character for the standard melodramatic script. Sapho's following includes a devoted *cavalier-servant*, Fabien, who stands ready to obey her every command. To him alone she will disclose her plot to dishonour the entire Campbell family by seducing Paul to his ruin: 'Mais il me faut plus que ... son honneur' [...]. '[Fabien] recula épouvanté, le regard de Sapho avait une expression sinistre' (248–9) (But I need more ... I need ... his honour [...]. [Fabien] recoiled, horrified. Sapho's gaze bore a sinister expression).

By now the reader may have guessed that Sapho is none other than Marie Laurent. As Sapho, she has become an independent woman of means, proud of her power in a way not as overtly expressed in francophone women's writing perhaps since Staël's astonishing Corinne. 'J'ai [...] une grande fortune,' she comments, 'je suis arrivée à ce moment de la vie, après lequel j'ai longtemps soupiré: être la maîtresse de son coeur et de ses actions, avoir des amis de son choix, n'est-ce pas le bonheur?' (257) (I have [...] a large fortune. I have arrived at that stage in life for which I have longed for ages: to be the mistress of one's heart and one's actions; to have the friends of one's choice: is that not happiness?). Even Corinne, having arrived at precisely this point in her plot, had decided to give it all up and follow the morose lord, Sir Ralph, back to his native England.

Sapho, however, will not be stopped in her quest for vengeance. As melodramatic as the revenge plot may be, even in this early novel by Chabrillan, the unmelodramatic questions of the nature of good and evil and the respective weights of responsibility and social injustice are posed, and posed with anguish, but with no answers: 'c'est qu'en effet [...] je suis une nature étrange et qui ne peut se définir elle-même; j'ai beau regarder en moi, je ne vois que des ombres. Qu'est-ce qu'un rêve? Est-ce le présent ou le passé? Qu'est-ce qui est la réalité de ma vie? Est-ce le bien, est-ce le mal?' (261–2) (it's true [...] that I have a strange nature which cannot define itself. I try to look inside myself, but I see only shadows. What is a dream? Is it the present or the past? What is the reality of my life? Is it good; is it evil?). These are the issues which the Countess de Chabrillan's fiction will address obsessively. In *La Sapho*, the questions are all formulated, but the self remains explicitly opaque to analysis, and there seems to be no attempt at self-exoneration: what prevails is the blind need to punish. Indeed, retribution lies at the heart of this novel's 'work.'

If, in its insistence on vengeance, *La Sapho* rejoins the melodramatic plot, nonetheless the sense of agency and power bestowed upon the feminine persona here is remarkable indeed. Sapho conceives an elaborate plan to ruin and dishonour the Campbell family, a plan she

choreographs and stages in a way which will visit every possible humiliation on each member of the family. Paul Campbell has ruined himself buying Sapho jewellery, property, and art. Furthermore, she has
manipulated him into writing promissory notes on which he has forged
the signature of a family member. He receives an anonymous letter inviting him to what will be, unbeknown to him, the scene of reckoning.

Moreover, Sapho has managed to acquire incriminating correspondence between Léonie Campbell (née Pallier) and a lover. Our determined
stage director stands ready to reveal the Pallier daughter's adultery, a
disclosure which would also blur the boundary separating the virtuous
from the fallen woman. Léonie, too, has received a mysterious letter,
inviting her to a rendezvous. Next to be summoned by a letter, old
Monsieur Pallier is brought in to witness the dishonour of his daughter
and his son-in-law's criminal forgery, itself a grim reminder of the letter
he himself had forged so many years ago to such disastrous consequence
for Marie Laurent: 'Il [Monsieur Pallier] était venu pour commander, il
fut obligé de prier' (314) (Monsieur Pallier came to give orders; he was
obliged to beg).

Lady Campbell, the cold mother, has also been summoned to witness
the double dishonouring of her sons Richard and Paul. The anonymous
letter written to her had mentioned the false signatures of the Campbell
family name, and she is determined to buy them back, cost what may.
Finally, Richard has been 'invited' to appear in order to witness the ravages and dishonour he has brought down upon his erstwhile lover,
Marie Laurent. Sapho savours this little reunion in these terms: 'Ah!
Richard, bourreau de mon coeur! Je te verrai souffrir à mon tour! Je te
dirai le chemin que Marie a dû suivre pour devenir Sapho. Comme la
vie déflétrie est longue' (282) (Ah! Richard, my heart's tormentor! I shall
watch you suffer in my turn! I shall tell you about the path which Marie
has had to follow to become Sapho. How long is a life which is sullied
and withered).

In contrast to the complete vulnerability and powerlessness of young
Marie Laurent, Sapho has become, through her efforts exclusively, the
stage director in her own theatre of revenge : 'La mise en scène était
préparée' (304) (The stage was prepared). In broad daylight, she has her
sumptuous London residence brilliantly illuminated to spotlight the
scene during which she unveils her true identity. The spectators, confused at first, soon become participants in this little drama wherein
each will be required to expose his or her role in the downfall of Marie
Laurent. Sapho luxuriates in the public humiliation which she has been

orchestrating for so long and is now administering. She remains adamant and implacable in doling out the blame. To her lover Paul, who had prepared a secure future for her by signing over his remaining assets, she shows the door: 'Vous plaisantez, Sapho, oubliez-vous les sacrifices que je vous ai faits?' 'Non, mais c'est parce qu'il ne vous en reste plus à faire que je vous quitte. Vous n'exigez pas qu'une femme comme moi ait du coeur. Je ne vous ai jamais aimé, je ne vous l'ai jamais dit; par la même raison que vous nous quittez sans regret lorsque notre beauté passe, nous avons le droit de vous quitter lorsque vous êtes ruinés' (311) ('You are joking, Sapho. Are you forgetting the sacrifices I made for you?' 'No, but it is because there are none left to make that I am leaving you. You don't expect a woman like me to have a heart? I never loved you; I never said I did. For the same reason you leave us with no regrets when our beauty fades, we have the right to leave you when you're ruined'). To Monsieur Pallier, who wishes to buy back his daughter's amorous correspondence, Sapho is relentless: 'Ces lettres sont si curieuses que je ne vous connais pas le droit d'en priver la postérité' (314) (These letters are so curious that I do not grant you the right to deprive posterity of them).

It is to Richard, however, that the full weight of responsibility devolves. Never, declares Sapho, will she forgive him: '"Jamais," répondit Sapho avec un mouvement énergique; "Marie est morte, vous l'avez tuée"' (307), concluding that 'si je suis un monstre, c'est vous qui m'avez créée. Adieu, Richard, défendez-vous mieux de ma haine que je ne me suis défendue de votre amour' (308) (Never. Marie is dead. You killed her [...]. If I am a monster, you created me. Adieu, Richard. Defend yourself better from my hatred than I defended myself against your love). If the justice sought by Céleste de Chabrillan in the course of her lifetime with respect to the social conditions leading to her own prostitution remains elusive, she can at least mete it out in fiction. She does so with relish!

Nonetheless, the work of the text is not confined to accomplishing this purely destructive fantasy, although it is critical that the vengeance fantasy be played out in fiction in order for Chabrillan to move on in her life and in her writing. A couple of the subsidiary plots involving other characters sketch out potentially productive solutions to the thorny question of personal moral responsibility, which, if completely unequivocal in Sapho's case (as a victim, she *was* seduced and abandoned by Richard), is more ambiguous in the case of Céleste Vénard, who opted, with her mother's permission, it is true, to register herself as a prostitute at the age of sixteen. Somehow, if Chabrillan is to enjoy peace of mind, she will need to revise her personal history.

There are other issues under negotiation in this early novel by Chabrillan. The most prominent one, at least in terms of sheer textual space, is the Sapho/Lélia/mother figure constellation. It has been seen that the character Lélia alternates between lucidity and the kind of de-mentia which, in literature at least, can reveal deep and often otherwise unspeakable truths. In a trancelike state, Lélia evokes childhood memories of her mother, now lost to her, and asks Sapho if she has a mother: '"Moi," murmura Sapho d'une voix tremblante, "Dieu me l'a reprise."' '"S'il te l'a reprise,"' retorts Lélia, '"c'est que tu étais une mauvaise fille."' "Oh! Non," murmura Sapho en cachant sa figure dans ses mains pour pleurer' (284) ('As for myself, God took mine.' 'If he took her back, it's because you were a bad daughter.' 'Oh! No,' murmured Sapho hiding her face in her hands to cry).

The less sinister aspect of Sapho's plot has been to reunite one mother/daughter duo and to shed some light on the family origins of her ardent supporter, Fabien. Yet another letter has summoned one Madame Smith (who was discovered to be Lélia's lost mother) to the final reckoning scene. From behind a curtain (as befits the stage director), Sapho witnesses their reunion: 'elle [la mère] a deviné toutes les idées errantes de son enfant, elle a dit comme elle, lui donnant raison sur tout; au lieu d'une folle, on eût dit qu'il y en avait deux; elles sont heureuses; il n'y a que la tombe qui ne vous rende pas votre mère' (295) ([the mother] guessed all the rambling ideas of her child; she spoke like her; she agreed with her on everything. Instead of one crazy woman, one might have said there were two. They are happy: only the grave cannot return your mother to you). Thus a mother/daughter restoration scene is staged, one which leaves the door open to familial reconciliation as long as the parties involved are still alive.

As for Fabien, Sapho has done some research on his unknown origins as well. What she learns – knowledge she is thus empowered to transmit – is that Fabien's father was none other than her own 'protector,' who had seduced Fabien's mother, a young Irishwoman. Explains Sapho to Fabien: 'Ma mère, la tienne, Fabien, étaient le reflet presque invisible de deux pâles étoiles qui sont disparues en ne laissant de traces que dans nos coeurs' (316) (Your mother and mine, Fabien, were the nearly-invisible reflection of two pale stars which disappeared leaving traces in our hearts alone). Pallid stellar reflections and flowers gathered up only to be negligently tossed away: these are the images the novel employs to describe the vulnerability of underprivileged women. Try as she might, Sapho cannot make sense of *this* world, where good and evil are topsy-turvy, and wherein the *real* causes of misery and wrong appear to go unrecognized: 'J'ai souvent demandé à Dieu pourquoi il y avait des êtres plus heureux les uns que les autres; pourquoi l'un mourait de faim tandis que l'autre était écrasé par l'abondance; rien ne m'a repondu' (316–7) (I have often asked God why some beings were happier than others; why one died of hunger while the other was crushed under abundance; nothing answered me).

By novel's end, Sapho has avenged herself completely: her mission is nearly accomplished. Nonetheless, a few narrative threads need to be tied up, and other 'work' remains to be done. The plot comes to completion when an irate lover (a rival of Fabien) suddenly bursts into the room and attempts to shoot Fabien. Sapho interposes herself, receiving instead the fatal bullet. Her death scene and its aftermath conclude this novel, one of whose final issues will be the question of forgiveness. Indeed, as she lies dying, Sapho's final wish is to write: 'Donnez-moi de quoi écrire' (322) (Give me something to write with). She scribbles down her testament and then continues to argue with the faithful Fabien and her brother Pierre about the proper disposition of the many incriminating letters which she has been at such pains to collect. Even in her dying breath, she refuses clemency toward Paul Campbell, urging her survivors (and heirs) to deliver his forgeries to the police authorities. Apparently wracked by the need for vengeance until the very end, Sapho expires, having requested burial next to her mother's grave.

Yet Fabien cannot believe that Sapho would leave the world still clinging to thoughts of revenge; and, in a way, he is right. The two men open the testament, which, as written word, truly *is* the last word, superseding her orally expressed wishes. With some relief, they discover her instructions to deliver the compromising letters back to their authors. What, then, it must be asked, is the point of having Sapho refuse to pardon (orally) only to contravene her own nearly simultaneously expressed written wishes in her will? At the strictly narrative level, the narrator explains away the contradiction by attributing her mental state as she neared death to delirium, although this is not terribly convincing. In fact, this simultaneous 'yes' and 'no' allows the author/narrator to have her cake and eat it too. As a compromise construction, the contradiction signifies that an important issue (here forgiveness) is under psychological negotiation. Through the oral refusal to pardon, Sapho brings her vengeance plot to its logical completion.

Far more significant, however, is the other message being proposed here: namely, *that the act and product of writing supersede other acts*. And, as we shall see, it is on this latter truth that the Countess de Chabrillan is pinning her hopes.

Sapho's considerable fortune is to be divided among Pierre, Fabien, and Madame Smith, for the care of Lélia. Madame Smith 'restores' Lélia to innocence ('à force de soins, de caresses, elle la rendit obéissante et docile comme un enfant') (329) (through care and caresses, she made her as obedient and docile as a child), and Pierre and Fabien sail off for Australia: 'La nuit s'abaissa sur la mer, comme le rideau d'un théâtre lorsque le drame est fini' (331) (Night descended over the ocean, like the curtain in a theatre when the drama is over). And indeed, in the theatre of revenge, this drama has been completed.

In writing this novel, Céleste de Chabrillan has accomplished much. Besides meting out punishment to the author of every crime which brought harm to Marie Laurent, propelling her onto the long path of dishonour, there are several scenes of reparation and restoration. It is significant that these reparations are conducted at the level of characters *other than Sapho*, as if the plotting and execution of vengeance (or justice) were all that could be accomplished in one novel with direct regards to its heroine. But it is equally important that these gestures of restoration be sketched out as credible and indeed potential plots for future writing even if they do not – for the time being – relate to the novel's heroine. Thus a mother/daughter reunion is vicariously envisioned through Madame Smith and her daughter Lélia, who has herself been restored to an Edenic childhood in which she may be imagined free to tread a less disastrous path than the one Lélia (or Sapho, or Céleste Vénard) had travelled. In such a way, the silhouette of the dutiful daughter rests on the horizon of possibility, even if Sapho herself cannot repeal her *own* past. Indeed, she is not even allowed to survive her narrative of vengeance. Too much about her, for the present at least, remains unelucidated. As she herself had acknowledged: 'Je suis un mystère pour moi-même.'

The same type of melodramatic splitting of good and bad daughter exists at the level of maternal projection. With the 'real' mother (Madame Laurent) dead, the mother figures presented in the novel are polarized, with the cold Lady Campbell set out against the warm and maternal Madame Smith, who will nurture Lélia back to innocence. Nor are acts of reparation beyond the pale in this novel: even the primal seducer, the old libertine who has ruined more than one woman's life, has been shown making amends in the form of *post facto* cash compensations.

What is being suggested ever so tentatively through these various reparation scenes is that rehabilitation is possible. Moreover, to her surprise, Céleste de Chabrillan has discovered that writing is assuaging her bitterness:

Étudier le jour, écrire la nuit, rien ne m'arrêtait.
   Je me suis mise à ce travail et j'y ai trouvé un intérêt qui m'a surprise et enchantée. En repassant ma vie, j'étais étonnée de voir les amertumes s'en adoucir. Je découvrais en moi des ressources dont je ne m'étais pas doutée. (*Mémoires* 4: 178)

Studying during the day, writing at night; nothing stopped me.
   I took up this work and I found in it an interest which surprised and delighted me. In thinking over my life, I was astonished to see its bitternesses soften. I discovered within myself resources which I had not suspected.

For Chabrillan, herein lies the wonderful promise of fiction. It is in the theatre of writing that the work of self-rehabilitation will be most thoroughly achieved. In her life, the Countess de Chabrillan will carry out positive acts of reparation such as the founding of a school for girl orphans, but the *real* work of self-exoneration will take place bit by bit, through the elaboration of dilemmas (such as the above contradictions or polarizations) followed by their slow, laborious, and ultimately satisfactory resolution.

A 9 January 1856 journal entry written in Australia (transcribed in *Un deuil au bout du monde*) demonstrates Chabrillan's determination to follow this path: 'Je ne sors plus; j'écris beaucoup. J'ai fait et refait dix fois un roman sur les voleurs d'or. Je ne sais où le cacher, dans la crainte que Lionel ne le trouve' (100) (I no longer go out. I am writing a lot. I have done and ten times redone a novel on gold thieves. I don't know where to hide it in fear that Lionel will find it). Moreover, she is explicit and conscious of what she wishes to achieve through fiction: 'Enfin, j'aime mieux que tout ce que je fais soit perdu que d'avoir à me dire un jour: Ah! si j'avais eu plus de courage, j'aurais peut-être pu arriver à quelque chose; si la volonté d'être l'enfant de ses oeuvres n'est pas un vain mot, qui sait si dans quelques années on ne pardonnera pas à Lionel de m'avoir épousée' (100) (In the end, I prefer it if everything I do is lost rather than having to say to myself one day: Ah! If I had had more courage, perhaps I could have amounted to something. If the will to be the child of one's works is not a futile phrase, who knows whether or not, in a few years, Lionel will be forgiven for having married me). From the very outset of her writing career, then, the Countess de Chabrillan aspires to forge the literary voice necessary to the project of self-rebirthing. What a rare and powerful image for a daunting project!

This analysis of *La Sapho* has demonstrated what happens when the lens of writing passes from the beholder to the beheld. In Chabrillan's prose, the conventional flower/seduction image is uprooted and the reader is afforded the perspective from the flower's point of view: 'Le voyageur qui a son but ne s'arrête pas pour épargner les pauvres fleurs des champs qui sont sous ses pieds. Dieu les a créées, le soleil les fait vivre, mais il ne les défend pas: il semble que tout soit inventé pour le caprice de l'homme' (*Sapho* 279) (The traveller who has his goal does not stop to spare the poor wildflowers under his feet. God created them; the sun makes them live, but he does not defend them. It seems that everything has been invented for the whims of man).

It is probably in Zola's 1880 novel *Nana* that the hysteria surrounding the 'powerful' courtesan figure reached its apogee. In one sense, the Sapho persona created by Chabrillan in 1858 prefigures Zola's (future) representation in that the female protagonist does achieve Nana's level of wealth and influence. But Sapho attains this exalted vantage point and power not due to some natural and essential viciousness of character typical of Zola's voracious virago, but exclusively in order to be in a position to rectify the injustices of a society in which 'tout semble inventé pour le caprice de l'homme.' Whereas Zola's Nana and her sister demi-mondaines managed to crush an entire regime between their thighs, Sapho's mission as the flower consumed is to avenge all those young women for whom prostitution may have been the sole means of survival.

It is not too much of a stretch in time to conjure up one of those Toulouse-Lautrec paintings of the man in a top hat ogling the dancers on stage through his elegant monocle. The eyepiece points to the direction of the male gaze and thus to the objectivization of the women being observed. However, because the glass is detached from the man's eye and doubles it, as it were, the viewing subject is reverberated and generalized, becoming Every Man gazing. Imagine now Sapho equipped with her own lorgnette, peering back from the stage at the many men indulging in acts of predatory viewing. Such is the unique reverse perspective offered in the fiction of Céleste de Chabrillan.

5 Plotting Exoneration

La Sapho is a key work in Chabrillan's literary production, and it is no accident that it occurs early on in her writing itinerary. Although the Countess would shy away from using the demi-monde in her other novels, it is easy to see why she spotlighted it in *La Sapho*. This is the novel which afforded her the full expression of her rage: rage at what had happened to her personally and, beyond that, at the social realities which propelled young women into lives of sexual servitude. Equally attractive for her, no doubt, was the prospect of vicarious vengeance, which she could derive through her characters and the situations in which she placed them. All in all, writing *La Sapho* must have been a powerfully cathartic experience for Céleste de Chabrillan. With her fury at least partially assuaged, our nascent writer was freed up to treat other subjects.

From 1857 through 1885, Chabrillan penned ten novels, four of which were reissued and at least one of which was fashioned into a play. These include *Les voleurs d'or* (1857), *La Sapho* (1858), *Miss Pewel* (1859), *Est-il fou?* (1860), *Un miracle à Vichy* (1861), *Émigrantes et déportées* (1876), *La duchesse de Mers* (1881), *Les forçats de l'amour* (1881), *Marie Baude* (1883), and *Un drame sur le Tage* (1885). During the fifteen-year hiatus separating *Un miracle à Vichy* from *Émigrantes et déportées*, Chabrillan developed her skills as a playwright, composing and staging at least ten plays. The date of her final novel – 1885 – coincides with the end of her career in the theatre, a fact which is highly significant, as the last chapter of this book will demonstrate. And if there is a single significant event which marked Chabrillan's writing career and altered her creative trajectory, it was the death of her mother in 1874. To the end, their relationship had remained conflicted.

The goal of the current chapter is twofold. The first part is devoted to a general description of Céleste de Chabrillan's artistic evolution as a writer and to the themes which recur throughout her work. Because one of the projects of *Writing with a Vengeance* is to introduce an extraordinary woman writer, an overview of the central concerns articulated in her fiction is necessary. These themes – chiefly related to oppression – will be explored without regard to the sequence of their appearance since, indeed, they span her oeuvre.

The second part of this chapter, on the other hand, attends closely to the permutation of certain key elements of story line over time. For what one realizes in reading the Countess's fiction in its entirety is that beyond the narrative logic governing individual plots, there are 'kernels' of narrative incessantly being retold, albeit in different formulations. This is where chronology of composition moves to the fore of the analysis. Why – we shall be asking – is so much selective narrative rehashing taking place? Where is it leading?

Since the topic of the demi-monde was marginalized by Chabrillan in her writings subsequent to *La Sapho*, one might well wonder what part of Chabrillan's experience remained that could be recounted. The response lies in her life of travel, indeed a rich resource. Three of her novels are situated, at least partially, in Australia. *Un drame sur le Tage* takes place in Lisbon, while there are others whose action is placed in London. And then there is *Marie Baude*, a later novel featuring Parisian bohemia and the working classes. Like most writers, Chabrillan used venues with which she was personally familiar, drawing her characters from across the range of classes, all of which she had been exposed to first-hand due to the socially transgressive nature of her former trade. If her tales take their characters from all classes, however, the perspective she brings to bear on the world she creates is resolutely one of working-class awareness.

As the Countess advanced in her apprenticeship to writing, there is a clear evolution in style and narrative plotting. Plot resolution in some of her early works (*Les voleurs d'or* [1857] or *Miss Pewel* [1859]) relies heavily on coincidence. With time, however, her style became consistently lighter, and it is fair to say that two of her later novels, *La duchesse de Mers* (1881) and the beginning of *Marie Baude* (1883), have passages which sparkle with wit. These two later novels will be treated in this chapter, which will also revisit *La Sapho* occasionally when it is important to stress the linear chronology of Chabrillan's writing.

In general, the situations of her novels tend to the melodramatic, vengeance being one of the central themes. This is particularly true of her early work. Much evil is afoot in these worlds, which teem with rapes, seductions, thefts, counterfeits, and even homicides. Furthermore, the women characters are armed and violent in ways rarely seen in fiction of this period. Sapho sports a revolver (as did Mogador)[1] and shoots very accurately, whereas mad Jenny of *Miss Pewel* kills by the blade. Personal life, narrative, and melodrama are threads which are closely intertwined beginning with her early writing.

The elements of melodrama, linked both to her personal past on the boulevard du Crime and to her class appear throughout Chabrillan's oeuvre. Gradually, however, the melodramatic aspects of her writing wane as her writing skills become more refined and as she herself becomes less angry and more reconciled with her past. In her late novel *La duchesse de Mers*, a Countess advises the Duchess on how to end her liaison with her noble, albeit broke, lover: 'Ne cherchez pas à finir votre roman de moeurs, comme finissent les vieux mélodrames. Nous n'avons plus de vengeurs, n'ayons plus de remords inutiles' (17) (Don't seek to end your novel of manners the way melodramas finish. We no longer have avengers: let's not entertain useless remorse anymore either). Guilt and vengeance are thus indissociably linked, for if there has been a need for vengeance, it is because those who have put the ex-prostitute Mogador in the position of feeling guilty must be punished. Ultimately, though, what will be the most important for Chabrillan in her writing is that *the very concept of guilt* itself must be challenged. Even as early as her third novel, *Miss Pewel*, the melodramatic tenor is consistently overridden by philosophical and moral considerations such as the role of forgiveness and the nature of justice, an ethical perspective which complicates – and even subverts – melodrama's facile polarities. As for her characters, while they are heavily polarized in her early novels as good or evil, they become more nuanced with time.

Twenty-eight years separate the Countess's first novel, *Les voleurs d'or* (1857), and her final narrative, *Un drame sur le Tage* (1885), and there is a world of difference between them. From the awkward plotting of her beginnings as an author, she has learned to assemble well-constructed narratives whose resolutions issue cogently from their narrative premises. For, in the course of Chabrillan's development as a writer, something interesting happens to her female characters. Compared with the Sapho persona, so obviously an authorial projection, the later novels feature two or even three strong women figures – not always sympathetic, but whose personality flaws may be justified by their experiences as victims of social injustice. Thus, as Céleste de Chabrillan ages, and as she begins to see herself retrospectively with a sense of detachment at different stages of life, her women characters multiply and embody, diversely, various of the Countess's traits and moral dilemmas. For instance, in *Les forçats de l'amour* (1881), the eldest of the three strong female characters, the mysterious and powerful Mistress Branck, tells the middle-aged woman Diana Wolf: 'Que de peines se donnent nos romanciers à chercher des fictions quand ils n'auraient qu'à écrire mes mémoires' (175) (How much trouble our novelists take looking for fictions when all they would have to do is write my memoirs). The projection of the Mogador persona onto one of her characters is not difficult to discern here.

Concurrently with the strong woman figures and the emphasis on a working-class perspective, the novels touch on issues which one would be hard-pressed to find in other fiction of this period. In *Les voleurs d'or*, for example, a young woman who has been raped becomes pregnant. The expression of her feelings about this 'alien' presence in her body plus the frank admission of her desire to abort it are astonishing: 'Ce n'est point un enfant que je vais mettre au monde, c'est un reptile [...] et je voudrais l'arracher de mes entrailles. Mille fois j'ai voulu tenter ma délivrance' (212) (It is not a child which I am going to bring into the world; it's a reptile [...] and I would like to tear it from my womb. A thousand times I have wanted to deliver myself of it).[2]

Céleste Vénard's life of mountainous social highs and cavernous lows gave her a remarkable vantage point from which to view the arrogance of undeserving privilege. Autodidact though she may have been, she nonetheless grasped perfectly well that privilege is an affair of gender, class, and race, and her narratives abound in characters who are only too conscious of whom their society benefits the most.

Because the solidarity with the underprivileged is so pronounced in her fiction, it merits particular attention. The novelistic worlds created by our author are heavily – though not exclusively – populated by the working classes and the urban poor: hat makers, washerwomen, sailors, street vendors, beggars, weavers, embroiderers, domestic servants, grooms, butlers, and many more. Although scoundrels and rogues abound, they come from all classes. Where class difference is an issue, the text usually empathizes with the lot of the underdog. One of Chabrillan's most telling descriptions of the toll which long-term servitude can exact on a person's very being is to be found in *La Sapho* apropos of a maid, Rosalie: 'Lorsqu'on est obligé pour vivre de se plier sous la volonté d'autrui, on n'a plus le droit d'avoir une idée. Elle était devenue ce que deviennent beaucoup de serviteurs à la longue: l'exécuteur de la pensée des autres. On n'a rien à soi, pas une heure [...] on ne peut ni rire ni pleurer sans qu'on vous le permette' (147) (When, in order to live, one is obliged to bend to the will of others, one no longer has the right to have an idea. She had become what most servants become in the long run: the executor of others' thoughts. One has nothing to oneself, not even an hour [...] one can neither laugh nor cry unless you are authorized to do so). The pronominal slide from the generic 'on' to the 'vous' abruptly shifts the discourse from the impersonal objective into the personal subjective mode, where suddenly the reader is forced to shoulder the uncomfortable burden of victimization.

In *La duchesse de Mers*, the Duchess's maid hesitantly asks her mistress if she may attend the funeral of her own illegitimate child. The compassionate Duchess, herself remorseful about an adulterous liaison in which she has long been involved, exclaims: 'Ah! vous êtes tout excusés, vous, pauvres enfants que rien n'avertit, que rien ne protège, tandis que nous [...]' (49) (Ah! You can be excused for anything, poor children whom nothing warns and nothing protects, whereas we [...]). The sympathies and authorial identifications here are fairly clear: what we also glean from this quote is how often the hypocrisy and double standards of the period must have resulted in dismissals for domestics who found themselves in these situations.

There are many other snapshots of the social conditions which lead to 'vice.' For instance, in *La Sapho,* the text describes the dreadful mistreatment of sailors as a way of explaining their legendary drunkenness. And in one chilling episode of the memoirs, Céleste Mogador and la Reine Pomaré are leaving a restaurant in the wee hours of the night. The Parisian landscape is desolate, and the urban rag pickers are hard at their work when a woman streetsweeper brushes dust onto Pomaré's legs. La Pomaré's upbraids her and receives this response: 'Tiens! Voyez-vous ça, madame l'embarras! [...] J'ai été un peu mieux que toi, ma petite, et un peu plus huppée; mais j'étais pas fière avec le pauvre monde' (*Mémoires* 1: 302) (Well, look at that, Madame Complaint! [...] I was a little better looking than you, my little one, and a bit more classy. But I was never proud with poor folks). This is one of the constant reminders in the *Mémoires* that dust returns to dust and whores end up on the dissection slab.

One of the most poignant class-related reproaches expressed in Chabrillan's oeuvre is the way the rich squander the education that would be so precious to the poor. The narrator of *La duchesse de Mers* makes a wry comment on dandy Achille de Marembry's affected lower-class dialect: 'ce mauvais genre a tellement plu et pris, que la langue morte des petits voyous du vieux boulevard du Temple est ressuscitée avec les enjolivements de l'argot des filous; pendant que les uns cherchent à s'instruire, à s'élever par le travail de l'esprit, d'autres cherchent à descendre, à s'abaisser' (21) (this bad lingo appealed and was adopted with the result that the dead language of the small bullies from the boulevard du Temple was resuscitated and embellished with the slang of petty thieves. While some seek to learn, to rise through the work of the mind, others seek to descend, to lower themselves). There is little doubt as to which category the Countess belongs. Marie Baude, a silent and self-silencing character who finally does not send an important letter because she so fears having made 'quelque faute d'orthographe grossière' (240) (some gross spelling error) explains to her rival, Adrienne, how she has acquired such instruction as she has: 'ma chère […] je glane un peu partout […] c'est de cette manière que les niveaux s'égalisent; vous sortez de vos pensionnats dégoûtés de vos études; nous qui regrettons de ne pas les avoir faites, nous vous imitons dans ce qu'il vous reste de mieux' (240) (my dear […] I glean a bit from everywhere […] this is how levels equalize. You leave your boarding schools disgusted with your studies; we regret not having done them. We imitate what remains the best in you). Thus beyond the clear awareness of the disparities born of class privilege, the Countess sees the way to attenuate these differences: education.

Chabrillan's fiction is not centrally preoccupied with issues of race. Indeed, she herself was anti-Semitic, although, perhaps more unusually, she was also keenly aware of this fact. When a brilliant young Jewish composer fell in love with her, she rejected him because of his faith, noting nonetheless that given her past, she should have been the last person to harbour such prejudices: 'à moi moins qu'à toute autre personne il appartient d'avoir des préventions' (*Mémoires* 2: 73) (I should be the last person to have biases).

In her anti-Semitism, the Countess is very much of her time, when such attitudes were probably more the rule than the exception. She is less of her time, however, in some of her remarks regarding the indigenous peoples of the world to whose spoliation and extermination she bore witness in her travels. In the second instalment of her memoirs, *Un deuil au bout du monde*, Chabrillan relates how, at the Cape of Good Hope, the English were treating the Kaffir king whom they had taken captive with great brutality: 'Eh bien, je trouve odieuse cette manière de procéder avec un ennemi vaincu, quel qu'il soit' (Well, I find this way of dealing with a conquered enemy – whoever it may be – odious), predicting that: 'Toutes ces peuplades qu'on pourchasse sans cesse pour les déposséder, se révolteront un jour; les Cafres ont déjà commencé, d'autres finiront, et ce sera une guerre d'extermination dans laquelle ce sauvage aura droit d'être féroce parce que l'homme civilisé a été cruel' (55) (All these peoples who are being endlessly pursued in order to be dispossessed will rise up in revolt one day. The Kaffirs have already begun; others will finish, and it will be a war of extermination in which the savage will have the right to be ferocious because civilized man has been cruel). The imperialist notions of primitivism versus civilization may remain in place in her thinking, but Chabrillan retains the same empathy with the racially oppressed as she does in the case of gender and class.

Un deuil au bout du monde was translated into English by two Australians, likely because it constitutes an extraordinary document of early frontier life in Australia.[3] The Countess finds the aboriginal population frankly repulsive: 'la tête démesurément grosse, les cheveux hérissés et crépus, [...] la poitrine bombée parce qu'ils tiennent toujours leur coudes pointus en arrière' (112) (heads disproportionately large, hair frizzy and standing out [...] chests thrust forward because they always hold their elbows pointed behind them [...]). They eat the colonizers' garbage along with raw worms which abound in the bark of trees. It is more than a 'civilized' woman can stomach, and here again she predicts the disappearance of this indigenous people: 'on en rencontre de moins en moins [...] à mesure que les villes se forment, ils reculent, et je crois qu'ils disparaîtront bientôt' (115) (one encounters fewer and fewer of them [...] as towns grow, they are retreating, and I think that they will disappear soon).

Let us now turn to questions of social injustice and to the unusual perspective which Chabrillan's novels offer of the social 'down under,' and finally, to her one novel, *Les forçats de l'amour*, to confront the issue of white domination of other races. Céleste Vénard, the future Countess de Chabrillan, did not possess the systematized consciousness of the social inequities characteristic of some of her female contemporaries such as George Sand, Olympe Audouard, and Suzanne Voilquin. If Mogador practised the free love (well, hardly free) advocated as a liberation by some of the *saint-simoniennes*, it would only be to her great regret subsequently. So it was that while Céleste yearned to join the fold of bourgeois respectability, the Saint-Simonians and other social reformers

were looking hard to expand the parameters of acceptable female behaviour and action. In Chabrillan's apparent conservatism, however,
one should not overlook the fact that none of these more intellectually
emancipated women had suffered social stigmatization to the degree
that Céleste Mogador had. And she remained scarred by it, in body,
spirit, and soul.

As a child of eight, Céleste had witnessed first-hand the great violence of the Lyons insurrection. For the remainder of her life, she would
harbour a fear of working-class uprisings, although in 1870, she would
befriend one of the more notorious revolutionaries of the Commune
movement. In the 1848 Revolution, she did her utmost to protect her
future spouse, Lionel de Chabrillan, an obvious potential target of en-
raged proletarian mobs, particularly as he helped to dismantle the bar-
ricades which mushroomed in the various *quartiers* of Paris.

Nonetheless, Céleste Vénard had a very real consciousness of social
oppression, and it was born of constant and reiterated instances of personal humiliation. Her exposure to the nobility made her keenly aware
of the injustice of privilege. Her permanent ostracism from respectability by the culture at large fuelled her anger against societal hypocrisy.
The frequent victimization of poor women by men and the powerlessness of these women to improve their lot led her to an awareness of her
society's oppression of women. And although Céleste does not manifest a class consciousness per se, her fiction is full of cameo narratives
of individual workers and their daily tragedies.

What part, then, did the consciousness of gender oppression take
when worked into her writing? On the level of the narrative elaboration
of gender-based injustices, the two novels published in rapid succes-
sion, *Les forçats de l'amour* (1881) and *Marie Baude* (1883), present two
contradictory articulations of the question. Remarkably enough, the
first novel (*Les forçats*) actually sets up an unjust situation which the
author will then rectify in the subsequent novel.

Les forçats is a distinctive novel in that it features three strong female
characters: a young woman of colour (*Noée*), a middle-aged woman
(Mistress Wolf), and an elderly woman (Mistress Branck). Céleste de
Chabrillan, now fifty-seven years old, has at last acquired sufficient detachment from the wounded writing self of *La Sapho* to have acquired a
lucid retrospective view of herself at three distinct periods of her life.
Let us recall that in the staging of vengeance which was *La Sapho*'s
'work,' Sapho had said, over and over again, that her 'self' remains
completely opaque to her: 'c'est qu'en effet [...] je suis une nature

étrange et qui ne peut se définir elle-même; j'ai beau regarder en moi, je ne vois que des ombres' (261–2) (in fact [...] I have a strange nature which cannot define itself; in vain do I look within myself: I see only shadows). But that was in 1858, over twenty years earlier.

Although there are a number of male characters in *Les forçats*, only one qualifies as the protagonist: Albin Desjardins, the son of a wealthy shipping magnate based in Le Havre. Albin is setting off on the *Éclair* under Captain Faure on a kind of maritime world tour meant to complete his apprenticeship in the navigation industry. As was the case in Chabrillan's own trip to Australia, the *Éclair* nearly wrecks off the Cape of Good Hope, where it is forced to put in for repairs that will take a month to complete.

Les forçats de l'amour is Chabrillan's only novel to take up the question of racial oppression, but it does so with extraordinary vehemence. Here, as elsewhere, character names are significant: the whiteness connoted by Albin's name points to race as one of the novel's major preoccupations. While at the Cape, the passengers are lodged at a hotel where they are frequently entertained by the French consul. Albin, whom the narrator describes as having a 'légereté qui faisait le fond de son caractère' (45) (carelessness which formed the basis of his personality), is immediately attracted to the hotel maid, a Malaysian woman named Noée. For Albin, Noée is an easy prey: she is young and innocent, with an ear unaccustomed to the dulcet tones of the seducer from the West. Captain Faure, who has been keeping a watchful eye on his protegé Albin, counsels the latter not to attempt the seduction on racial grounds: 'Noée n'est pas une jeune fille, c'est une Malaise [...]. Pour moi les femmes de couleur n'existent pas' (68) (Noée is not a young woman. She's a Malaysian [...]. For me, women of colour do not exist). Disregarding the Captain's advice, Albin seduces Noée, a seduction which results in her suicide. Albin, a young man of privilege who has never had to give the consequences of his actions a second thought, is very disturbed by this death.

The Noée subplot of *Les forçats* is clearly redolent of George Sand's early novel *Indiana*. Therein, the Creole servant Noun is seduced by the young noble Raymon, who actually loves her mistress, Indiana. Raymon's thoughtless actions, which ran roughshod over Noun's feelings, result in her suicide, and she is found, a black Ophelia, floating in a pond. Sand's *Indiana* is thus a probable intertext of *Les forçats de l'amour*. This noted, Chabrillan demonstrates a far greater empathy with the hatred and rancour of the racially oppressed than Sand had shown in *Indiana*. In fact, Chabrillan has even created a character, an East Indian, to embody this rancour. Le Lion, as he is called, is in love with Noée and cautions her regarding Albin's intentions: 'Pour moi, tu es belle [...] pour lui tu es une femme de couleur' (66) (For me, you are beautiful [...] for him you are a woman of colour). On realizing what Noée has done, le Lion climbs the mountain from which his beloved had hurled herself, shadowed by Albin. When Albin understands that le Lion has loved this woman all along, he asks him for pardon. But le Lion has only contempt for him: '"Nous sommes si peu, nous autres, gens de couleur, qu'on peut nous sacrifier impunément," répondit le Lion avec une dignité qui écrasa moralement Albin [...]. "Je jure de la venger sur la race entière des blancs"' (161) ('We people of colour matter so little that we can be sacrificed with impunity,' responded le Lion with a dignity which crushed Albin morally [...]. 'I swear to avenge her on the entire white race').

All too soon, Albin's attentions focus on Diana Wolf, a married woman who is far less naive than the innocent Noée. In fact, Diana is not presented as a sympathetic character, particularly toward the novel's beginning. Noting that Mrs Wolf can be cruel to women she views as rivals, the narrator relativizes her behaviour by comparing it to that of men: 'Si ce caractère vous paraît extraordinaire chez une femme, on le comprendra peut-être en mettant en regard celui des hommes qui aiment la guerre, voir couler le sang qui donne la mort à leurs semblables' (69–70) (If this character trait seems to you to be extraordinary in a woman, it can perhaps be better understood when compared with that of men who love war and love to see the blood of their fellow humans shed). Mrs Wolf and Albin begin an affair of which Captain Faure, by secret letter, informs her husband who is in Australia. Meanwhile, Diana Wolf is pregnant, and when they dock in Sydney and Mr Wolf comes to claim her, the identity of the father becomes abundantly clear.

The events in Australia are a maze of peripeteia which allow, amid other things, the character of strange Mistress Branck to be elucidated. Ultimately Mr Wolf dies and Albin has sailed homeward with the ever-solicitous Captain Faure, thinking Diana has been reconciled with her husband. Instead, the latter, pregnant and ill, has set off herself in search of her lover, the father of her child.

Albin Desjardins returns a hero to Le Havre and the paternal hearth. His father, meanwhile, has arranged for him to marry a cousin, and the indecisive Albin, giving little thought to Diana Wolf, marries. Wolf, drugged and duped by ship captains (who seem to be the novel's evil genies), dies on board a ship docked in Le Havre. By novel's end, even the amoral Captain Faure regrets his participation in 'toutes les folies dangereuses du fils de son armateur pour lequel il n'y avait ni remords, ni châtiment' (278) (all the dangerous follies of the shipper's son for which there was neither remorse nor punishment). What *Les forçats de l'amour* presents to the reader familiar to the conventions of Western narrative is nothing less than the underside of the male novel of initiation – that is to say, the toll taken on *others* by the protagonist's itinerary toward homecoming and maturity.

'Neither remorse nor punishment': the narrator's final words seal the novel's message of the unaccountability of male privilege. Two women have perished as a direct result of Albin's behaviour, 'mais ni douleurs, ni regrets, ni chagrins, ne pouvaient troubler même à la surface ce bonheur nonmérité et si parfait' (279) (but neither pain, nor regret, nor chagrin could trouble even the surface of this perfect and undeserved happiness). *Les forçats de l'amour* ends with the triumph of injustice. There is no doubt that Céleste Mogador experienced gender- and class-related injustice with white-hot anger. If *Les forçats* ends on the triumph of inequity, her next novel, *Marie Baude*, addresses – and indeed redresses – this very injustice while settling a personal score to boot.

The Countess de Chabrillan stood well beyond the pale of orthodoxy both with regard to the subjects she chose to treat and in terms of her consistent solidarity with the underclasses. In this respect, she is a writer of courage and great conviction. It was in fact precisely this moral commitment which led her to donate her property in Le Vésinet to the Sisters of Saint-Charles in 1875. However, this generous gift made in order to establish an orphanage for young girls was accepted only on the condition that the name of its benefactress not figure officially in its founding. For how could an ex-Mogador possibly be permitted to underwrite a charitable institution? By 1875 then – and probably well before – Céleste must have realized that the society in which she lived would never admit her into the ranks of respectability.

The realization that her society would forever withhold pardon from her would bring a new meaning to the function and power of Chabrillan's writing process. Henceforth only the act of writing could hold out the hope of personal redemption, now clearly out of reach in other areas of her life. Personal transformation of this magnitude never takes place overnight, but, in fact, from its inception the Countess's work had already begun to lay the foundations of exoneration. From now on, through various strategies of equivocation, her works will negotiate and debate issues of responsibility, calling into question verdicts of guilty while occasionally offering characters solace from the torment of blame. Slowly, through shifting iterations of the same dilemma, Céleste de Chabrillan will undertake the reconstruction of a new story all her own.

The central thesis of the remainder of *Writing with a Vengeance* is that with each novel on her itinerary, the ex-Mogador will make limited progress toward self-pardon. Sometimes there will be backsliding in a subsequent work which may revisit the same issue as if to consolidate earlier gains. Gradually and laboriously, however, each act of writing moves her further along the trajectory of self-acceptance. What this type of incremental evolution implies is that whereas each novel stands alone as a piece of fiction in its own right with its own particular themes and internal logic, each work also – and more importantly – constitutes a 'chapter' in a master plot whose narrative stakes far exceed those of the individual novels. Let us now observe as the Countess's fiction works through the paralysing questions of remorse, retribution, and responsibility.

Thus it is that guilt makes itself felt relentlessly in ex-Mogador's work. Every single novel has at its heart the wrongdoing of one – and often of several – characters. This is the thematic matrix from which all other issues emanate. The crimes may range from adultery to robbery and even to murder, but they are always the pivotal question of the narrative. By situating several of her novels in Australia, besides providing fascinating reading for her contemporaries, Chabrillan has selected a kind of territorial alter ego of herself. As a penal colony, the country is populated by convicts serving out their sentences, or ex-convicts having already done so. There are as well the myriad seekers of fortune and immigrants leaving their native countries to escape misfortune or the reach of the law. Finally, there are the representatives of the British crown charged with maintaining order in the country and its prisons, with exploiting the land as well as ensuring that the new Australian 'race' remains white.

In many ways, then, Céleste de Chabrillan must have sensed a shared identity with the country. Founded as a space to contain guilt and crime – a sort of *maison close* of the British Empire – expiation through forced labour, although technically possible, was in reality socially impossible. Not only did ex-convicts remain social outcasts for life, their position as untouchables redounded upon their progeny.

Thus, in an uncanny parallel to ex-Mogador's predicament in France, the Australian convict was essentially unrehabilitatable.

In fact, *Les voleurs d'or* presents an intermediate caste: those sent to Australia with only light sentences to serve out. These 'emancipists,' as they were termed, hoped to be integrated into the mainstream colonial culture. In vain, however, 'il en fut autrement. Ils furent méprisés' (92) (it did not turn out that way. They were held in contempt). Even more cruel, however, was the fate reserved for the innocent descendants of the ex-convicts: 'L'homme qui fréquentait le fils ou le petit-fils d'un convict était exclu de la société; les préjugés devenaient si forts, la séparation si absolue et si tranchée, que la vie de chacun était scrutée avec soin et qu'on se livrait les uns aux dépens des autres à une véritable inquisition' (92) (The man who frequented the son and the grandson of a convict was excluded from society. The prejudices had become so strong, the separation so absolute and distinct, that the life of each person was scrutinized with care, and a veritable inquisition was carried out by some at the expense of others).

The 1859 *Miss Pewel*, situated entirely in Australia, features a female character, Mary Acton, whose mother had changed her last name unbeknown to her daughter: her father had been an ex-convict allowed entry to certain towns only and was 'reduced' to earning his living by doing business 'avec les noirs' (275) (with the blacks). This is the tainted source of Mary Acton's fortune which, in fact, precludes her marriage into respectability. While actually innocent, Mary is viewed as 'semi-guilty' – one of the many borderline formulations of the guilt/innocence problem typical of Chabrillan's fictional strategies of equivocation.

In *Miss Pewel*, where almost every character has a secret crime to his or her credit, one of the outcomes is the exculpation of some of those considered guilty, followed by the lifting of opprobrium from the shoulders of the innocent descendants. As virtually the only untainted character in the novel, Lucie alone is empowered to dispense absolution to Mary Acton (whose only flaw was to be her mother's daughter): 'Peu importe d'où vient la créature,' she proclaims, 'de qui elle est fille, quand elle est grande par le coeur; respectez-la, aimez-la [...]' (305) (What difference where the creature comes from, whose daughter she is: when she has a great heart, respect her; love her). In this quote, the projection of the Mogadorian persona onto Mary Acton comes abruptly and sharply into focus through the choice of 'creature,' a term reserved in Céleste's lexicon for the prostitute. It is not a term appropriate to

Mary Acton, herself virtuous. The use of 'creature' is symptomatic of Chabrillan's personal investment in this character.

Absolved by Lucie's pronouncement, then, Mary is free to wed Lucie's brother André. But André's mother had a guilty secret of her own, one of which he, too, was unaware. While his sister Lucie is legitimate, André is the offspring of an adulterous liaison. In this novel, two mothers are discovered to harbour guilty secrets, secrets which radically alter the lives of their children for the worse, plunging them into disrepute. Mary, despairing, exclaims, 'Ah! ma mère, ma mère, ne puis-je donc penser à vous sans vous maudire?' (266) (Ah! My mother, my mother: can I not think of you without cursing you?), while André, her intended, wonders 'laquelle des deux mères était la coupable?' (279) (which of the two mothers was the guilty one?).

In this, Chabrillan's third novel, the possibility of maternal guilt is raised for the first time. In the previous work, *La Sapho*, the daughter figure (Sapho) assumes the complete burden of culpability. Throughout her life, Céleste would be tormented by the question of which of the two of them – mother or daughter – should be held responsible for the 'moral suicide' which was her slide into prostitution. The shifting of positions on this question from one novel to the next is an example of equivocation and negotiation of this painful issue, which, not coincidentally, will only be resolved in her final novel, *Un drame sur le Tage*, written well after her mother's death.

Miss Pewel is an early work, composed when Chabrillan could reasonably hope for moral resurrection, and the narrator ends on this happy note: 'Le coeur fait quelquefois fausse route, le destin a tant à faire, qu'il ne peut pas nous guider tous à la fois. Donnez au coeur le temps de reconnaître son erreur, de revenir lui-même. Tant qu'on n'est pas mort, on peut espérer' (317) (Sometimes the heart takes the wrong path. Destiny has so much to do that it can't guide us all at the same time. Give the heart time to recognize its error, to come back on its own. As long as one is not dead, one can hope). Alas, the optimism of this hope, so poignantly expressed in 1859, will be slowly eroded as time wears on and societal pardon remains elusive for Chabrillan.

Another major theme explored in *Miss Pewel* is that of forgiveness. Already in *La Sapho* we saw that the question of pardon – both pardon of the wayward daughter Lélia as well as forgiveness by the daughter-figure Sapho of those responsible for her fall into prostitution – was tentatively broached. The subsequent novel, *Miss Pewel*, on the other hand, embraces the project of forgiveness fully. The titular character (published under the title of *Une méchante femme* in its 1877 second edition) had been seduced and deserted as a young woman. She has chosen *not* to forgive, and lives a life of increasing bitterness given over to sordid plotting. It is perhaps appropriate, then, that Miss Pewel meets a violent end, stabbed by a madwoman. Such, apparently, are the rewards of the incapacity to forgive. If the articulation of pardon in Miss Pewel through pardon of the children figures André and Mary constitutes an evolution with respect to *La Sapho*, the troubling puzzle of maternal guilt has barely made it onto the table. In terms of the overall masterplot, much narrative work remains to be done on this question.

Marie Baude (1883) is a product of Chabrillan's maturity. Its immediate predecessor, *Les forçats de l'amour*, was discussed earlier in terms of its major themes: gender- and race-related oppression. The novel ends (it will be recalled) with the triumph of injustice: Albin Desjardins returns home to a hero's welcome with all the rewards of the male novel of initiation, including an advantageous marriage. How did a writer like Chabrillan, so angry about the inequities of her culture, and so capable of retribution-through-fiction, allow her novel to end in this manner?

One of the resources which fiction writing opens up to its practitioners is the capacity to 'rectify' history. Many of Balzac's pages present readers with fictional repeals of certain parts of the Napoleonic Code which he considered politically disastrous, such as the abolition of primogeniture. Chabrillan, too, avails herself abundantly of this liberating potential. If *Les forçats* ends disconcertingly for the reader who is familiar with other of the Countess's novels, it is because it must be considered to be part of a larger plot. As we shall see, its successor novel, *Marie Baude*, will pick up where *Les forçats* left off.

Marie Baude's action takes place in artistic bohemia, which is liberally populated by the working classes. The narrative sympathies are clearly with the small tradespeople. When Marius from Bordeaux enquires of Madame Carnet as to the whereabouts of his painter-friend, Albert Laville, Madame Carnet muses: 'C'est un noble [...]. Voilà pourquoi c'est si mal élevé; ça vous appelle portier, au lieu de dire concierge!' (*Baude* 4) (It's a noble [...]. That's why it has no manners. It calls you porter instead of saying concierge!). Chabrillan also pokes gentle fun of Parisians as Marius once again asks directions, this time of a police officer: 'Voilà certainement un provincial' (Surely this man is from the provinces), thinks the policeman, 'les Parisiens ne nous saluent pas; à peine nous disent-ils "merci," quand ils ont besoin de nos services' (4) (Parisians don't greet us; they hardly say 'thank you' when they need our services).

It is clear by the tone set in her penultimate novel's opening that Céleste de Chabrillan has made enormous strides in her writing. The subject of *Marie Baude* is serious, but the narrative itself is nonetheless infused with humour and levity. Furthermore, a linguistic playfulness has made its appearance in the Countess's storytelling techniques. The same Madame Carnet predicts to Alphonse that this friend's latest painting will probably raise some eyebrows at the upcoming salon: 'C'est joliment touché [...] Ah! je m'y connais. Depuis vingt ans que je fais des ménages *d'artisses* [...] (3) (It's got some pretty touches [...] Ah! I know something about this. Twenty years I've been cleaning house for *artisses*).

If the essence of the novel form lies in its propensity to blend a range of discourses such that these form a textured and variegated web, one which 'performs' at the linguistic level the social and historical interactions of a given culture at a given time, then Chabrillan has surely attained the technical sophistication of a good novelist. This alone is a magnificent achievement for someone who was semi-literate until the age of twenty-seven, who was an autodidact, and who could stand in the shelter of no literary tradition.

Let us return now to that aspect of *Marie Baude* which can be read as a response to Chabrillan's own challenge, articulated in the denouement of her previous novel, *Les forçats de l'amour*, as the victory of injustice and male unaccountability. The two artists already presented form part of the light side of *Marie Baude*'s plot. Marie Baude and her intimate friend, Jeanne, work as their models. Perhaps not surprisingly, given what we know about bohemia's plots, the artists' fates remain 'comic.' Like Rodolphe, Schaunard, and Colline of *Scènes de la vie de bohème*, they will survive and, indeed, will marry in the end. Marie Baude, on the other hand, is both victim and perpetrator of violence and disaster. She, like Sapho, lives with and protects a woman with whom her real relationship is, at the very least, ambiguous. She, like Sapho, is capable of violence and will die. She, like Mogador, is presented as completely unschooled and so ashamed of her grammar and spelling that, unlike the Countess, she will not write, thereby condemning herself to an emotional muteness which, unable to find expression, is doomed to erupt in violence.

Albert, who is educating the provincial Marius into the ways of Parisian life, describes Marie and Jeanne to him thus: 'C'est une Parisienne du faubourg du Temple ... mais sa mère a eu quatre enfants de pères différents .... Une excentricité vivante, cette grande fille-là; une enveloppe vulgaire, mais un cœur d'or. Elle a pour Jeanne une tendresse vraiment maternelle. Jeanne, d'ailleurs, n'est pas solide et je crois bien qu'elle s'en va de la poitrine' (19) (She's a Parisian from the faubourg du Temple ... but her mother had four children by different fathers .... A living excentricity, that big girl, a common exterior, but a heart of gold. She has a real maternal tenderness for Jeanne. Jeanne is not solid anyway, and I think she's dying of a chest ailment). The narrator takes over to explain that Mariotte (Marie Baude) was apprenticed to a laundress when her mother died. A kindly neighbour houses Mariotte but dies soon thereafter, leaving the young woman her entire fortune of two thousand francs. With this money, Marie secures a modest room in a boarding house.

Enter the unsavoury Jules Signard, a new neighbour, who is just reporting to their landlady on the marvellous day he has spent at the morgue ('c'est le dernier mot du mélodrame, l'Ambigu n'est rien à côté' (94) [it's the last word in melodrama. The Ambigu [theatre] is nothing next to it]). Jules is a man of facile speech with a past which includes being the organ of propaganda for people of all political stripes as well as a stint as a brilliant impresario in Montmartre: in short, he is the seducer par excellence.

And seduce her he does: with considerable precipitation when he learns of Mariotte's small treasure. Then when Signard reaches the end of her funds, he leaves Mariotte. Another neighbour, Jeanne, helps her through this dark period. Alas, Marie Baude has fallen irrevocably in love with this shyster, and her mute and brooding acceptance of his behaviour bodes no good: 'Mariotte ne répondit rien, mais son regard était devenu sombre; une colère sourde, terrible, commençait à gronder au fond de son coeur' (128) (Mariotte replied nothing, but her gaze became sombre; a deep and terrible anger began to rumble in her heart).

It should be added that Jules has just completed his second such adventure. Previously he had seduced a young woman from the provinces with promises of a glorious acting career in the capital, inciting her to steal the necessary funds from her mother. Thus financed, the couple had gone to Paris, where he left her to her own devices, which became prostitutional. The young woman turns out to be Marius's sister, Adrienne, and it seems ineluctable that she will meet Marie Baude eventually.

Earlier it was mentioned that in addition to responding to the unjust situation with which Chabrillan's previous novel had ended, the work of *Marie Baude* may also include settling some personal scores. Indeed, one would be hard-pressed not to see in the roguish character of Jules Signard a reference to Maître Jules Sénard, the prominent lawyer who won the litigation which the state had directed against Flaubert for the 'immorality' of *Madame Bovary*. (So grateful was Flaubert to his resourceful lawyer that he dedicated his masterpiece to him.) It is one of those ironies of history that Jules Sénard was the very lawyer representing the publisher Locard-Davi et de Vresse in their suit against Céleste de Chabrillan for breach of contract to publish her memoirs scarcely one year later. Since she was very bitter at having lost this case, whose outcome had irrevocably placed her in the public eye, casting the lawyer in the unsavoury role of Jules Signard – and doling out to him a disastrous fate – must have afforded Chabrillan some satisfaction. As in the case of *La Sapho*, fiction has its rewards.

Returning now to the twin themes of injustice and guilt, Marie Baude chances to meet Adrienne, and the two realize their shared history of seduction at the hand of their Jules. Together they concoct a plot to blackmail this man, although in the end, Adrienne will betray Mariotte in their agreement. Suffice it to say that the canny Jules plays the women off against each other. This situation is more than the devoted Marie Baude can bear, and her reason crashes under the pressure: 'Les veines de son cou étaient gonflées et ses muscles tendus. Il se livrait certainement en elle une lutte terrible entre la raison et la folie' (276) (The veins in her neck were bulging and her muscles tense. Certainly a terrible struggle was taking place within her between sanity and madness).

Blinded by madness and jealousy, Marie Baude rings the bell of Adrienne's residence so insistently that Jules, inebriated and in bed with Adrienne, hides in the kitchen, fearing Adrienne's protector, a rich banker. There, Jules falls into a drunken slumber. Mariotte enters Adrienne's bedchamber, accusing her of being 'une prostituée plus méprisable que celles […] dans les rues, où elles ne cherchaient parfois qu'un morceau de pain!' (284) (a prostitute more contemptible that those who have been in the street where sometimes all they were looking for was a piece of bread). There ensues a scene of physical violence in which Marie Baude demonstrates a power and an agency which defy all conventional representations of the feminine. First, she clutches Adrienne's throat with a grasp 'qui ressemblait à un collier de fer' (285) (which resembled an iron collar), taunting the victim with her ugliness ('Tu deviens laide aussi' (285) (You're becoming ugly too). Once Adrienne has collapsed into 'an inert mass' (286), Marie drags her body into bed, where, with 'un calme féroce' (a ferocious calmness) she knots a white scarf around the dead woman's neck, 'le serrant à plusieurs reprises de toutes ses forces' (286) (tightening it several times with all her strength).

When we consider that the conventions of French theatre – which traditionally forbade the display of violence on stage – dictated that Othello's strangulation of Desdemona be softened to 'mere' suffocation under a pillow, Marie Baude's powerful act of homicide shocks from the perspectives of both representation and gender. It is true that the novel is a genre which accommodates greater realism than other literary forms. Still, Marie Baude's horrific act stands out as remarkable at the very least and probably unique in women's writing of this period. Even today it would be the stuff of tabloid news.

Not content with the strangulation, however, Chabrillan treats her readers to the gruesome post-mortem depiction: 'la bouche de la malheureuse soeur de Marius s'ouvrit toute grande, et sa langue enflée, violette déjà, en sortit à moitié' (287) (the mouth of Marius's unfortunate sister opened wide, and her swollen tongue, already violet, extended half way out). The act of violence committed by Marie Baude under the veil of madness constitutes an act of vengeance against male privilege and unaccountability because Jules Signard will serve as the scapegoat.

What is most extraordinary in the ending of this novel is that the despicable Signard – surely guilty of so many other offences – finds himself cornered into taking responsibility for this murder, of which he is, in fact, innocent! Meanwhile, Mariotte has fled and is rambling insanely along the *quais* of the Seine. Jules awakens in the kitchen and staggers into bed, little suspecting that next to him his mistress lies dead. He awakens late in the morning to the appalling spectacle. But just then the maid enters the bedchamber, draws the apparently inevitable conclusion, and sends for the police. Other evidence appears to corroborate his guilt, and, realizing that all the appearances are against him, Jules signs a declaration of guilt. His name 'Signard,' with its derogatory '-ard' ending, points to his demise, which will be sealed with his *signa*ture. Chabrillan has successfully framed him while at the same time administering a punishment-through-fiction of Flaubert's canny lawyer Jules Sénard.

Despite her madness, however, the Mariotte character is not exonerated in the narrative. Before throwing herself into the Seine, she asks God why He forsook her and 'Il lui sembla qu'une voix mystérieuse lui répondit (It seemed to her that a mysterious voice answered): "Dieu t'avait donné un guide pour t'enseigner le devoir et le bien; pourquoi n'as-tu pas suivi les conseils de la mère Caron?"' (307–8) (God gave you a guide to teach you duty and the good. Why did you not follow the advice of mother Caron?). 'C'est vrai' (It's true), she murmurs, and before ending it all, begs God for His misericordia.

Shifting now to the perspective of Chabrillan's overarching plot, we must ask how this ending can be read within the trajectory of her writing? From the 'local' point of view of this particular novel's narrative economy, the ambiguities and equivocations around the question of guilt and innocence which we have seen at play in every novel since *La Sapho* are still much in evidence. Jules Signard, while guilty of a host of unethical actions which have had devastating effects on the lives of others, has actually been convicted of an act of which he was, in fact, innocent. Marie Baude, who has been treated with great injustice, has nonetheless *not* been exonerated for all that: with respect to the heroine, then, the problem of victimization and the nature of guilt and innocence remain murky in this penultimate novel of Céleste de Chabrillan.

However, in detaching these recurrent themes from their immediate narrative environment to consider them with respect to the 'work' of a masterplot, the inculpation of the 'innocent' Jules Signard might be considered to be a response to the ending of her previous novel, *Les forçats de l'amour*, in which Albin Desjardins, responsible for the death of two women, had remained spotlessly white, as his name would suggest. In this reading, not only does Chabrillan respond to the kinds of situations, injustices, and humiliations with which her life was bedevilled, she actually sets up situations inter-novelistically, as it were, which posit the injustice in the first instance, the better to rectify it subsequently in another novel. It is a tactic which affords her full mastery of the kind of situation over which she, in her life, was powerless.

Notwithstanding the novelist's godlike prerogative to construct stories with controllable outcomes, certain questions – such as the nature of evil – remain beyond the pale of mastery, at least for Céleste de Chabrillan. Underlying the 'smaller' categories of oppression which surface with increasing frequency in her later works is a broader ethical and theological issue: namely, how to explain the gross injustices that abound in this life. 'J'ai souvent demandé à Dieu,' Sapho had mused, 'pourquoi l'un mourait de famine tandis que l'autre était écrasé par l'abondance; rien ne m'a répondu' (316–17) (I have often asked God why one dies of hunger while the other is crushed by abundance; nothing answered me).

While posing this question often, Chabrillan's writings generally seem to be inconclusive on the explanation of evil. For Céleste, who remained in her life a believer, even asking the question is tantamount to challenging divine authority. More than once God is asked, and silence ensues: 'rien ne m'a répondu.' We shall see that in her final novel,

Un drame sur le Tage, the completely virtuous Fernande desperately wonders: 'Pourquoi Dieu m'abandonne-t-il [...]? Me fait-il responsable des fautes commises par ma mère?' (187) (Why is God abandoning me [...]? Is he holding me responsible for the errors committed by my mother?). Finally, tried beyond her capacities, she exclaims that she could end up 'par me révolter même contre la justice de Dieu' (252) (by revolting even against the justice of God). Sometimes God is described as a laissez-faire creator, as is the case of the women-flowers in *La Sapho*, created by God but not defended by Him. One strategy for letting God off the hook, as it were, is to pin the responsibility for injustice on Providence, Chance, Fate, or Destiny. Chabrillan, no doubt in her need to preserve a belief in God, often has recourse to these agencies. For instance, after the Duchess de Mers has committed suicide, her step-daughter explains that 'nous avons tous des existences marquées, la faute en est à la destinée et non à nous' (*Duchesse* 245) (we all have marked existences. The fault for that lies with destiny and not us). And later, as if guilt must absolutely be assigned to something or someone, she says 'la Destinée fut seule coupable [...]. Que pouvons-nous à cela? Rien, n'est-ce pas?' (273–4) (Destiny alone was guilty [...]. What can we do about that? Nothing, isn't that so?).

Readers of *Madame Bovary* will recall seducer Rodolphe's cynical invocation of Destiny to explain to Emma why he must leave her, or again the cruel irony of Charles Bovary's explanation to himself ('C'est le destin') of his wrecked life. Of course, none of the catastrophes of Flaubert's novel can be attributed to some vague fortune: herein lies the terrible irony and irresponsibility hidden behind the novel's use of the term 'destiny.' But in Chabrillan's works, where the assignment of guilt is all-important, imputing tragic error to destiny is a compromise solution which is only partially satisfactory.

In a long article by Chabrillan which appeared in 1871 in the newspaper *La Réaction*, she exhorts those who have committed grave errors not to waste their time on 'Our Fathers' or 'Hail Marys.' The way upward for prostitutes will only come by dint of hard work: 'Puisqu'il [Dieu] voit tout et qu'il les a laissées choir si bas, il ne se baissera certes pas pour les ramasser. C'est à nous de nous aider' (Since God sees everything, and has allowed them to fall so low, He will certainly not stoop to pick them up. It is up to us to help ourselves). At the end of her life, would the Countess have retained this optimism toward redemption through merit that she exhibits in 1871? We know only that the hard labour of writing was to become her solace and comfort over the next fifteen years.

6 Chabrillan's Final Novels, or The Uses of Fiction

Et personne maintenant, sachez-le bien, ne me fera plus souffrir ni baisser la tête. L'avenir est à moi, puisqu'il ne reste de la créature que ses oeuvres
(Countess de Chabrillan, *La Réaction* 1871)

Know this: nobody will make me suffer or lower my head any longer. The future is mine, since the only thing remaining of the creature is her work.

In the long newspaper article published in *La Réaction*, Céleste de Chabrillan has publicly announced that her literary achievements have eclipsed her ignominious self, now dead. And in truth, the list of her accomplishments by this time is considerable. With five novels and a set of memoirs to her credit, she has also contributed to the war effort by successfully organizing Les Soeurs de France under official state patronage. She has composed, produced, and performed at least nine plays at six different Parisian theatres and has acted as director of the Folies-Marigny theatre in 1865.

Even so, the above obituary of her former self is perhaps an example of wishful writing. Unquestionably, her work of personal rehabilitation must have progressed significantly for her to announce the death of her prostitute-persona ('la créature'). Indeed, if the five novels she has published by this time are an indication, all the ugly issues have been articulated in print, and the work of the negotiation of guilt and forgiveness through narrative has been seriously engaged.

Nonetheless, ten years later in her 1881 novel *Les forçats de l'amour*, the question of the indelible past resurfaces. The novel, it will be recalled, features three strong women characters. Each commands her own subplot, and each represents the Countess at least partially at different moments of her life. The elder Mistress Branck, whose sobriquet 'la Tempête' denotes her strength, had committed 'presqu'un crime' in England. This 'near-crime' had simply amounted to stealing wages due to her from her reticent employer. The latter had her deported to Australia to serve out her sentence, another example, first, of an injustice to which the underprivileged fell victim and, second, of a crime which really isn't one, like Céleste's 'fall' into prostitution when few other adequate employment opportunities existed.

In any case, Mistress Branck, who had earlier mentioned that her memoirs could inspire writers of fiction, claims that 'il m'a fallu user trois existences, changer trois fois de nom' (I needed to go through three existences; change my name three times) in order to forget the period when she bore the title of 'la Tempête.' And now during this particular sea voyage, someone has remembered it! '"Le passé," murmura-t-elle en retombant lourdement dans son fauteuil. "Ah! Le passé n'a pas d'âge"' (Les forçats 174). ('The past,' she murmured falling heavily back into her chair. 'Ah! The past has no age'). Her sense of defeat is palpable. The Countess is no doubt wondering: from Vénard, to Mogador, to Chabrillan, which of the three names will prevail?

Because the past presents itself as exasperatingly indelible in so many of her books, there are also corresponding moments of oblivion in which characters are able to enjoy brief reprieves from shameful personal histories. La Sapho, when she had been the young, seduced Marie Laurent, awakens from a coma following her attempted suicide: 'à ses yeux le passé était une ombre impénétrable' (140–1) (in her eyes, the past was an impenetrable shadow). Sapho herself will not be forgiven her past: it is too early in the Countess's itinerary of literary self-rehabilitation for absolution of the prostitute-protagonist. That absolution, however, is played out vicariously through the Lélia subplot. For Lélia is this novel's 'madwoman in the attic,' or at least of the second floor, and she is 'folle tout à fait' (222) (completely crazy).

Madness, well known to be a female literary and operatic affliction, proves a useful narrative tool for Chabrillan. First, it is a zone in which the past can be erased. It is also a zone which lies outside the domain and dictates of logic and as such constitutes a space where anything can happen. In the Countess's fiction, women go mad simply when the level of injustice to which a character has submitted is too high for reason – any woman's reason – to endure intact. Some of these ruptures of the rational result in the female character committing brutal murders,

murders which are condemned at one level of the text but treated with considerable understanding at other levels. In fact, the state of madness is often the state which enables the truth to out: it constitutes a gigantic textual symptom of the insanity of social injustice.

When Mélida of *Les voleurs d'or* gives birth to the child of her rape, she remains *'folle'* for several months after delivery, as if both her body and her mind were unable to withstand the assault made upon them. When Jenny, the maid and mistress of aristocratic scoundrel Albert, loses her child in a storm, her intelligence snaps sufficiently for her to speak the truth about her oppression: 'Voleur! [...] tu ne me battras plus' (*Pewel* 170–1). (Thief! [...] you'll not beat me anymore). Soon thereafter, still crazed, she will stab her erstwhile lover to death. And we have seen Marie Baude victoriously and even voluptuously strangling her rival in love and then witnessing with pleasure when the homicide is attributed to the evil Jules Signard. How crazy are these women really? On the one hand, their temporary insanity absolves them to some extent of their crimes. On the other, we the readers have watched the double-binding situations which these characters have endured and can understand how the only sane mental defence is precisely a lapse into madness. It is also Lélia's madness which allows her to return to her Edenic childhood and mother: 'elles sont heureuses; il n'y a que la tombe qui ne vous rende pas votre mère' (*Sapho* 295) (they are happy; only the grave cannot return your mother to you).

At long last, we arrive at the heart of Chabrillan's fiction – the mother – lost, guilty, loving, distant, traitor, or even child seller: her nature and identity are debated throughout Chabrillan's oeuvre. Fathers are virtually absent but bad mothers are plentiful: Lady Campbell the chilly (*La Sapho*); Lady Bolmer, who lied to her son about his paternity (*Miss Pewel*); Marie Baude's mother, who favoured her son over her daughter; and Mary Acton's mother, who had changed her name to disastrous consequence for her daughter, whose final words are 'Ah! Ma mère, ma mère, ne puis-je donc penser à vous sans vous maudire!' (*Pewel* 266) (Ah! My mother, my mother. Can I not think of you without cursing you!). We shall see what Chabrillan's final novel, *Un drame sur le Tage*, holds in store for the maternal figure.

Nonetheless, for all the examples of bad mothers, 'good' mothers occur in at least equal number and take numerous forms. There are the substitute mothers who take abandoned daughters under their maternal wing: Madame Joseph of Chabrillan's first novel, *Les voleurs d'or*, helps young Louisa, and Madame Caron adopts Marie Baude in difficulty.

Some mothers are falsely considered guilty: *Un miracle à Vichy* (1861), besides featuring a strong daughter who is learned and composes music, also clears the reputation of the Marquise de Chasais, who had long (and falsely) been considered an adulteress. All possible permutations of the dilemma of 'who is guilty: mother or daughter?' can be found articulated across the Countess's ten novels.

A particularly interesting instance of this process of guilt negotiation can be found in *La duchesse de Mers*. The Duchess had long entertained a liaison with the Marquis de la Villaray and, even after breaking off the relationship, has a great deal of remorse about it. More than anything, she wants to hide the knowledge of the affair from her beloved step-daughter Berthe, another strong daughter figure. Through a series of machinations by the cuckolded Duke and the fortune-seeking Marquis, the latter becomes betrothed to Berthe. The pain at witnessing her step-daughter wed to her own ex-lover, whom she knows to be a disreputable gambler on the lookout for a dowry, combined with her husband's cruel requirement that she *not* alert Berthe, leads the Duchess to commit suicide, leaving behind her a letter for Berthe in which she reveals all. Like a Greek chorus, the maid Julie doles out the words of pardon: 'Elle a souffert pour que Dieu lui pardonne sa faute' (244) (She suffered so that God might pardon her error). The guilty mother is thus exonerated in the text, even as the daughter, now aware of the plot behind her impending marriage, forcefully resists the Marquis, ultimately bringing him to his doom.

This particular version of the mother/daughter guilt dilemma places the blame squarely on the mother. To the daughter, an Antigone figure, falls the task of taking vengeance and redeeming her mother's reputation and memory. The function of redemption had become evident earlier in the novel when it appeared (falsely) that Berthe had died. The distraught Duchess had reacted thus: 'Elle est morte! [...]. Dieu n'a pas permis que cet ange me rachetât plus longtemps de mes fautes!' (*Duchesse* 144) (She is dead! [...]. God has not permitted this angel to redeem my errors any longer!).

Because Chabrillan's art has developed so appreciably by 1881, it is no longer possible to sense an authorial investment in one character alone. This multi-voicedness is also characteristic of her contemporaneous novel *Les forçats de l'amour*. Chabrillan's fiction now functions on multiple registers, complete with the humorous remarks of the domestics about their masters, and the not-so-humorous remarks by the narrator on the dehumanization of the mind wrought through servitude.

Indisputably there is something of the Countess in both the Duchess de Mers and her daughter figure Berthe, but these characters also have identities all their own. What remains unchanging in this novel, however, is the extraordinary need both to exculpate and to punish. The text reverses the situation of Céleste's youth, when it was, in fact, the daughter who registered to become a prostitute and the mother who agreed to it.

Guilt, guilt everywhere, and nary a sign of pardon. Guilty daughters (*La Sapho*), daughters guilty, but under extenuating circumstances (*Marie Baude*), daughters and sons falsely considered guilty (*Miss Pewel*). Guilty mothers, too – guilty of not loving their daughters enough (*Marie Baude*), of adultery (*duchesse de Mers*), falsely considered guilty (*Un miracle à Vichy*). Is no relief in sight for the anguished characters populating Chabrillan's fictional world?

Reversal of responsibility for her 'fall,' as she would always refer to it, will be possible only through the painstaking elaborations of this guilt-and-innocence scenario with its endless permutations and performances. Crucial to Chabrillan's rewriting of her personal story is the death of her mother which occurred in 1874. As of this date, there was no more physical presence to impede Céleste from reconstructing the scenario in her own favour. But it is nonetheless significant that, although the Countess has managed to refashion much of her personal narrative through fiction, it is still too much of a stretch to lay full blame on the mother in *La duchesse de Mers*, published in 1881. (It is worth noting that the surname 'Mers' is a homonym of the French word for mother.) Hence the novel's parting conclusion: 'La Destinée fut seule coupable […]. Que pouvons-nous à cela? Rien, n'est-ce pas?' (*La duchesse* 273–4) (Destiny alone was guilty […]. What can we do about that? Nothing, isn't that so?).

N'est-ce pas? Destiny remains a force to be invoked in order to explain the otherwise inexplicable: the triple outrage of injustice, of a past far too indelible, and of a mother who ought to have been more protective but was not. Let us now turn to Chabrillan's final novel published in 1885 to take the measure of the 'work' achieved though her fictional itinerary. It will be recalled that her career as playwright also essentially ended in 1885 with the five-act drama *Pierre Pascal* and the very telling open letter published with that play.

It is Céleste de Chabrillan's final novel, *Un drame sur le Tage*, which at last rectifies all the wrongs and resolves, once and for all, the terrible dilemma of guilt and innocence. *Un drame* takes place in Lisbon. To the ubiquitous Mogadorian themes of the mother/daughter guilt dilemma, the seemingly inescapable reach of the past, and the gratuitous 'merit' of aristocracy, an extraordinary new dimension has been added: the concept of a nobility of spirit equivalent to that of class. To summarize the plot as briefly as possible, Fernande Beauvallais has married the elderly Marquis de Gontier, who is unaware, as indeed she is herself, that 'il y avait bien quelque chose à redire sur le compte de sa mère, mais cela remontait à son séjour à Paris, et, depuis quinze ans qu'ils habitaient Lisbonne, les on-dit avaient à peu près cessé' (10) (there was something with which her mother could be reproached, but that dated back to her time spent in Paris, and, after the fifteen years they had been living in Lisbon, the rumours had more or less ceased). The Marquis has two grown children by a previous marriage, the evil Raoul and the spoiled Marthe, the latter engaged to be married to Count Gaston de Servigny, the nephew of the Duchess de Servigny.

Leaving his wife, the Marquise Fernande, in Lisbon, the Marquis and his daughter Marthe voyage to Paris to firm up the marriage arrangement with his friend, the Duchess. Two events occur in their absence: the arrival in Lisbon of one Count de Dargebrune, who quickly acquaints himself with Fernande's mother, Madame Beauvallais; and the appearance of Count Gaston de Servigny, unaware that his intended is in Paris visiting his aunt.

The virtuous Marquise has been left behind in Lisbon to her own devices. Both Counts are taken with her. The unscrupulous Dargebrune, having understood that the Marquise's mother has heavy gambling debts, proposes to the mother a diabolical contract: that she make her daughter Fernande available to him (through invitations) in exchange for large sums of money. Later, when Fernande learns of this arrangement, she confronts her mother: 'Quelle femme êtes-vous donc pour avoir conçu l'idée d'un marché aussi odieux?' (141) (What kind of woman are you to have conceived the idea of such an odious deal?). By now the reader will have understood the function of this mother character within the broader context of Céleste de Chabrillan's master narrative.

If Madame Beauvallais had been prepared to sell her daughter indirectly, however, she herself is succumbing, in a sense, to her past, for her own mother had indeed been imprisoned for selling her. As with Australian ex-convicts, the sins of forefathers and -mothers are unjustly visited upon their descendants. But unlike the novels of, for instance, Zola, where the modern-day Furies of family illness and genetic defects pursue members down though the generations, the rampage of these ills – more social than genealogical in the Countess's case – is broken.

Fernande is adamant: she will not suffer for her mother's mistakes, as her mother had unfortunately been forced to do for her mother before her.

Back to the love plot: the Count Gaston, who is honourable unlike Dargebrune, has also fallen in love with Fernande de Gontier. She realizes this and, sensing in herself similar feelings, flees the Count at every opportunity. Meanwhile in Paris, the Marquis, Fernande's husband, has died suddenly. This abrupt and convenient demise opens up the novel's plot to new possibilities. The scheming son Raoul now plans to force his stepmother Fernande out of the familial chateau once his sister Marthe has been married off to Gaston de Servigny, the Duchess's nephew and sole heir. But Raoul had not reckoned with the strength and conviction of self-worth which Fernande possesses. When the servant, Salver, exclaims to Raoul: 'Ah [...] vous n'êtes pas digne de porter le titre de votre père!' (248–9) (Ah [...] you are not worthy to bear your father's title!), Fernande intervenes 'avec autorité' with 'Non! mais j'en suis digne, moi!' (No! But I myself am worthy!).

Let us savour for a moment this extraordinary claim of self-worth. All the heroines in Chabrillan's fiction have manifested a remarkable strength of character. Yet none thus far has been able to affirm unequivocally 'I am worthy,' much less 'I am worthy of bearing my aristocratic title.' Sapho was the equal of Victor Hugo's famous Hernani character in being 'une force qui va,' but even if she had been the victim of a terrible social injustice, she remained unpardonable in the narrative.

Other women characters were similarly strong (Mistress Branck had even commanded a band of escaped convicts), but all had some stigma attached to them. In the later of the Countess's novels, stigmas have been successfully overcome, if not erased: such is the case of the proletarian Julie of *Émigrantes et déportées* (1876), who had professionally sold her 'heart' in the past but who manages to find conjugal happiness and acceptance in the genial sailor, Roule-toujours. Thus far, however, the work of rehabilitation through fiction has never been so complete as to present a female protagonist of incomparable dignity with no moral blemish whatsoever unless that blemish reside ... in the person of her mother! Only by shifting the blame entirely onto the mother figure can Chabrillan – the daughter – rise, rehabilitated, from the ashes of her past. Through the slow elaboration over time of innumerable scenarios involving mother, daughter, and guilt, the Countess de Chabrillan has at last achieved one of the resolutions of her master plot. All guilt has been shifted onto the mother, and the daughter has been wholly exonerated.

But the work to be done in *Un drame sur le Tage* does not stop here. It is not enough to have arrived at moral respectability and self-empowerment, for judgment *by the world* is still out. For instance, Fernande may have claimed herself worthy of the title she bears, but others do not recognize this nobility as legitimate. The character to be convinced in this regard is the Duchess de Servigny, the very incarnation of nobiliary values.

The first obstacle the Duchess de Servigny poses to the marriage of her nephew to Fernande de Gontier is, again, the mother question: 'Vous n'êtes pas coupable personnellement, on ne choisit pas plus sa mère que sa marraine, *mais* [...]' (251–2, emphasis added) (You are not personally guilty. One does not choose one's mother any more than one's godmother, *but* [...]). It is as if the novel could not shout the daughter figure's exoneration loud or long enough. In still another conversation, Gaston de Servigny must interrupt his aunt to exclaim: 'Mais elle n'est pas coupable!' (255) (But she is not guilty!). The judgment of 'not guilty' emerges like a refrain, spouting from the mouths of character after character.

The next question to be resolved is that of whether the heroine, a commoner, has the right to bear a title. In all of Chabrillan's novelistic fiction, this is the first appearance of this particular issue, one which in fact brought her considerable misery once she had taken the Chabrillan family name. It will be recalled that the Chabrillans repeatedly attempted to bribe her to drop their name once her husband had died. Minister de Lesseps had even summoned her to his office and attempted to convince her to do the same, ostensibly influenced by the family. Further, in an attempt to intimidate her, the Paris police commissioner called her in and, pulling out her dossier with its incriminatory registration number, threatened to incarcerate her as if she were still a registered prostitute. It was a bluff – again motivated by the Chabrillan family – for, as she pointed out to the commissioner, Lionel de Chabrillan had secured her freedom from the infernal register in 1852.

For the Countess de Chabrillan what was at stake in holding onto her married name was nothing less than the preservation of an entirely new personal and professional identity, one which represented her as the author of a significant oeuvre as well as the author of good works such as the founding of the Soeurs de France and the home for orphan girls who had no employment prospects.

How can one explain the fact that the question of the right to bear a noble title does not surface until her final novel? If Chabrillan's master plot constitutes a meticulous negotiation of personal issues with the perspective of forging a new identity, she could not affirm that identity until the project of liberation from the past had been achieved. With *Un drame*, the time has come to capitalize on the exculpation which has been so long in the making. As has been the case in previous novels, the notion is first entertained by a character of credibility before being taken up seriously by the characters whose opinion on the question matters the most. In *Un drame*, it is a doctor, summoned to care for Fernande, who tells her: 'La vraie noblesse, mon enfant, n'appartient pas à celui que l'a trouvée dans son berceau, mais à celui qui la mérite' (254) (True nobility, my child, does not belong to him who found it in the cradle, but to him who merits it).

If a member of the Chabrillan family had chanced to read this novel, how she or he must have seethed! But Chabrillan the writer has more up her sleeve, for what she is about to do is to put this statement into the mouth of the Duchess de Servigny herself, surely a transparent stand-in for the Counts and Countesses de Chabrillan who have made her life miserable. In a moment of compassion, the 'duchesse [de Servigny] baissa la tête; elle comprit enfin que madame de Gontier avait une véritable valeur personnelle, et qu'elle avait eu tort de la traiter de si haut' (254–5) (Duchess of Servigny lowered her head. She finally understood that Madame de Gontier had real personal worth, and that she had been wrong to treat her so condescendingly).

By the time she has completed her final novel, Céleste de Chabrillan is no longer young. At sixty-one, her sense of authority, of authorhood, and of her own self-worth has led her to create a heroine who makes astonishing demands for herself. Thinking back now to the Sapho character created some twenty-seven years earlier, she was a woman of force and energy – true – but a character who was also the deliverer of vengeance and retribution. And one recalls how she had hidden her head in shame and sobbed when her friend had suggested that she must have done something wrong in her life. Sapho settled her scores with those who had ruined her life and reunited a number of people and families, but she herself remained beneath elevation. Fernande de Gontier, on the other hand, is certified by the text to be pure and possessed of well-merited nobility, and she claims for herself the right to happiness. Standing firm on her eligibility to marry Gaston de Servigny, she exclaims: 'je ne peux plus, je ne veux plus renoncer à ma part de bonheur en ce monde!' (269) (I no longer can nor do I wish to give up my share of happiness in this world!). As Mogador had always said, 'Vouloir c'est pouvoir' (Where there's a will, there's a way).

Before discussing the somewhat perplexing ending of *Un drame sur le Tage*, it will be useful to review the history of Chabrillan's coming-into-writing, making a final assessment of what, for her, have been the uses of fiction. As she is writing her memoirs in 1851, she describes the shame of her semi-literacy: 'Ainsi, je suis honteuse de mon ignorance, je brûle du désir d'apprendre […]. Quand j'essaye d'apprendre à écrire, et que ma main n'obéit pas à ma volonté, je me pince le bras au point d'en porter les marques' (1: 275) (Thus I am ashamed of my ignorance. I burn with the desire to learn […]. When I try to write and my hand does not obey my will, I pinch my arm to the point that it bears marks).

Chabrillan's fiction includes a number of women who lack the most elementary of educations. For Marie Baude, even reading poses difficulty: 'Après avoir épelé presque tous les mots, elle reprit couramment' (*Baude* 132) (After having spelled out almost all the words, she reread them fluently). Another Marie, the young woman seduced by the nobleman before her saphic metamorphosis, had been too ashamed to write: 'Marie ne lui avait jamais écrit, la pauvre fille avait donné tout son temps au travail; elle savait écrire, mais si mal qu'elle n'avait jamais osé envoyer une ligne à Richard; il y a des femmes qui ne savent pas que le mot: "je t'aime," peut s'écrire de toutes les manières' (*Sapho* 131–2) (Marie had never written to him; the poor girl had given all her time to work. She knew how to write, but so poorly that she had never dared to send a line to Richard. There are women who do not know that the phrase 'I love you' can be written in any way). As for Mary Acton of *Miss Pewel*, she had spent her sea voyage to Australia pulling herself out of illiteracy: 'C'est pendant les six mois que dura notre traversée, que j'appris à écrire et à lire' (273–4) (It was during the six months that our crossing lasted that I learned how to write and read).

In any case, writing for the Countess de Chabrillan is associated from the beginning with judgment and self-defence: 'Je me défendais mieux' (I defended myself better), she writes of a trial in which she is involved, 'en écrivant qu'en parlant' (*Mémoires* 4: 175) (by writing rather than speaking). What she had not anticipated, however, was that she would come to enjoy it: 'je finis par prendre goût à ce griffonage' (4: 175) (I ended up developing a taste for this scribbling). She had not realized that the act of putting pen to paper would actually bring her relief from bitterness. Nor could she have dreamed that the process by which she elaborated her fictions would, over time, exorcize her personal demons.

It is unclear whether or not Céleste de Chabrillan was aware that over the ensemble of her work there was an overarching narrative whose 'plot' entailed the slow negotiation and reparation of her personal shame. The resolution of this master plot, elaborated, as we have seen, using a host of different strategies, has been self-absolution. Such, at least, has been the argument of the preceding pages. Crowning her cast of strong women protagonists, often tainted and bearing some unspeakable moral burden, is the dignified and virtuous Marquise Fernande de Gontier. The anguished ambivalence surrounding the mother figure, sometimes projected in the text as protective and good, sometimes as guilty, has resolved itself in *Un drame sur le Tage* into a mother deemed unequivocally guilty of attempting to sell her own daughter to a man. Here, finally, is the revision of Céleste's personal story which her oeuvre has taken so long to establish. The mitigating circumstance in this case is that this guilty mother is only repeating what had been done to her. The perpetuation of past wrongs onto the innocent generations which follow opens up Chabrillan's narratives to the contemplation of the ravages of social injustice and undeserved privilege. This is perhaps one of the most extraordinary aspects of her work. It is constantly taking the measure of personal responsibility for individual acts against the backdrop of poverty, lack of opportunity, inequities in the law, and the privileges of the few.

If it is impossible to determine Chabrillan's awareness of the psychological strategies by which her novels have freed her from the burden of her past, Chabrillan's overt and conscious concept of how her writing functions is that it enables her to transcend her Mogadorian self through accomplishments. Far more has been at stake than financial survival: all along, it has been a question of parthenogenesis through writing. Gone is the 'creature' of yesteryear: Chabrillan has actually re-birthed herself into a new identity. And it is clear that her explicit and steadfast goal has been the transcendence of her prostitutional self by sheer dint of achievement. Propositioned by the French statesman to drop her new name and title in exchange for money, she had been adamant: 'Il [Lionel] m'a donné son nom, je le porterai jusqu'au jour de ma mort, et je ferai tant, qu'il me survivra' (*Un deuil* 249) (He [Lionel] gave me his name. I will bear it until the day of my death and I shall ensure that it (he) survives me).

An 1856 journal entry recorded in *Un deuil au bout du monde* confides that she has completely given herself over to study and writing: 'J'écris beaucoup' (I am writing a lot), she notes in the hope that '*la volonté d'être l'enfant de ses oeuvres* n'est pas un vain mot' (100, emphasis added) (*the will to be the child of one's works* is not in vain). Whereas so many writers, female and male alike, depict their books as children, painfully issuing into the world after the ordeal of intellectual gestation, for Chabrillan, it is her many books and plays which have culminated in her own rebirthing. Céleste Vénard – the daughter of a mother who betrayed her; Chabrillan – the writer with virtually no intellectual genealogy: she has had to become her own mother, and in so doing, has given birth to a new self. The forging of this new identity has thus been a circular process. And within the circularity in which daughter becomes the mother of her own rebirthing, linear time is abolished, and with it, the past is buried. The result? Chabrillan simply is. By 1885, Chabrillan's master narrative has been brought to term.

From this vantage point, then, let us survey the ground which has been covered in order for Chabrillan to generate her writing self. First, the issues to be dealt with have had to be laid out on the table, as it were. As long as these obstacles remained unarticulated, the work of the text could not go forward. Thus in the early novel *La Sapho*, the shame attached to prostitution is expressed. This is probably the most fundamental problem to be confronted. As we have seen, this novel gives free rein to the anger of the woman who has been victimized and has been forced into making her living by selling her body.

Within the context of nineteenth-century French fiction, this point of view with its accompanying rage is absolutely unique. With the exception of Sand's novel *Isidora*, all other literature, including documentary 'literature,' trains its gaze upon the prostitute as object, a perspective perfectly embodied, for instance, in the many Degas paintings which portray sad line-ups of brothel inmates as viewed from the perspective of an anonymous gentleman, usually portrayed as assessing the lot from a front edge of the painting.

Part of the initial work of Chabrillan's novels will be to appease her own rage once it has been expressed. And it is with clear delectation that *La Sapho* accomplishes this task through its staging and performance of vengeance. Wrongdoers are brought before the court of fiction for all to see. Their acts are enumerated in as painful a way as possible; they are forced to recognize their actions publicly and to make amends for them. In the melodrama which is her life, Sapho (and Mogador) must hoist themselves onto a sufficient level of power and authority so as to be able to dole out the retribution. But in this early novel, exculpation of the central daughter figure cannot even be envisioned. Judging from her later works, such exoneration appears to require that responsibility be shifted onto the mother. Still, just as it was important for the existence of anger to be acknowledged, so too is daughterly forgiveness floated on the horizon of possibility through the Lélia subplot, almost like a shadow play.

La Sapho is clearly the text of catharsis within Chabrillan's oeuvre. The following novel, Miss Pewel, stresses the value of forgiveness. Once the rage has been expressed, the prospect of pardon is far easier to contemplate. In Miss Pewel, the 'bad woman' is she who cannot forgive, and for this intractable bitterness she will pay with her life. By the end of this novel, two mother figures have been indicted by their offspring, who are themselves pronounced innocent by the novel's sole representative of legitimacy. Still, to indict is merely to accuse. This is another instance in which an issue to be 'debated' by subsequent texts is articulated as simple possibility, and left at that.

In the seven novels which follow and which span the period between 1860 and 1885, the question of who is guilty, mother and/or daughter, is negotiated in every possible permutation. Nonetheless, it is not until 1885 in her final novel, Un drame sur le Tage, that a satisfactory response to the question is achieved. In fact, the reason Un drame is her final novel is precisely because a satisfactory resolution has been arrived at. Thereafter no further utterance need be made. Vicariously through her own fictional production, the Countess de Chabrillan has forgiven herself, has – through fiction – been pronounced innocent by others, and has created a new identity, arriving, finally, at a love of self.

Taken separately, these novels – from Miss Pewel to Un drame – spin out a host of different formulations of guilt and innocence: for example, a (learned) daughter pattern with a mother figure thought to be guilty of adultery, but whose reputation is restored in the end (Un miracle à Vichy); or a woman of easy virtue forgiven, accepted for what she is now, and married into respectability (Les deux soeurs). On the other hand, Les forçats de l'amour, while also a reflection on guilt and innocence, presents the reader with the three faces of Chabrillan: Noée, the young and innocent victim; Mistress Wolf, the mature woman who admits her sexual desire with an astonishing frankness ('et si j'ai fait mon devoir avec une régularité qui contraste un peu avec mes habitudes, c'est que j'y trouvais une satisfaction personnelle') (92) [(and if I have done my duty with a regularity which contrasts a bit with my habits, it is because I found in it a personal satisfaction)]; and, finally, the enigmatic Mistress Branck, who declares that her memoirs constitute the stuff of fiction.

The 1881 Forçats does not really probe the troubled waters of maternal or filial guilt. What it does do, however, is to posit and consolidate a triple identity which can be likened to the manner in which the Countess de Chabrillan conceives of herself: Céleste Vénard/Mogador/Chabrillan. What the three fictional women share is a remarkable strength of character. At this point, Céleste de Chabrillan has entered old age. She has achieved a sense of perspective with respect to her own life, has now published her memoirs twice, and, though never a shrinking violet, has been further fortified by having spent the past two decades writing and producing plays and even, for a time, directing a theatre.

Marie Baude appears in 1883. The equivocation surrounding the mother/daughter question continues. This novel censures one mother figure only to spotlight the benevolent qualities of another. The daughter persona, Marie Baude, has a mind which collapses under the strain of the injustice to which she has been subjected. Having killed her rival in love, she is wandering the streets crazed when the thought comes to her that her substitute 'good' mother had given her the necessary tools and money to conduct her life respectably. Here, it would seem, the scales of judgment tilt in favour of filial guilt.

This condemnation of the daughter will be reversed in Chabrillan's next and penultimate novel, *La duchesse de Mers*. Although the mother figure of this novel is treated sympathetically, she is no less guilty (of adultery) for all that. A new element surfaces in this particular telling of the guilt/innocence story. Not only is the stepdaughter Berthe a forgiving daughter, the novel makes it clear that one of the functions of the daughter is to redeem her mother through her own purity and nobility of spirit. Thus, before Chabrillan embarked on the final novel, the master narrative under elaboration presents maternal culpability salvaged by a daughter who is strong, magnanimous, and ultimately victorious. Such is the strong position which will serve as a springboard for her final piece of writing.

We are now in a position to contemplate the somewhat problematic ending of *Un drame sur le Tage*. Within Fernande de Gontier, the daughter figure, are assembled all the character traits which bode success and, now that she is widowed, point to marriage with Count Gaston de Servigny: virtue, courage of conviction, and the resolve to lead a happy life. All registers of the text seem to proclaim her innocence as well as her differentiation with respect to her mother, the venal Madame Beauvallais. Furthermore, Fernande's nobility and merit have been recognized by virtually the entire cast of characters, culminating in the class-conscious Duchess de Servigny, who is forced to revise her opinions and eat her words. And with this novel, the final piece of Chabrillan's personal puzzle has fallen into place. At last – at long last – all the guilt for the 'fall' into prostitution has been laid squarely on the shoulders of the mother, she of the shady past who was willing to arrange encounters between her married daughter Fernande and the Count de Dargebrune in exchange for money. The inculpation of the mother figure (with allowances made for the fact that her own mother had sold her) and the concomitant exoneration of the daughter thus complete the revisionist narrative of Chabrillan's past.

In the light of this final achievement, then, how is the reader to understand the Marquise de Gontier's decision *not* to marry Gaston de Servigny and to retire, instead, within the walls of a Trappist convent? Since signs of religious fervour in Chabrillan's oeuvre are rare to say the least, the text does not authorize us to read into this resolution a sudden conversion. Nor should we place it within the well-worn feminine literary tradition in which a female protagonist takes refuge from the world through self-claustration. The Countess de Chabrillan was never one to shrink from a challenge.

The key to understanding this final retreat of *Un drame sur le Tage* lies in the term 'Trappist,' with its obvious connotation of silence. It is not that Céleste de Chabrillan has feared being silenced. On the contrary, since the first publication of her memoirs in 1854, she has never ceased speaking out and denouncing the oppressive conditions which have directly resulted in the mangled and tainted lives of so many working-class women. This retreat should be read as the victorious conclusion of Chabrillan's master narrative, the central goal of which has been to rewrite the circumstances of her fall into prostitution in such a way as to be credible to herself.

The new and revised story's credibility has not come easily and, indeed, has required declension in myriad different forms across the entire body of Chabrillan's novelistic production. The many hesitancies, reversals, and denials which characterize the slow forging of her modified narrative are necessary in a psychological sense, for they translate the anguished internal debate surrounding the question of guilt and legitimacy. And what is ultimately the most important element in the constant retelling of her story is the credibility of the revised plot which has been under construction over so many years and through so many novels. For if Chabrillan is without a doubt writing for a readership, her most attentive reader is herself.

Far from constituting a gesture of resignation, then, Fernande de Gontier's final choice of silence corresponds to Chabrillan's sense that her work of self-rehabilitation has at last been achieved through her writing. No more need be said. She has reconciled herself with her past by rewriting it and, as a woman with a new identity, can look to the future with a new vision and, indeed, move forward in life with her new – if laboriously reconstructed – self. And she claims as much in her open letter to Monsieur Bessac published with her final drama, *Pierre Pascal* which also dates from 1885: 'Les bravos du public ont affirmé ma confiance en la valeur de mon *travail* et m'ont rendu toutes mes espérances pour l'avenir' (The bravos of the audience have affirmed my confidence in the value of my *work* and have revived all my hopes for the future). In a word, favourable public judgment has been passed on her behalf. Such, it would seem, are the uses of fiction.

Conclusion

So ends the story of the Countess de Chabrillan, born Céleste Vénard and baptized into infamy under the name of Mogador. The three identities of this remarkable woman constitute in and of themselves a narrative with its beginning in the working classes, a lengthy middle episode of notoriety, and an ending of a personal reincarnation of sorts.

The real narrative, of course, is not quite so simple. Céleste's fall from grace occurred when she was barely sixteen years of age. Not for forty-five long years would she at last lay down the pen, her anger assuaged, enemies punished, hypocritical society unmasked for what it was, and the mother figure rendered responsible for the daughter's plunge into the inferno of prostitution.

Perhaps if her culture had been capable of accepting her and her many sisters, Chabrillan would never have left us the literary legacy which she did. Or perhaps she would have written other novels, different plays. Still, it is unlikely that her culture could have embraced her as respectable under any circumstances for its institutions had too much riding on keeping the prostitute in her place and enforcing her silence.

For one thing, its most prominent and reputable men would have risked being exposed in compromising positions. Often. For another, the protection of legitimacy with the family suddenly having become urgent with the enactment of the Napoleonic Code, the stakes involved in guaranteeing married women's respectability were higher than they had ever been. The divide separating the *monde* from the demi-monde could remain porous for men as long as it remained absolute and impassable for women. Or more precisely, women could only move in one direction: downward.

Happily for Céleste, what the world refused her she was able to find in the symbolic field. This is the other story which has been told in

Writing with a Vengeance: that of the enormous power which is available through the process of writing fiction. Ian McEwan's 2001 novel *Atonement* stages, in fiction, a similar process of expiation through writing. His heroine Briony had falsely accused a family friend of rape, with horrific consequences for the young man and others. Like Céleste Vénard, Briony was young – an adolescent – when she committed her defining act. Both these women are doomed to move through the fog of ambiguity surrounding the degree of their own personal responsibility and the level of implication of their respective societies, which easily supported their actions because it was culturally convenient to do so. In her twenties, Briony composes a short story, a thinly veiled version of her own dilemma, which the publisher rejects with all-too-probing questions regarding the protagonist's motivation and the implausibility of the ending. Briony is thus forced to reconsider the narrative construction which had sufficed to pacify her conscience until then.

Decades later, near the end of her career as a distinguished novelist, she is still rewriting the story, which, over the years, has evolved into an act of reparation. She has explained – though not justified – her own youthful crime to herself, and her revised plot has transfigured the people most harmed by her crime into noble characters whose destiny now is to live forever through fiction. The power of writing lies in its process.

Guilt was surely the great motivational force behind Céleste de Chabrillan's writing. For good reason it stands at the forefront of every single novel she composed. But it was a guilt only partially shouldered by her for it was complicated by her sense that her culture was in strong collusion with the events which had damned her. In a sense, Chabrillan's final novel, *Un drame sur le Tage*, perfectly recaptures the painful ambiguities of her situation, all the while reconfiguring the players and the action in her favour. The daughter figure has at last emerged as powerful, dignified, noble, and morally immaculate, whereas the mother is made to bear the guilt which, for the first time since the long-ago *Sapho*, is of a clearly prostitutional nature. And the mother is partially exonerated because of her society's role in making her who she was.

Self-acceptance through writing hardly came easily to Céleste de Chabrillan: indeed it could not. The scorn and contempt for venal women in nineteenth-century France rendered them so abject to themselves and others that to redeem oneself was to move a mountain. This is the magnitude of the task which she confronted and mastered. Few men or women of this period or any other have ever achieved so much.

Notes

Introduction

1 In this regard, one thinks of the social activist Flora Tristan with her
  odyssey to Peru in 1833–4: a quest for her inheritance. She published an
  account of the journey, *Les pérégrinations d'une paria*. She is also the author
  of *Promenades dans Londres* (1840), which devotes a section to the unregulat-
  ed prostitution in that city.
2 There is some evidence that Cora Pearl was registered with the Paris
  police, sadly, after her spectacular career was over (Rounding 292). In fact,
  the trajectory of most of the celebrated venal women of Paris was almost
  always downward at the end of their lives.
3 In her memoirs, fifty is the figure which is given. However, the newspaper
  article published in the 7 March 1858 *Gazette des tribunaux*, which reported
  the verdict of the trial as well as its background, claimed that of 2000
  copies which had been printed, only 300 had gone unsold.
4 For excellent discussions of the culture and importance of the *cabinet de
  lecture*, see both *Lire à Paris au temps de Balzac* by Françoise Parent-Lardeur
  and James Scott Allen's *Popular French Romanticism*.
5 In fact, Alain Corbin had already arrived at the same conclusions: 'Malgré
  l'immensité de la bibliographie, on en vient finalement à déplorer l'absence
  de récits ou de mémoires rédigés par les prostituées elles-mêmes' (85)
  (Despite the immensity of the bibliography, in the end, one is forced to
  deplore the absence of tales or memoirs written by prostitutes themselves).
6 We have just noted that ex-Mogador wrote ten novels.
7 As the reader now knows, Mogador's case proves this assertion to be
  erroneous.
8 Her first series has been translated by Monique Fleury Nagem and is
  entitled *Memoirs of a Courtesan in Nineteenth-Century France* (2001).

Although one can appreciate the fact that a translation is available at all, this translation is unfortunately based on an edition which takes great liberties with the original version. Such liberties include the addition of subtitles which are often smutty, a tone which is absolutely dissonant with the original text. The second series, which includes her years spent in Australia, has been translated, aptly, by two Australians, Patricia Clancy and Jeanne Allen, and was published by Melbourne University Press in 1998 under the title of *The French Consul's Wife: Memoirs of Céleste de Chabrillan in Gold-Rush Australia*. And the wonders of Google enable one to discover that the French department of that same university has developed a language-learning interactive text based on Mogador's Australian saga.

9 I thank my colleague Madeleine Cottonet Hage for drawing my attention to this book.

10 Let me clarify that Cora Pearl's account of how she was waylaid by a 'nice man' promising her goodies at a very young age and her subsequent and, she alleges, lifelong contempt for many men is part of the more sombre side of her recital.

11 The case of Britain is a counterexample to this generalization. There, the emphasis was put not on a system of management but on personal reform, both of the client and the sex worker. Florence Nightingale had seen the 'French system' at work during the Crimean War and concluded that it was merely a way to increase syphilitic (and doubtless moral) contamination.

1. The Wages of Shame

1 Unless otherwise noted in the text, all reference to the first set of memoirs will be to the 1858 edition.

2 As James Smith Allen points out in *Popular French Romanticism*, prior to the 1833 laws mandating public elementary education, literacy skills 'were social status symbols, the tools of the middle classes, the elements of *la civilisation*.' Céleste was in fact deeply ashamed of her semi-literacy, although it was hardly uncommon among her peers. Smith also reports that in 1819, only one-fifth of all Parisian children had benefited from a primary education.

3 In his genealogy of the Moreton de Chabrillan family, Laine includes Lionel alongside his other siblings but lists no spouse for him. It would seem that even in semi-official records there was an attempt to expunge Céleste's legitimate marital connection to him.

4 As Chartier and Martin note in their *Histoire de l'édition française*, during the Second Empire, 'On était revenu au système de la saisie administrative qui existait sous le Premier Empire […]. On invoqua l'article 10 du Code d'instruction criminelle qui donnait aux préfets le droit de faire tous les

actes nécessaires [...] pour justifier la saisie d'un journal ou d'un ouvrage quelconque avant sa publication et en dehors de toute poursuite judiciaire' (3: 50) (One had returned to the system of administrative seizures which existed during the First Empire [...]. Article 10 of the Code of Criminal Instruction was invoked, giving prefects the right to do whatever was necessary [...] to justify the seizure of a journal or any kind of work before its publication and outside of all legal actions).

5 It is exceedingly difficult to trace the history of publication of the *Mémoires* in part because a great deal of misinformation on the subject has circulated. What seems to have occurred is the following: the 1854 *Mémoires* were seized by the state after a limited number had appeared. This seizure was *not* motivated by censorship – as some have contended – but was, rather, the temporarily successful outcome of the Countess's request of Prince Napoleon to halt publication. However, the publishing house, not to be done out of its 'scoop,' sued the Countess ex-Mogador for breach of contract and won its case. The outcome of the trial was reported in *Le Journal des débats* of 7 March 1858.

6 It should be noted that *Madame Bovary* had already appeared in serialized form the previous year in the *Revue de Paris*. The Countess de Chabrillan always complained that the Chabrillan family had prevented her from negotiating contracts to serialize. Not only was this form of writing extremely lucrative, it also could provide advance publicity for the novel once it appeared in book form.

7 The sighting referred to is reported by Thérèse Marix in an article in the November 1938 issue of the *Revue de Musicologie* entitled 'Séjour de Bizet au Vésinet' d'après les "Mémoires inédits" de Céleste Mogador, comtesse de Chabrillan' (142–50).

8 I was able to discover several manuscript letters by Chabrillan at the Bibliothèque nationale in Paris. All of these letters are undated. The letter to Dumas fils must date from her retirement. There are, in addition, three letters she wrote to photographer and friend Félix Nadar. Two of these, written evidently before she retired, are requesting that he return her Australian album and her letter from Antoine Fauchery. Did Céleste de Chabrillan have a photographic album of her years spent in Australia? If so, what a pity it has been lost.

2. Worlds Apart: Mapping Prostitution and the Demi-monde

1 Unfortunately, statistics on the number of prostitutes in Paris vary considerably. One can always count the number of women who were registered, but many prostitutes plied their trade outside the regulatory system. In his 1836 magnum opus *De la prostitution*, Parent-Duchâtelet counted 3131.

Adler claims that 125,000 were registered in 1864. Many women, however, simply did not register and took the risk of incarceration.

2 In a 22 April 1859 letter to George Sand, publisher Jules Hetzel describes the following encounter with Alfred de Musset, Sand's erstwhile lover: 'J'ai une fois à 4 heures du matin rencontré Alfred à la porte d'une maison de filles de la rue Saint-Marc, il pleurait. Il avait été si ignoble dans cette maison qu'on l'avait flanqué à la porte' (cited in Guéno et al., *Sand et Musset* 186) (One time I encountered Alfred at 4 o'clock in the morning outside the door of a brothel in Saint-Marc Street; he was crying. He had been so ignoble in the brothel that he had been thrown out).

3 Corbin notes that cause for arrest could be provocation in public (ill defined and subjectively assessed), being in groups of whores, drunkenness, and numerous other behaviours (157).

4 I wish to point out that Adler's assertion is at odds with what Jill Harsin claims in her meticulous work *Policing Prostitution*. Since Mogador's testimony seems to bear out Adler's claim of the difficulty of leaving the life of prostitution, I have retained this account.

5 See, however, Robert Darnton's recent article in the *New York Review of Books*, 'Finding a Lost Prince of Bohemia,' in which he reports having discovered an avatar of bohemia in a two-volume novel dating from 1790 entitled *Les bohémiens*.

6 The entire plot of Dumas's 1855 play *Le demi-monde* revolves around the efforts of one respectable nobleman to reveal the fact that the betrothed of his best friend has a tainted past and thus cannot be married. He manages to thwart the marriage, and this is the 'happy ending.'

7 See my article 'Paternity and DNA' (1998) for a thorough discussion of Balzac's novella with respect to the Civil Code.

8 See Margaret Rosenthal's book *The Honest Courtesan* for an account of the public/private divide in Venetian society of the Renaissance and the ways in which Veronica Franco transgressed and challenged that divide.

9 In his *Courtesans and Fishcakes*, Davidson discusses the invisibility of Athenian citizen/wives within the broad spectrum of Athenian life of the classical period. Hamel's more focused analysis of the trial of courtesan Neaira brings to the fore what the stakes were in ensuring that courtesans *could* not cross over the line of socio-political legitimacy. This is not the place to examine the relationship between political legitimacy and the claustration of women in detail, but there are very interesting parallels which exist between the Athenian practice of feminine claustration (and the related existence of an extensive and highly available demi-monde) and the similar situation which arose in France between 1840 and 1900.

The parallel suggests that even though the two situations are no doubt historically determined, some structural similarities do exist.

10 On this point, see Berlanstein 38.

11 It was not until 1929 and the discovery of penicillin that cures for syphilis could be effected.

12 Walter Benjamin, who conducted vast amounts of research on this period as part of his project on the advent of modernity, cites a compatriot's claim that 'a certain Chicard [...], premier cancan dancer at the Mabille ball [...] maintains he dances under the surveillance of two police sergeants whose sole responsibility is to keep an eye on the dancing of this one man' (*Arcades Project* 497). In fact, Chicard would later found a *bal* of his own.

13 Jane Avril reports that the Moulin Rouge replaced the older Reine Blanche (111n60).

14 The manuscript of this composition for piano and cello is held in the Frederick R. Koch Collection of Yale University's Beineke Rare Books Collection.

3. Fictions of Prostitution

1 Bernheimer's explanation for the dread of the venal woman centres around a classical Freudian psychoanalytical understanding of the literature. Briefly put, his contention is that the many artistic treatments of prostitutes in nineteenth-century France which seek to silence, contain, mutilate, or dissect the venal woman's body stem from a primal – and evidently collectively primal – need to parry threats of castration allegedly posed by the prostitute. Whether or not one subscribes to the notion of fear of castration, it can at least be read in a more 'secular' way as a male fear of loss of power, authority, and legitimacy.

2 Seigel's remarks on the *grisette* are among the most illuminating of the ample literature on this topic: 'That the *grisette* was already [perceived as] receding into the past in the 1840s tells us what kind of a myth hers was. A fantasy image constructed out of the misunderstanding of one sex and class by another, it had to be projected onto the past because it found few opportunities for realisation in the present' (42).

3 Cited in Francis Lacassin's preface to *Les mystères de Paris* (21).

4 It should be clarified that abolitionism refers to the social movement which sought to abolish the system by which prostitution was regulated. It does not refer to abolishing prostitution itself.

5 The novel version, however, includes a morbid, sordid exhumation of her body.

6 An entire chapter of *Nana* is devoted to a horse race featuring a horse unsubtly named Nana. In Lorrain's *La maison Philibert* [1904], whose milieu is much more lower-class, there is a constant chatter about the 'livestock' as well as the 'poultry' and the 'game.'

7 The couturier in question can only be a reference to the famous fashion establishment of Worth, who catered to both the respectable and the less so.

8 She goes on to note that young male prostitutes took on the names of the most notorious courtesans, for example 'la Pougy' to evoke Liane de Pougy. But as a professional dancer, she was greatly offended to learn that one of these men 'qui […] me ressemblait, se faisait appeler Jane Avril!' (72) (who […] looked like me, called herself Jane Avril!). It took some degree of notoriety to be thus parodied, and reputations of this type do not readily fall into eclipse as one realizes in reading William Peniston's study of male homosexuality in nineteenth-century France: herein he reports that one Arthur Dechatillon was recurrently arrested in the 1870s. His drag nom de guerre was none other than la Mogador (163). Twenty years after her retirement from the trade, Céleste de Chabrillan's reputation lingered on – at least in a certain demi-monde.

9 Had Baudelaire realized this, he would not have wondered: 'Pourquoi, l'homme d'esprit aime les filles plus que les femmes du monde, malgré qu'elles soient également bêtes? – À trouver' (*Mon coeur mis à nu* 1283) (Why does the man of wit like whores more than respectable women even though they are equally stupid? – To find out). If all women, regardless of class, are equally stupid, why indeed prefer the company of whores unless it be that they confirm one's convenient assumptions about who is inherently intelligent and who is not, and – more signifi-cantly – who can transcend the body and who is stuck bearing its burden.

10 For an account of how French women of the seventeenth century invented the novel as a genre, see Joan Dejean's *Tender Geographies*.

11 Some of the first feminist historians to explore this issue were Carole Pateman (*The Sexual Contract*), Joan Landes (*Women and the Public Sphere in the Age of the French Revolution*), and Geneviève Fraisse (*Muse de la raison: la démocratie exclusive et la différence des sexes*). More recent treatments have tended to be more nuanced, some insisting on the fact that, while the public/private divide of early French democracy was certainly gendered, French women nonetheless managed to project themselves into the public sphere in a variety of ways including through publication. See for example the various essays comprising Alison Finch's *Women's Writing in Nine-teenth-Century France*.

12 Parent-Duchâtelet had noted this in 1836, but at least he ascribes this trait to their need to render themselves oblivious to their terrible trade.
13 I wish to thank Isabelle Hoog Naginski for making me aware of this novel. Sand's view of the prostitute was also a conflicted one, albeit in a different way from those of her male counterparts. Her own mother had been a venal woman (though hardly a registered prostitute) when her father, then in the army, married her.

5. Plotting Exoneration

1 It may seem odd that Mogador would know how to handle a gun. In fact, she was known to be a crack shot. Some of the more spacious *bals publics* – those which had large gardens – also had shooting galleries. The Élysée-Montmartre was an example. We may conclude that she gained her experience and competence (in these matters as in others) in these amusement parks.
2 Abortion is not an unknown topic in literature of the period, but it is the frank approach to it in Chabrillan's novel which is being emphasized here. In Sue's *Les mystères de Paris*, the most evil character, a doctor, is an abortionist. His profession is never openly stated, and it is only through all manner of euphemisms that it becomes clear at all. Needless to say, it is represented as the worst possible of crimes.
3 Patricia Clancy and Jeanne Allen's annotated translation (*The French Consul's Wife*) is an excellent resource because it contextualizes Céleste de Chabrillan's narrative of her Australian experience between 1854 and 1856. The notes and appendices provided in this translation are invaluable.

Works Cited

Novels, Memoirs, and Selected Works by the Countess of Chabrillan (in chronological order)

Adieux au monde: Mémoires de Céleste Mogador. First edition, 1854. 5 vols. Paris: Locard-Davi et de Vresse.

Mémoires de Céleste Mogador. Second edition, 1858. 4 vols. Paris: Librairie Nouvelle.

Mémoires de Céleste Mogador. Third edition, 1876. 2 vols. Paris: Librairie Nouvelle.

Memoirs of a Courtesan in Nineteenth-Century Paris. Trans. Monique Fleury Nagem. Lincoln: University of Nebraska Press, 2001.

Les voleurs d'or. Paris: Michel Lévy, 1857.

La Sapho. Paris: Michel Lévy, 1858. [*Un amour terrible. (Sapho)*. Second edition, 1876; third edition, 1897.]

La Sapho. Paris: L'Harmattan, 2007.

Miss Pewel. Paris: Bourdilliat, 1859. [Republished by Calmann-Lévy as *Une méchante femme*, 1877.]

Est-il fou? Paris: Bourdilliat, 1860. [Republished by Calmann-Lévy, 1881.]

Un miracle à Vichy. Vichy: Bougarel fils, 1861.

La Réaction, newspaper article, 1871.

Émigrantes et déportées ou Les deux soeurs. Michel Lévy, 1876. Calmann-Lévy, 1887.

Un deuil au bout du monde: suite des mémoires de Céleste Mogador par la comtesse de Chabrillan. Paris: Librairie Nouvelle, 1877.

The French Consul's Wife: Memoirs of Céleste de Chabrillan in Gold-Rush Australia. Trans. Patricia Clancy and Jeanne Allen. Melbourne: Melbourne University Press, 2003.

La duchesse de Mers. Calmann-Lévy, 1881.

Les forçats de l'amour. Calmann-Lévy, 1881.

Marie Baude. Calmann-Lévy, 1883.

Un drame sur le Tage. Calmann-Lévy, 1885.

Pierre Pascal: un drame au Tréport. Paris, 1885. With open letter to Ulysse Bessac, 31 August 1885.

Manuscripts

Chabrillan, Céleste de. Letters to Félix Nadar (3). Ms. NAF 24278 ff 668–73. Bibliothèque nationale de France.

– Letter to Alexandre Dumas fils. Ms. NAF 14664 ff 1–4. Bibliothèque nationale de France.

Secondary Sources

Books

Adler, Laure. *La vie quotidienne dans les maisons closes: 1830–1930*. Paris: Hachette, 1990.

Alhoy, Maurice. *Physiologie de la lorette*. 1841. Paris: Aubert, n.d.

Allen, James Smith. *Popular French Romanticism: Authors, Readers, and Books in the Nineteenth Century*. Syracuse: Syracuse University Press, 1981.

Aron, Jean-Paul. *Misérable et glorieuse: la femme du XIXe siècle*. 1980. Paris: Éditions complexe, 1984.

Artus, Maurice. *L'Élysée-Montmartre: 1807–1900*. Paris: Société 'Le vieux Montmartre,' 1910.

'Aux Bibliophiles.' *Catalogue de cabinet de lecture*. 1896. M-2700. Bibliothèque nationale de France.

Avril, Jane. *Mes mémoires*. Paris: Phébus, 2005.

Balzac, Honoré de. *La fille aux yeux d'or. Histoire des Treize, Ferragus, La fille aux yeux d'or*. Paris: Garnier-Flammarion, 1988.

– *Le père Goriot*. Paris: Garnier-Flammarion, 1995.

– *Splendeurs et misères des courtisanes*. Paris: Flammarion, 1973.

Banville, Théodore. *Mes souvenirs*. 1882. Paris: Éditeurs d'aujourd'hui, 1980.

Barrière, Théodore, and Lambert Thibault. *Les filles de marbre*. Paris: Michel Lévy, 1853.

Baudelaire, Charles. *Mon coeur mis à nu. Oeuvres complètes de Baudelaire*. Paris: Pléiade, 1961.

– 'Le peintre de la vie moderne.' *Curiosités esthétiques, L'art romantique et autres oeuvres critiques de Baudelaire*. Paris: Garnier, 1986. 453–502.

Bellanger, Marguerite. *Confessions de Marguerite Bellanger: mémoires anecdot-iques*. Paris: Librairie Populaire, 1882.

Benjamin, Walter. *The Arcades Project*. Trans. Eiland and McLaughlin. Cambridge: Harvard University Press, 1999.

– *Charles Baudelaire: Un poète lyrique à l'apogée du capitalisme*. Paris: Payot, n.d.

Berlanstein, Lenard. *Daughters of Eve: A Cultural History of French Theater Women from the Old Regime to the Fin de Siècle*. Cambridge: Harvard University Press, 2001.

Bernhardt, Sarah. *Ma double vie: mémoires*. Paris: Charpentier et Fasquelle, 1907.

Bernheimer, Charles. *Figures of Ill-Repute: Representing Prostitution in the Nineteenth Century*. Cambridge: Harvard University Press, 1989.

Biographie des écuyers et écuyères du Théâtre national et du Cirque-Olympique par un flâneur. Paris: L'Éditeur du Répertoire dramatique, 1846.

Brooks, Peter. *Reading for the Plot: Design and Intention in Narrative*. New York: Alfred A. Knopf, 1984.

Byrne, Paula. *Perdita: The Literary, Theatrical, Scandalous Life of Mary Robinson*. New York: Random House, 2004.

Champfleury, Jules. *Les aventures de Mademoiselle Mariotte*. 1853. Paris: Charpentier, 1874.

Chartier, Roger, and Henry Jean Martin. *Histoire de l'édition française*. Vol. 3. *Le temps des éditeurs: Du romantisme à la belle époque*. Paris: Fayard, 1990.

Cholley, Jean. *Courtisanes du Japon*. Paris: Picquier, 2001.

'Cinq Mille Volumes.' *Catalogue de cabinet de lecture*. 1863. M-2700. Bibliothèque nationale de France.

Claudin, Gustave. *Mes souvenirs: les boulevards de 1840–1870*. Paris: Calmann-Lévy, 1884.

Clayson, Hollis. *Painted Love: Prostitution in French Art of the Impressionist Era*. New Haven: Yale University Press, 1991.

Corbin, Alain. *Les filles de noce: misère sexuelle et prostitution au XIXe siècle*. Paris: Flammarion, 1978.

Curtiss, Mina. *Bizet and His World*. New York: Alfred A. Knopf, 1958.

D'Aurevilly, Barbey. 'La vengeance d'une femme,' in *Les Diaboliques*. Paris: Garnier, 1963.

Davidson, James. *Courtesans and Fishcakes: The Consuming Passions of Classical Athens*. New York: HarperCollins, 1997.

DeJean, Joan. *Tender Geographies: Women and the Origins of the Novel in France*. New York: Columbia University Press, 1991.

'Delorme.' *Catalogue de cabinet de lecture*. 1871. M-2700. Bibliothèque nationale de France.

Delvau, Alfred. *Les cythères parisiennes: histoire anecdotique des bals de Paris.* Paris: E. Dentu, 1864.

– *Henry Murger et la Bohème.* Saint-Germain-L'Auxerrois, 1866.

– *Mémoires d'une honnête fille.* [written with Céleste de Chabrillan]. 2nd ed. Paris: Achille Faure, 1865.

Dijkstra, Bram. *Idols of Perversity: Fantasies of Feminine Evil in Fin-de-Siècle Culture.* New York: Oxford University Press, 1986.

Dottin-Orsini, M., and D. Grojnowski, eds. *Un joli monde: romans de la prostitution.* Paris: Laffont, 2008.

Duchêne, Roger. *Ninon de Lenclos ou la manière jolie de faire l'amour.* Paris: Fayard, 2000.

Dumas, Alexandre. *Filles, lorettes et courtisanes.* Paris: 1843.

Dumas fils, Alexandre. *La dame aux camélias.* Paris, 1852.

– *Le demi-monde.* Paris: Michel Lévy, 1855.

Finch, Alison. *Women's Writing in Nineteenth-Century France.* Cambridge: Cambridge University Press, 2000.

Flaubert, Gustave. *L'éducation sentimentale.* 1869. Paris: Gallimard, 1965.

– *Madame Bovary.* Paris: Garnier-Flammarion, 1986.

Fraisse, Geneviève. *Muse de la raison: la démocratie exclusive et la différence des sexes.* Paris: Alinéa, 1989.

Fusco, Domenico. *Bibliografia ragionata del 'Gamiana' di de Musset.* Torino: Berruto, 1953.

Gaillard, Marc. *Paris au temps de Balzac.* Etrepilly: Presses du village, 2001.

Gautier, Théophile. *Histoire du romantisme.* Paris: Flammarion, 1939.

– *Lettres à la Presidente.* Paris: Champion, 2002.

Gavarni. *Les lorettes,* in *Oeuvres choisies.* 1.1. Paris: J. Hetzel, 1846.

Gelfand, Elissa D. *Imagination in Confinement: Women's Writings from French Prisons.* Ithaca: Cornell University Press, 1983.

Girardin, Delphine de. *Chroniques parisiennes: 1836–1848.* Paris: Des Femmes, 1986.

Gluck, Mary. *Popular Bohemia: Modernism and Urban Culture in Nineteenth-Century Paris.* Cambridge: Harvard University Press, 2005.

Golden, Arthur. *Memoirs of a Geisha.* New York: Random House, 1997.

Goncourt, Edmond de. *La fille Elisa.* 1877. Paris: Flammarion, 1956.

Goncourt, Edmond de, et Jules de Goncourt. *Journal: mémoires de la vie littéraire: 1851–1865.* Vol. 1. Paris: Laffont, 1989.

– *La lorette.* Paris: Du Lerot, 1853.

Griffin, Susan. *The Book of the Courtesans: A Catalogue of Their Virtues.* New York: Broadway, 2001.

Guéno, Jean-Pierre, Diane Kurys, and Roselyne de Ayala. *Sand et Musset: les enfants du siècle.* Paris: Éditions de la Martinière, 1999.

Guillemot, Gabriel. *Le bohème*. [*sic*] Paris: Chevalier, 1868.

Gullickson, Gay. *The Unruly Women of Paris: Images of the Commune*. Ithaca: Cornell University Press, 1996.

Hamel, Debra. *Trying Neaira: The True Story of a Courtesan's Scandalous Life in Ancient Greece*. New Haven: Yale University Press, 2003.

Harsin, Jill. *Policing Prostitution in Nineteenth-Century Paris*. Princeton: Princeton University Press, 1985.

Hawthorne, Melanie. *Rachilde and French Women's Authorship*. Lincoln: University of Nebraska Press, 2001.

Heilbrun, Carolyn G. *Writing a Woman's Life*. New York: Norton, 1988.

Hemmings, F.W.J. *Theatre and State in France, 1760–1905*. London: Cambridge University Press, 1994.

Hickman, Katie. *Courtesans*. New York: HarperCollins, 2003.

Houbre, Gabrielle. *Le livre des courtisanes*. Paris: Tallandier, 2006.

Houssaye, Arsène. *Les confessions: souvenirs d'un demi-siècle, 1830–1890*. 6 vols. Paris: Dentu, 1885–91.

Huart, Louis. *Physiologie de la grisette*. 1841.

Hugo, Victor. *Ruys Blas; Les burgraves; Marion de Lorme*. Paris: Flammarion, n.d.

Huysmans, Joris Karl. *Marthe, histoire d'une fille*. Paris, 1876. Paris: Le Cercle du livre, 1955.

Iwasaki, Mineko. *Geisha, A Life*. New York: Atria Books, 2002.

Jaget, Claude ed. *Prostitutes – Our Life*. Trans. Anna Furse, Suzie Fleming, and Ruth Hall. Bristol: Falling Wall, 1980.

Kelly, Dorothy. *Fictional Genders: Role and Representation in Nineteenth-Century French Narrative*. Lincoln: University of Nebraska Press, 1989.

Lacombe, Hervé. *Les voies de l'opéra français au XIXe siècle*. Paris: Fayard, 1997.

Laine. *Généalogie de la maison Guigues de Moreton de Chabrillan complétée par les notes du comte F. de Chabrillan*. Paris: Champion, 1913.

Landes, Joan. *Women and the Public Sphere in the Age of the French Revolution*. Ithaca: Cornell University Press, 1988.

Lasowski, Patrick, ed. *L'espion libertin ou le calendrier du plaisir: histoires, adresses, tarifs et spécialités des courtisanes de Paris*. Paris: Philippe Picquier, 2000.

Leclerq, Pierre-Robert. *Céleste Mogador: une reine de Paris*. Paris: La Table Ronde, 1996.

Le Hir, Marie-Pierre. *Le romantisme aux enchères: Ducange, Pixéricourt, Hugo*. Amsterdam: John Benjamins, 1992.

Lorrain, Jean. *La maison Philibert*. Paris, 1904. [staged as play in 4 acts by Georges Normandy, Jose de Berys et Nore Brunel. Paris: Moulin de la Chanson, 1932.]

Lyons, Martin. *Readers and Society in Nineteenth-Century France: Workers, Women, Peasants*. New York: Palgrave, 2001.

Mainardi, Patricia. *Husbands, Wives, and Lovers: Marriage and Its Discontents in Nineteenth-Century France*. New Haven: Yale University Press, 2003.

Manning, Jo. *My Lady Scandalous: The Amazing Life and Outrageous Times of Grace Dalrymple Elliott, Royal Courtesan*. New York: Simon and Schuster, 2005.

Mardoche, Jacques, and Pierre Desgenais. *Les Parisiennes*. Paris: Dentu, 1882.

Margadant, Jo Burr. *The New Biography: Performing Femininity in Nineteenth Century France*. Berkeley: University of California Press, 2000.

Martin-Fugier, Anne. *La vie élégante ou la formation du Tout-Paris, 1815–1848*. Paris: Fayard, 1990.

Matlock, Jann. *Scenes of Seduction: Prostitution, Hysteria, and Reading Difference in Nineteenth-Century France*. New York: Columbia University Press, 1994.

Maupassant, Guy de. 'Boule de suif.' *Contes choisis*. New York: Doubleday, 1961.

– 'La Maison Tellier.' *Contes choisis*. New York: Doubleday, 1961.

– *Les tombales*. *'La Parure' et autres scènes de la vie parisienne*. Paris: Flammarion, 2001.

McEwan, Ian. *Atonement*. New York: First Anchor Books, 2003.

Mérimée, Prosper. *Arsène Guillot*. *Carmen; Arsène Guillot; L'abbé Aubain; La dame de pique*. Paris: Plon, 1936.

– *Carmen*. *Carmen and Other Stories*. Trans. Nicholas Jotcham. Oxford: Oxford University Press, 1989.

Milner, Max. *Le romantisme: 1820–1843*. Vol. 1. Paris: Arthaud, 1973.

Mollier, Jean-Yves. *Michel et Calmann Lévy ou la naissance de l'édition moderne, 1836–1891*. Paris: Calmann-Lévy, 1984.

Monselet, Charles. *Figurines parisiennes*. 1854. Paris: Jules Dagneau, Libraire-Éditeur. Refait par Du Lérot, éditeur, 1990.

– *Petits mémoires littéraires*. Paris: Charpentier, 1885.

Moser, Françoise. *Vie et aventures de Céleste Mogador, Fille publique, femme de lettres et comtesse (1824–1909)*. Paris: Albin Michel, 1935.

Moses, Claire Goldberg. *French Feminism in the Nineteenth Century*. Albany: State University of New York Press, 1984.

Mossman, Carol. 'Paternity and DNA.' *Paternity and Fatherhood: Myths and Realities*. Ed. Lieve Spaas. London: MacMillan Press, 1998. 40–8.

Murger, Henry. *Scènes de la vie de bohème*. 1851. Paris: Garnier, 1929.

Murger, Henry, and Théodore Barrière. *La vie de bohème: pièce en cinq actes, mêlée de chants*. Paris: Imprimerie Dondey-Duprey, 1849.

Musset, A.D.M. [*sic*] *Gamiani ou deux nuit d'excès*. Réimpression conforme au texte original ornée des douze gravures de Déveria et Grévedon. Extrait des *Mémoires de la Cesse de C+* (Elisabeth Céleste Vénard, Cesse Lionel de Chabrillan). Paris: Les Amis de l'Époque romantique. N.d.

– *Mimi Pinson: Profil de grisette*. 1845. *Mimi Pinson et autres contes*. Paris: La Girouette, n.d. 275–320.

Nerval, Gérard de. *La bohème galante*. Paris: Michel Lévy, 1856.

Noël, Leon. *Histoire de Murger pour servir à l'histoire de la vraie bohème, par trois buveurs d'eau*. [Lelioux, Nadar, Noël.] Paris: Hetzel, 1862.

Offenbach, Jacques. *La Chabrillan Polka* for cello and piano. 'Polka composée expressément pour Madame la comtesse de Chabrillan.' Ms Frederick R. Koch Collection. Yale Beineke Rare Books, n.d.

– *La vie parisienne*. 1866.

Parent-Duchâtelet, Docteur Alexandre. *De la prostitution dans la ville de Paris considérée sous le rapport de l'hygiène publique, de la morale et de l'administration*. 1836. 2 vols. Paris: 1837.

Parent-Lardeur, Françoise. *Lire à Paris au temps de Balzac: les cabinets de lecture à Paris: 1815–1830*. Paris: Éditions de l'École des hautes études en sciences sociales, 1999.

Parsons, Deborah L. *Streetwalking the Metropolis: Women, the City and Modernity*. Oxford: Oxford University Press, 2000.

Pateman, Carole. *The Sexual Contract*. Stanford University Press, 1988.

Pearl, Cora. *Mémoires de Cora Pearl*. Paris: Jules Lévy, 1886.

Peniston, William A. *Pederasts and Others: Urban Culture and Sexual Identity in Nineteenth-Century Paris*. New York: Haworth Press, 2004.

Pernoud, Emmanuel. *Le bordel en peinture*. Paris: Adam Biro, 2001.

Pichois, Claude. *Le romantisme: 1843–1869*. Vol. 2. Paris: Arthaud, 1979.

Pierrefitte, P.L. de. *Histoire du théâtre des Folies Marigny: 1848–1893*. Paris: Tress et Stock, 1893.

Pougy, Liane de. *My Blue Notebooks*. Trans. Diana Athill. New York: Tarcher/ Putnam, 2000.

Privat d'Anglemont, Alexandre. *Paris anecdoté*. Paris: Delahays, 1865.

Proust, Marcel. *Contre Sainte-Beuve, précédé de 'Pastiches et mélanges' et suivis de 'Essais et articles'*. Ed. Pierre Claras et Yves Sandre. Paris: Gallimard, 1971.

Puccini, Giacomo. *La bohème*. 1896. London: Dover, 1962.

Renault, Louis. *La 'Traite des blanches' et la conférence de Paris: un point de vue international*. Paris: A. Pedone, 1902.

Richardson, Joanna. *The Bohemians: 'La Vie de Bohème' in Paris 1830–1914*. New York: A.S. Barnes, 1969.

– *The Courtesans: The Demi-monde in Nineteenth-Century France*. 1967. Reissued by Phoenix Press, London, 2000.

– *La vie parisienne, 1852–1870*. New York: The Viking Press, 1971.

Roqueplan, Nestor. *La vie parisienne*. Paris: 1857.

Rosenthal, Margaret. *The Honest Courtesan: Veronica Franco, Citizen and Writer in Sixteenth-Century Venice*. Chicago: University of Chicago Press, 1992.

Rosmarin, Léonard, *When Literature Becomes Opera: Study of a Transformational Process*. Amsterdam: Rodopi, 1999.

Rounding, Virginia. *Grandes Horizontales: The Lives and Legends of Four Nineteenth-Century Courtesans*. New York: Bloomsbury, 2003.

Rozier, Victor. *Les bals publics à Paris*. 3rd ed. Paris: Gustave Havard, 1856.

Rude, Maxime. *Confessions d'un journaliste*. Paris: Sagnier, 1876.

Sand, George. *Indiana*. Paris: Gallimard, 1984.

– *Isidora*. Paris: Éditions des femmes, 2000.

– *Lélia*. 2 vols. Paris: Aurore, 1987.

Seigel, Jerrold E. *Bohemian Paris: Culture, Politics, and the Boundaries of Bourgeois Life, 1830–1930*. New York: Viking, 1986.

Showalter, Elaine. *Sexual Anarchy: Gender and Culture at the Fin de Siècle*. New York: Viking, 1990.

Silverman, Willa Z. *The Notorious Life of Gyp: Right-Wing Anarchist in Fin-de-Siècle France*. New York: Oxford University Press, 1995.

Stains, Théodore. *Paris dansant ou les filles d'Hérodiade: folles danseuses des bals publics: le Bal Mabille, la Grande-Chaumière, Le Ranelagh, etc.* Paris: Bréauté, 1845.

Sue, Eugène. *Les mystères de Paris*. 1842–3. Paris: Laffont, 1989.

Thiesse, Anne-Marie. *Le roman au quotidien: lecteurs et lectures populaires à la belle époque*. Paris: Seuil, 2000.

Tristan, Flora. *Pérégrinations d'une paria*. Indigo et Côté-femmes, 1999.

– *Promenades dans Londres: L'aristocratie et les prolétaires anglais*. 1840. Paris: Indigo et Côté-femmes, 2001.

Vaudoyer, J-L. *Alice Ozy ou l'Aspasie moderne*. Paris: Tremois, 1930.

Verdi, Giuseppe. *Verdi's La Traviata*. Ed. Burton D. Fisher. Opera Classics Library. Coral Gables: 2001.

Wagner-Martin, Linda. *Telling Women's Lives: The New Biography*. New Brunswick: Rutgers University Press, 1994.

Wilwerth, Evelyne. *Neel Doff: A Biography (1858–1942)*. Trans. Renée Linkhorn. New York: Peter Lang, 1997.

Zola, Émile. *Nana*. 1880. Paris: Flammarion, 2000.

Articles

Arsenal 4 RO 12921: Collection of newspaper clippings and articles on Mogador including one by René de Pont-Jest in 1894 (newspaper untitled) (now in Bibliothèque nationale de France, site Richelieu).

Arsenal 4 RO 12953: Collection of newspaper theatre reviews, mostly without author, journal name, sometimes with date; Paris: 1844–9 (now in Bibliothèque nationale de France, site Richelieu).

Cassan, Catherine. 'Catalogues de cabinets de lecture.' Bibliothèque nationale de France. 5 (1989).

Chabrillan, Lionel de Moreton. *Mémoire à messieurs de la Cour impériale de Bourges*. Paris: Didiot, 1853.

Corbin, Alain. 'Le temps des maisons closes.' *L'Histoire* 264 (2002): 48–53.

Darnton, Robert. "Finding a Lost Prince of Bohemia." *New York Review of Books* 55.5 (2008): 44–8.

Davy, Lynda A. 'La croqueuse d'hommes: images de la prostituée chez Flaubert, Zola et Maupassant.' *Annales* 42.6 (1987): 59–66.

Lever, Maurice. 'Courtisanes et filles galantes.' *L'Histoire* 264 (2002): 46–7.

Lintz, Bernadette C. 'Concocting *La dame aux camélias*: Blood, Tears, and Other Fluids.' *Nineteenth-Century French Studies* 33.3–4 (2005): 287–307.

Marix, Therese. 'Séjour de Bizet au Vésinet, d'après les "Mémoires inédits" de Céleste Mogador, Comtesse de Chabrillan' in *Revue de Musicologie* 68 (November 1938): 142–50.

Marrone, Claire. 'Male and Female *Bildung*: The *Mémoires de Céleste Mogador*.' *Nineteenth-Century French Studies* 25.3–4 (1997): 335–47.

'Mémoires de Mlle Céleste Vénard dite Mogador. Traité pour la publication avec MM. Jacottet et Bourdilliat. Demande de résolution.' Audience du 6 mars [1858]; 1re chambre; *Gazette des tribunaux* 7 mars: 1858, 1.

Palacio, Jean de. 'La féminité dévorante: sur quelques images de la manducation dans la littérature décadente.' *La Revue des Sciences Humaines* 168 (1977): 601–18.

Whitmore, Harry E. 'Readers, Writers, and Literary Taste in the Early 1830s: The *Cabinet de lecture* as Focal Point.' *Journal of Library History* 13.2 (1978): 119–30.

Woestelandt, Evelyne. 'Le corps vénal: Rosanette dans *L'Éducation sentimentale*.' *Nineteenth-Century French Studies* 16.1–2 (1987–8): 120–31.

Manuscript Source

Chabrillan, Félicité de Levis-Mirepoix, comtesse, A. de Chabrillan. Ms correspondence with Ferdinand Bac. Bibliothèque nationale de France. [14158/54] 1915–46.

Journals Consulted

L'Artiste
Le Charivari
Le Corsaire-Satan
La Gazette des tribunaux
La Presse

Index